State
and
Society
in the
TAIWAN
MIRACLE

An East Gate Book

State and Society in the TAIWAN MIRACLE

Thomas B. Gold

M. E. Sharpe, Inc.

Armonk, New York/London

In Memory of E. H. G.

East Gate Books are edited by Douglas Merwin
120 Buena Vista Drive, White Plains, New York 10603

Copyright © 1986 by M. E. Sharpe, Inc.

Available in the United Kingdom and Europe from M.E. Sharpe,
Publishers, 3 Henrietta Street, London WC2E 8LU.

Library of Congress Cataloging in Publication Data

Gold, Thomas B.
    State and society in the Taiwan miracle.

    Bibliography: p.
    1. Taiwan—Economic conditions—1945-   . 2. Taiwan—Politics
and government—1945-   . 3. Taiwan—Social conditions. I. Title.
HC430.5.G65   1985   338.951′249   85-2350
ISBN 0-87332-349-1
ISBN 0-87332-399-8 (pbk.)

Printed in the United States of America

Contents

Preface   vii

Abbreviations   xiii

1. Explaining the Taiwan Miracle   3

2. Taiwan Prior to Japanese Colonization   21

3. Taiwan Under Japanese Rule   32

4. Chaotic Interregnum   47

5. Rehabilitation and Import-Substitution Industrialization, 1950–1959   56

6. Export Orientation and Political Quiet, 1960–1973   74

7. Industrial Upgrading and the Emergence of a Political Opposition, 1973–1984   97

8. State and Society in the Taiwan Miracle   122

Notes   135

Bibliography   147

Index   157

Preface

When writing about places as controversial as Taiwan, it appears to be common practice to put quotation marks about affirmative words such as "miracle" to inform readers of the author's profound skepticism about supposed achievements there. I have not put quotation marks around the word "miracle" in the title of this book for the simple reason that I think the people of that island nonnation have made miraculous progress at rapid growth, structural change, improved livelihood, and political democratization. I do not mean miraculous in the sense of a unique, nonrecurring God-given event, but rather as a wondrous recovery by dint of very human effort from a morass of destruction and despair.

I neither deny nor gloss over the past and present shortcomings of Taiwan's political system or the dangers inherent in its type of economic strategy. Part of the miracle is the fact that the ruling Chinese Nationalist Party (KMT), notorious for heading one of history's most corrupt, violent, and incompetent regimes during its days on the Chinese mainland, successfully undertook an internal reform, established a new relationship with Taiwanese society after brutalizing and alienating it, and spearheaded rapid economic growth with social and political stability. Another aspect of the miracle is the positive response of society to the limited but real opportunities offered it.

It required crushing defeat in one of this century's greatest popular revolutions to bring reform about, but how many other regimes in Asia, Africa, or Latin America, in circumstances far less desperate than those of the KMT in 1949, could muster the will to undertake such a cleansing and readjustment?

Although this book presents a case study of Taiwan, it is addressed as much to social scientists and others concerned with larger issues of development and underdevelopment as to Asianists. With few exceptions, the dominant theories in the field, aside from those of economists, were derived from studies of the failures and distortions of capitalist development strategies in Latin America. Theories and generalizations were not tested for East Asian cases. Virtually no one beside economists even analyzed East Asia, and, as I argue in the first chapter, the economists' studied neglect of politics has bequeathed a somewhat distorted and mystified picture of the "East Asian model" to scholars and planners outside the region. I hope through this book to bring the data from Taiwan and the other East Asian capitalist societies into the mainstream and to demystify the new economic orthodoxy about East Asian development.

The concepts of dependency and bureaucratic authoritarianism, which emerged from the Latin American field, are under severe attack now. Several countries, especially those in East Asia, share structural features of dependency but have avoided so far the same unfortunate consequences. And even in Latin America itself, the stalwart exemplars of bureaucratic-authoritarianism, such as Brazil, Argentina, and Peru, are now undergoing a definite return to democracy.

Rather than completely abandon these concepts, I have retained them here, critically to be sure, so as to make Taiwan a comprehensible case for the larger development community and at the same time to begin to reconceptualize the nature of development, dependency, and world system. The successful East Asian cases demonstrate clearly the potential benefits and dangers of consciously tying a nation's development to the world system and global product life cycle. They also show the costs and benefits of authoritarian exclusionary regimes at certain stages of this process; when they can be functional, when dysfunctional; and how change can be brought about.

This book represents an attempt on my part to come to terms with my two years of teaching and traveling in Taiwan from 1970 to 1972 as an Oberlin Shansi representative at Tunghai University. During that period, just as the economic takeoff was consolidated and the standard of living was rising rapidly, the external environment turned extremely nasty: Taiwan's withdrawal from the United Nations under pressure, the Nixon trip to mainland China, severed diplomatic relations with numerous Western countries, rising protectionism. Generalissimo Chiang Kai-shek's son, Chiang Ching-kuo, became premier. He was widely regarded as an ultra-authoritarian enemy of democracy and business, the Soviet-trained boss of the ubiquitous secret police. People lined up to emigrate, capital fled, liberals moaned.

By the time I returned in September 1977 to do research for my doctoral dissertation, Taiwan had weathered diplomatic isolation, the first oil crisis, industrial restructuring, and Chiang Ching-kuo's consolidation of power. Through enlightened policies aimed at uniting the populace and skillful manipulation of the media, he had transformed his public image to that of a warm and concerned man of the people. Two months after I arrived, Taiwan's democracy movement emerged and became an ineradicable part of the political scene.

I left at a time of despair and returned at a time of constructive ferment. Taiwan's society, economy, culture, and long stagnant political system were embarking on a fundamental, broadly based transition. For some, the pace was too slow; for others, any change was tantamount to inviting a Communist takeover. For a comparative sociologist steeped in cases of development failures, the contrast of Taiwan offered a remarkable laboratory for a longitudinal study to test theories of economic, social, political, and cultural change.

For my dissertation (Gold 1981), done under the guidance of Ezra Vogel, Orlando Patterson, and Theda Skocpol, I applied to Taiwan the *tri-pé* model derived from Peter Evans's (1979) excellent study of Brazil, *Dependent Development*. I looked at the interaction among the state, private capital, and multinational corporations, focusing on three industrial sectors, each of which characterized a different stage of Taiwan's development and incorporation into the international division of labor: textiles, electronics, and petrochemicals. I concluded that the same actors were key in both cases, but that the weights assigned to their roles differed widely between Brazil and Taiwan. This and the nature of the social structure, colonial legacy, state formation, and process of incorporation into the world system resulted in different outcomes. I argued that Evans's generalizations about the inherent consequences of dependent development did not apply to Taiwan or East Asia more broadly.

This book shifts the focus away from testing theories on Taiwan to asking how the Taiwan miracle came about and what is the best approach for explaining it. I use the data collected for the dissertation from archives, official sources, and approximately 150 interviews with government officials, businessmen, multinational corporation managers, scholars, journalists, gadflies, and political figures of all stripes, supplemented by return visits and updated interviews in 1982 and 1984.

Soon after I began to write the dissertation, I was selected as one of the first group of American exchange students to go to the People's Republic of China. I spent a year in Shanghai nominally studying modern Chinese literature. But I had arrived during China's Democracy Movement. Over the year, through hundreds of conversations in Shanghai and throughout the nation with people of all walks of life, I witnessed the profound self-doubt and questioning about thirty years along the socialist road and the aspirations for improved material and social life. I had intended not to discuss Taiwan, but found people on the mainland incredibly interested in what the KMT had wrought there after being chased off the mainland, destined for the garbage heap of history. This experience increased my appreciation of Taiwan's achievements.

In the course of that year, the Communists began publicly to criticize their development strategy. Without saying so, they began to adopt, at a macro level, some of the elements that had sparked Taiwan's rapid growth, especially an increased separation of economy and polity and party-state retrenchment across the board, granting people more scope to *fahui*, or to bring their enormous talents into play. The results, at first in the rural areas, then moving into the cities, were extraordinary. Extended visits in 1982, 1984, and 1985 have confirmed my conviction about the importance of the state-society relationship, especially in the economic realm, as fundamental for effecting development. The change in the Minnan area of southern Fukien province, from where most of the Taiwanese emigrated generations ago, is especially telling; it looks and feels like any Taiwanese backwater twenty years ago. Thirty-five years of socialist transformation are as yesterday when it is past.

Taiwan and mainland China are not directly comparable, but at a macro level, strategies of adjusting state-society relations within the constraints and potentialities of one's factor endowments, including culture and ideology, offer fruitful ground for future research.

As this book goes to print, Taiwan faces perhaps the greatest combined internal-external threat since 1950 to its continued survival as a de facto independent nation, and no one is in clear control. Most domestic discussions of the crisis focus on protectionism, lack of capital for local investors, onerous taxes, a massive banking and corruption scandal, and failure to upgrade the industrial structure as the reasons for the economic slowdown. The real cause of the economic crisis, of course, is political: Chiang Ching-kuo's failing health, his refusal to name a clear successor (or rule out potential candidates), and weak state leadership as the reformist People's Republic of China steps up its pressure for reunification. Although businessmen and society generally complain unceasingly about excessive state interference in their private affairs, whenever trouble brews they immediately look to the state to solve their problems. The vacillation and lack of firm leadership have exacerbated the current crisis and lack of confidence. No individual controls the military, party, and security networks the way the Chiangs have. There appears to be no forceful leader ready to step in and guide the island through this minefield. The present premier is seen as an unimaginative Shanghainese yes-man who speaks even worse Mandarin than the Chiangs, symbolic of his alienation from the populace. The Taiwanese vice-president has no mass base or clear support from the armed forces. The opposition is in disarray. Businessmen are getting their money and families out and refusing to commit the large amounts of capital needed for upgrading in accord with official plans. The PRC guaranteed Hong Kong fifty years of capitalism after reunification in 1997, but Taiwan's future is much less certain and businessmen are not curious enough to stick around to find out what will happen.

Ironically, the success of the PRC's economic reforms along the lines of Taiwan's example poses a greater threat to the island than force of arms. A Communist country with a mixed economy à la KMT-founder Sun Yat-sen's strategy—no matter what the Communists call it—would be tacit acknowledgment of the victory of the Taiwan alternative form of Chinese modernization and thus cut the legs out from under one of the KMT's main arguments against negotiating with the enemy and for justifying its continued monopoly of power over Taiwan. As it is, there is pressure from local businessmen and foreigners to open direct trade and investment across the Taiwan Straits. Clearly, the island faces a difficult transition. Fundamental, immediate restructuring of the two-tiered national-provincial governments, legislative and representative bodies, and leadership is called for.

The KMT has a tradition of undertaking difficult reforms in the face of challenges, and the time is ripe for another one.

In the course of writing the dissertation and this book—which was originally only to be a chapter in the revised thesis—numerous people shared insights and advice. I want to express my gratitude to those colleagues whose criticisms were of such great help: Alasdair Bowie, Fernando H. Cardoso, Cheng Tun-jen, Stephan Haggard, Chalmers Johnson, Guillermo O'Donnell, J. Samuel Valenzuela, Ezra Vogel, Andrew Walder, Tim Washburn, Martin K. Whyte, and Harold Wilensky. Discussions of theoretical and comparative issues with Chen Fu-mei, Cho Soon-Kyoung, Gary Gereffi, Hsin-huang Michael Hsiao, Hagen Koo, Chi Schive. Denis Simon, and Andrew Tanzer were of enormous value. The insights and introductions of K. T. Li, Lin Chien-shan, and Diane Ying were crucial to the project. I benefited from research assistance at the University of California, Berkeley, by Cheng Tun-jen and Lu Shih-hsiang. I assume full responsibility for any errors of interpretation. The manuscript was ably typed by Nadine Zelinski of Berkeley's Institute of International Studies, and the index prepared by Bob Freeland. Douglas Merwin and Anita O'Brien of M. E. Sharpe offered assistance and clarity. The dissertation research was supported by a Harvard Sheldon Traveling Fellowship. I also received assistance over the years from Julian Sobin as well as U. C. Berkeley's Center for Chinese Studies and Committee on Research. Academia Sinica in Taiwan provided facilities and stimulating colleagues. A research trip to Taiwan in 1984 was supported by a fellowship from the Wang Institute of Graduate Studies. My wife, Lucy Harris, has provided many years of encouragement.

Note on Romanization

I have used the Wade-Giles romanization system, for it is still employed, after a fashion, on Taiwan and will make names more easily recognizable.

T. B. G.

Abbreviations

ADL   Arthur D. Little, Incorporated
AID   (United States) Agency for International Development
AIT   American Institute in Taiwan
AWSJ   Asian Wall Street Journal, Hong Kong
CCP   Chinese Communist Party
CEPD   Council for Economic Planning and Development
CIECD   Council for International Economic Cooperation
       and Development
CUSA   Council on U.S. Aid
DFI   Direct foreign investment
ECLA   (United Nations) Economic Commission for Latin America
EPC   Economic Planning Council
EPZ.   Export Processing Zone
ERSO   Electronics Research Service Organization
ESB   Economic Stabilization Board
FCJ   Free China Journal, Taipei
FCW   Free China Weekly, Taipei
FEER   Far Eastern Economic Review, Hong Kong
GATT   General Agreement on Tariffs and Trade
GDCF   Gross Domestic Capital Formation
GDP   Gross Domestic Product
GRC   Government of the Republic of China
HUDD   Housing and Urban Development Department
IDC   Industrial Development Commission
ITRI   Industrial Technology and Research Institute
JCRR   Joint Commission on Rural Reconstruction

KEPZ	Kaohsiung Export Processing Zone
KMT	Kuomintang (Nationalist Party)
LDC	Less developed country
MAAG	Military Assistance Advisory Group
MITI	Ministry of International Trade and Industry (Japan)
MNC	Multinational corporation
MOEA	Ministry of Economic Affairs
NDP	Net Domestic Product
NYT	New York Times
OMA	Orderly Marketing Agreement
PLA	People's Liberation Army
PRC	People's Republic of China
R&D	Research and development
ROC	Republic of China
SRI	Stanford Research Institute
TNC	Transnational corporation
TPB	Taiwan Production Board
TPG	Taiwan Provincial Government
TSDB	Taiwan Statistical Data Book, Taipei
VACRS	Vocational Assistance Commission for Retired Servicemen
WSJ	Wall Street Journal, New York

State
and
Society
in the
TAIWAN
MIRACLE

1

Explaining the Taiwan Miracle

In November 1977, two months after I arrived in Taiwan to do the research for this book, the island experienced its first outbreak of popular antigovernment violence in thirty years. Fed up with the ruling Nationalist party's repeated crude attempts to rig the election for magistrate of T'ao-yuan County, a crowd of 10,000 people attacked the police station in the town of Chung-li, burned a police van, and went on a rampage.

This event was extraordinary for two reasons: one, that in Taiwan, a newly industrializing society noted for its strict authoritarianism and politically apathetic populace, a segment of the people had resorted to such an extreme and risky act to vent its frustration; and two, that a rapidly developing society had been free of social and political upheaval for such a long time.

In retrospect, the Chung-li Incident offers a unique key to understanding both the success and the shortcomings of Taiwan's development strategy wherein a strong authoritarian state guides and participates in rapid economic growth while suppressing the political activities of the social forces it has generated in the process. Chung-li represents the culmination of one historical stage in the interaction of these two strains and the beginning of a new one.

Departing from the standard economistic approach commonly used to explain Taiwan's economic miracle, this book offers a comprehensive sociological analysis, explaining Taiwan's unquestioned success by reference to the internal and external social, political, and economic contexts in which it occurred.

The Statistics on Taiwan's Miracle

The data on Taiwan's developmental experience up to 1982 are voluminous and can be accurately summed up with the government's own maxim, "growth with stability."

On the economic side, where development refers not only to GNP growth rates but also to structural change and deepening of industrialization, table 1 shows that

—GNP growth rates averaged 8.7 percent from 1953 to 1982, with a peak average of 10.8 percent for the years 1963–1972 (TSDB 1983:2). The 1982 value of GNP was twelve times that of 1952 (TSDB 1983:1).

—Industry grew at a spectacular rate, an average annual clip of 13.3 percent from 1953 to 1982 (TSDB 1983:2) to 42 times its 1952 value (TSDB 1983:1).

—The economy underwent a noticeable structural change as the contribution of industry outstripped agriculture and the leading sectors of industry changed as well, from processed food and textiles to electronics, machinery, and petrochemical intermediates. This indicates diversification and deepening of the economy.

—Trade surpluses occurred nearly every year since 1970 (TSDB 1983:184).

—Inflation was conquered, dropping from a murderous 3,000 percent in 1949 to 1.9 percent in the 1960s. Its resurgence has been regulated since the first oil crisis of 1974–75 (Kuo 1983:2).

—Gross Domestic Capital Formation has been financed almost entirely from gross domestic savings since the early 1960s (TSDB 1983:48).

—The gross savings rate has been above 20 percent of GNP every year since 1966 and more than 30 percent in ten of those years up through 1982 (TSDB 1983:49).

—Foreign reserves amounted to US $7 billion in 1980 (Prybyla 1980:75) and $15.7 billion at the end of August 1984 (*FEER*, October 4, 1984:72).

—Debt-service was a remarkably low 4.4 percent of exports in 1978 (World Bank 1980:135).

—The government showed budget surpluses every year from 1964 through 1981 (TSDB 1983:151).

On the social side, where development refers to changes in the occupational structure and per capita income as well as a host of indices denoting improved physical and abstract quality of life, table 1 indicates

—A positive record of equitable income distribution, with GINI coefficients[1] decreasing from .558 in 1953 to .303 in 1980 (Kuo 1983:96–97).

—Employment in the primary sector dropping from 56 percent in 1952 to 18.9 percent in 1982 and employment in manufacturing rising from 12.4 percent to 31.6 percent over the same years (TSDB 1983:16) with a negligible unemployment rate (TSDB 1983:14).

—Nine years of free compulsory education since 1968 and a literacy rate of 89.3 percent in 1979 (Hsi 1981:81).

—Other indicators of improved living standards, such as daily calorie supply of 2,805 per capita or 120 percent of requirement (World Bank 1980:153); infant mortality rate of 10.9 per thousand (HUDD 1981:57); life expectancy of seventy-two years (World Bank 1980:111); per capita income of US $1,229 in 1981 (HUDD 1981:7); 13.16 telephones per 100 people (HUDD 1981:51); and 212.3 television sets per 1,000 people (HUDD 1981:6).

—Domestic social and political tranquility from 1947 to the Chung-li Incident of 1977, including a smooth leadership transition after the death of long-time leader Chiang Kai-shek in 1975.

This is a remarkable record by any absolute or relative standard. The combination of economic and social development out of a morass of chaos and despair, compounded by one of the world's highest population densities—512.6 persons per square kilometer in 1982 (TSDB 1983:5), a crushing defense burden, and a dearth of natural resources (most notably, oil), justifies calling Taiwan's accomplishments a miracle. Table 2 illustrates Taiwan's accomplishments from a comparative perspective.

Answered and Unanswered Questions

How do we explain Taiwan's miraculous growth with stability? There are two questions to address: First, how did Taiwan attain and sustain such high *economic growth rates*? Second, how did Taiwan maintain *political and social stability* in the course of its economic takeoff?

Table 1

Indicators of Taiwan's Economy 1953–1982
Unit: % of growth

Year	(a) Population	(b) Real GNP	(c) GNP per capita	(d) Agricultural production	(e) Industrial production	(f) Consumer prices	(g) Exports	(h) Imports	(i) Per capita income at current prices
1953	3.8	9.3	5.8	9.4	24.8	18.8	35.1	8.7	29.2
1954	3.7	9.6	5.8	2.2	5.8	1.7	−26.9	20.0	5.5
1955	3.8	8.1	4.1	0.5	13.3	9.9	32.1	−4.8	14.6
1956	3.4	5.5	1.8	7.7	3.4	10.5	52.9	52.6	10.3
1957	3.2	7.3	4.0	7.1	13.0	7.5	25.4	9.6	12.4
1958	3.6	6.6	3.2	6.7	8.6	1.3	5.1	6.6	8.1
1959	3.9	7.7	4.3	1.8	11.7	10.6	47.8	50.2	11.2
1960	3.5	6.5	3.1	1.3	14.1	18.5	4.5	28.2	17.0
1961	3.3	6.8	3.5	8.9	15.5	7.8	30.9	19.4	8.8
1962	3.3	7.8	4.7	2.6	8.0	2.4	11.8	−5.6	6.9
1963	3.2	9.4	6.2	0.2	9.2	2.2	52.1	19.0	9.9
1964	3.1	12.3	9.1	12.0	21.1	−0.2	30.7	18.5	13.6
1965	3.0	11.0	8.0	6.5	16.3	−0.1	3.6	29.9	7.2
1966	2.9	9.0	6.1	3.3	15.6	2.0	19.3	11.9	9.1
1967	2.3	10.6	7.8	6.3	16.7	3.4	19.5	29.5	12.5
1968	2.7	9.1	6.5	6.8	22.3	7.9	23.2	12.1	13.6
1969	5.0	9.0	6.6	−1.9	19.9	5.1	33.0	34.3	13.1
1970	2.4	11.3	9.0	5.4	20.1	3.6	41.2	25.7	12.6
1971	2.2	12.9	10.6	0.5	23.6	2.8	39.1	21.0	13.8
1972	2.0	13.3	11.2	2.2	21.2	3.0	45.0	36.3	17.5
1973	1.8	12.8	10.7	2.7	16.2	8.2	42.8	43.9	27.3
1974	1.8	1.1	−0.7	1.9	−4.5	47.5	25.2	82.9	31.9
1975	1.9	4.2	2.3	−1.2	8.5	5.2	−5.7	−14.7	4.3
1976	2.2	13.5	11.2	10.0	24.4	2.5	53.8	27.7	16.9
1977	1.8	9.9	7.7	4.0	13.6	7.0	14.6	12.0	13.8
1978	1.9	13.9	11.8	−1.8	23.8	5.8	31.9	26.1	16.8
1979	2.0	8.1	6.0	5.3	8.0	9.8	23.6	30.5	18.1
1980	1.9	6.6	4.6	−1.0	9.3	19.0	22.9	33.5	22.0
1981	1.9	5.0	3.1	−0.6	4.0	16.3	16.5	9.4	14.8
1982	1.8	3.8	2.0	1.3	−1.7	4.0	4.2	−5.5	5.4[1]

Source: Columns a-h, TSDB (1983:2); column i, TSDB (1983:29).
Note: 1. Estimate.

Table 2 Taiwan in Comparative Perspective

Country or region	(1) Population (millions) 1978	(2) GNP per capita 1978:$	(3) GNP per capita avg. annual growth 1969–78:%	(4) GDP growth rate % 1960–70	(4) 1970–78	(5) Distribution of GDP (%) Agriculture 1960	Agriculture 1978	Industry 1960	Industry 1978	(Manufacturing)b 1960	1978	(10) Life expectancy at birth (years) 1978
Taiwan	17.1	1,400	6.6	9.2	8.0	28	10	29	48	22	38	72
South Korea	36.6	1,160	6.9	8.5	9.7	40	24	19	36	12	24	63
Singapore	2.3	3,290	7.4	8.8	8.5	4	2c	18	35	12	26	70
Hong Kong	4.6	3,040	6.5	10.0	8.2a	4	2c	34	31c	25	25c	72
Brazil	119.5	1,570	4.9	5.3	9.2	16	11	35	37	26	28	62
Argentina	26.4	1,910	2.6	4.2	2.3	17	13c	38	45c	31	37c	71
Chile	10.7	1,410	1.0	4.5	0.8	11	10c	38	29c	23	20c	67
Mexico	65.4	1,290	2.7	7.2	5.0	16	11	29	37c	23	28	65

Country or region	(6) Value of manufactured exports ($millions) 1963	1977	(7) Average annual rate of inflation 1960–70	1970–78	(8) Debt service as % of GNP 1970	1978	Exports 1970	1978	(9) Adult literacy rate 1975:%
Taiwan	129	7,925	4.1	10.3	1.4	2.6	4.5	4.4	82d
South Korea	39	8,480	17.5	19.3	3.1	3.9	19.4	10.5	93
Singapore	352	3,626	1.1	6.1	0.6	4.0	0.6	2.3	75d
Hong Kong	617	7,267	2.3	7.7	(.)	0.7	—	—	90
Brazil	45	3,141	46.1	30.3	0.9	2.2	13.5	28.4	76d
Argentina	79	1,349	21.8	120.4	1.9	3.5	21.5	26.8	94
Chile	22	145	32.9	242.6	3.1	7.3	18.9	38.2	88
Mexico	147	1,182	3.5	17.5	2.1	6.9	23.6	59.6	76

Source: World Bank 1980: Columns 1, 2, 3, 7, 9, 10:111, Column 4:113, Column 5:115, Column 6:133, Column 8:135.

Notes: a: for 1970–77, b: manufacturing is part of the industrial sectors, c: for 1977, d: for years other than 1975.

Most scholars both on Taiwan and abroad address the first question.[2] Some are seemingly most interested in reducing Taiwan's developmental experience to mathematical equations; others explain it primarily as a case of getting the relationship between domestic and international prices right; and a few point out that the state is an active participant in the economy, not merely a maker of policies and externalities. The explanation offered by economists can be summarized as follows.

Fifty years of colonial occupation by the developmentalist Japanese left a legacy of very productive if skewed agriculture, an island-wide infrastructure of roads, power, communications, etc., and investment in human resources. The infrastructure and small modern industrial sector were virtually wiped out by American bombing in the last years of the Pacific War. When the Japanese suddenly departed in 1945, and especially as the Communists took over the Chinese mainland, talented and dedicated Western-oriented Chinese officials, technocrats and businessmen from the mainland, filled the leadership vacuum that the native Taiwanese, always treated as a second-class race by the Japanese, were unqualified to fill. The mainland emigré elite, motivated by the official ideology of the Three Principles of the People, rapidly revived production to prewar peaks while stabilizing the political situation. At a critical juncture, American military and civilian aid provided a buffer to help control inflation; rebuild the economy; supply needed commodities, raw materials, and foreign exchange; and generally boost the confidence of the government and people. The Nationalist Chinese government is committed to development and social welfare, but it favors free-market principles. It practices fiscal conservancy to balance the budget and prevent renewed inflation. It led the Land Reform, did not neglect agriculture, protected infant industries when necessary but then wisely took the difficult step of reorienting the economy to exports via trade liberalization, price reforms, and other incentives. It created a good business climate for local and foreign investors. Taiwan's prime resource has been an abundant supply of cheap and disciplined labor, and the private sector and foreign corporations invested in labor-intensive rather than showcase capital-intensive industry, which helped to absorb labor and distribute income more equitably. Labor and other factor productivity grew rapidly. Taiwan used its comparative advantage in labor to compete successfully in world markets, and exports became the leading engine of growth. The people are by nature thrifty, hard-working, disciplined, and ambitious, and they place a high value on education.

This explanation covers the economic bases and goes a step beyond conventional neoclassical economic explanations by bringing the state in as an indispensable actor. It also leaves many unanswered but key questions, however, most of which relate to pinning down the reasons why Taiwan was so stable during this rapid economic takeoff. From what source, for example, did the Nationalist state derive its effective power? Why has it succeeded in bringing about development when other authoritarian states have failed and its own experience on the mainland was such a disaster? Has liberalization meant an end to state participation? How has it maintained social and political stability? What limits are there to the Nationalist state's power?

In addition, what effect did Taiwan's social structure have on development and vice versa? Why were workers, peasants, landlords, intellectuals, and the middle class so quiescent and cooperative? Have different social groups benefited disproportionately from Taiwan's type of economic growth strategy? As the social structure changes, what effect are new social forces having on the direction of economic growth and continued stability? Why has there been an upsurge in political movements for democracy since 1971, and especially since 1977?

What role have global political and economic structures played in Taiwan's development? Why did transnational corporations (TNC) invest in Taiwan and what was their impact on the economy and society beyond an infusion of capital and transfer of technology? Do TNCs from different countries behave differently and have different impacts?

In sum, although it goes beyond pure economistic explanations and brings in the role of the government, the standard economic approach does not delve further and ask how the structures and institutions that contributed to and shaped Taiwan's growth were formed, maintained, and have evolved.

At the opposite extreme from the economists, there are a small number of scholars who analyze Taiwan from a dependency or world-systems perspective.[3] As a rule, they start from outside Taiwan and situate it in global economic and political structures, first the Japanese empire, then the American-dominated modern world capitalist system. They attribute almost everything that has happened in Taiwan to external actors, denigrating the role of the Nationalist state and Taiwan's people beyond serving and responding to foreign masters. Taiwan would be nothing without Japanese imperialism, the U.S. Army, Agency for International Development, transnational corporations, international banks, and so on, the argument runs. Capital, technology, and demand are all externally derived. In this view, the state in Taiwan is a tool of foreign corporations, repressing its people, especially the proletariat, in the service of superexploitative global capital. Local entrepreneurs are compradors who sell out to their foreign masters.

These writers start with a preconceived model that they try to make Taiwan fit into. When it doesn't, they either reinterpret the facts to show that "so-called" development and equity are not really development and equity, or that Taiwan is an exception to all laws because of special circumstances. While they add a corrective to the narrow endogenous explanatory schema of the economists, drawing attention to social structure and exposing many of the costs of Taiwan's development path, their unwillingness to seek truth from facts, their use of rigid categories, and their undisguised antipathy seriously limit the usefulness and credibility of their argument.[4]

Fewer scholars have looked into the reasons for Taiwan's stability. The most common explanations focus on the declaration of martial law and the pervasive and multiform internal security system.[5] In some cases, the stability is linked with the need to provide a stable investment environment for TNCs, but it is always tied to the Nationalist party's overriding concern with preserving its power. The system is seen as frozen and inflexible from top to bottom. Other writers admit the authoritarian nature of the regime, but see the cause as much less sinister.[6] Their approach to the matter of stability emphasizes Taiwan's relatively equitable income distribution and mobility as defusing social tensions. For them, repression was necessary in the first instance to prevent communist subversion and mass revolt; the external threat is still quite real, so one-party rule and internal spying perform necessary functions. They see this not, however, as something inherent in the system, but as a stage already passing on the route to constitutional democracy. They accentuate the increased importance of electoral politics, emergence of an opposition, and recent democratization as proof. For them, the repressive apparatus performed a valuable function for stabilizing the society and helping to legitimize the regime, but current stability derives from shared interest among all social forces in preserving what they have built together, and from value consensus, especially anticommunism.

These analyses contain many valid points, but again they do not go far enough in exploring the connections among the repressive aspects, the social structure, economic growth, and external forces. Taiwan is hardly the only society under martial law—why has it been so effective and long lasting there and not elsewhere? Are workers quiescent purely because of repression or because of an improving standard of living? Is the state the willing tool of TNCs? Why did intellectuals remain out of politics for so many years?

A Comprehensive Approach

The questions I have raised are important in obtaining a deeper understanding of how Taiwan brought about spectacular growth with remarkable stability and in assessing the possibility of its serving as a model for other developing societies. It is clear that no single factor can be held up as the explanatory variable. On close examination, one sees that Taiwan's success was a product of the interaction of a number of forces—economic, political, and social; endogenous and exogenous; constructive and destructive; fortuitous and planned; ideological and pragmatic. No book or article has attempted to link all of these together in a comprehensive way; each offers unassailable truths but only partial explanations.

A further shortcoming is that the emotional and political nature of many studies of Taiwan, and indeed the entire discourse about the place—pro–Nationalist party, anti–Nationalist party, pro-reunification, pro-independence (left, right, nonaligned)—forces readers to take them with so many grains of salt as to render them nearly indigestible.

This book approaches the question of Taiwan's development from a different perspective. Inspired by Fernando Cardoso and Enzo Faletto's influential study, *Dependency and Development in Latin America*, I propose to offer what they call a "comprehensive analysis of development."

When formulating their "comprehensive approach" in the original Spanish version of the book in the mid-1960s, Cardoso and Faletto were reacting to both the American modernization models and the United Nations Economic Commission for Latin America (ECLA) critiques of those models as explanations for the failure of Latin American nations to develop. The "modernization" perspective posits two polar ideal types of societies, "traditional" and "modern."[7] In the vocabulary of Talcott Parsons' pattern variables, traditional societies have social organizations and value systems that are ascriptive, particularistic, diffuse, and affective, while modern societies are based on achievement-oriented, universalistic, specific, and affective-neutral qualities.[8] The components that make up modern societies derive from an abstracted description of what the authors conceived the United States and other Western societies to be. Underdeveloped societies are backward because they are traditional. This is a naturally occurring situation. By eliminating these traditional individual and structural traits (with the help of rational values, institutions, and technologies diffused from abroad), they can embark on a path that will replicate the experience of the West, and in the end they too will become modern. Scholars formulated stages through which all backward societies would pass on the journey to modernity, and they ranked nations by how far they had come according to their own particular set of criteria. Openness to Western economic and cultural forces has a positive, stimulative effect on this process. Explanations for China's failure to modernize, especially compared to Japan, commonly adopt this perspective.[9]

The ECLA economists criticized this approach as well as the prescription to base their economies on their comparative advantage in particular raw materials. They asserted that development efforts in their region were failing not because of indigenous tradition and lack of contact with the developed countries, but because of unequal terms of trade with those same countries. As a remedy, they prescribed diversification of trade and import substitution policies to establish indigenous industries. Forever relying on static comparative advantage in raw materials would achieve nothing.

But to Cardoso and Faletto (1979:viii), the ECLA critique did not go far enough, as it was "not based on an analysis of social process, did not call attention to imperialist relationships among countries, and did not take into account other asymmetric relations between classes." A variety of Latin American and other writers did explore these avenues beginning in the 1960s. They shifted the ground of inquiry from the individual nation-state per se to its links with global economic and political forces, arguing that no country's economy could be understood in isolation; hence the focus on the historical development of relations between the center or core of the world and the periphery, and how this unequal relationship, not traditional values, caused underdevelopment in the latter. In general, these authors saw this as a one-sided relationship, with core countries benefiting at the expense of the periphery. The dynamism in the system comes from the needs of the core; economic activity and the social and political changes in the periphery depend on stimuli from outside their own societies. From this fact comes the central concept of "dependency," which in the first instance describes an economic relationship:

> By dependency we mean a situation in which the economy of certain countries is conditioned by the development and expansion of another economy to which the former is subjected. The relation of interdependence between two or more economies, and between these and world trade, assumes the form of dependence when some countries (the dominant ones) can expand and be self-sustaining, while some countries (the dependent ones) can do this only as a reflection of that expansion, which can have either a positive or a negative effect on their immediate development. (Dos Santos 1970:231)

This is definitely not the same as dependence on raw materials or trade or interdependence in the modern world, with which it is often confused. It is a holistic concept including economic, political, social, and cultural dimensions that cannot be considered apart from the others.[10]

Although frequently unrecognized, there is a distinct diversity among writers who place the concept of dependency at the center of their analysis of development or underdevelopment.[11] I would draw attention to two important strains.

First is the group associated with Andre Gunder Frank which has become very influential in the United States. Intentionally combative, it is the source of what most Americans interested in the subject conceive of when they hear the term "dependency" or "dependency theory."[12] Frank attempts to construct a "theory of Latin American underdevelopment" (Palma 1978:898): economic dependency causes underdevelopment and renders capitalist development in the periphery impossible. The openness to capitalist economic and cultural forces from the core has not brought about development as the modernizationists predicted, but rather, exploitation and underdevelopment. The failure to develop is not due to originally extant "traditional" structures and culture but to the unequal, exploitative nature of the relationship between core and periphery. The core needs the periphery to maintain its status. In Frank's view, the only way to overthrow dependency and achieve genuine development is through socialist revolution and self-reliance.

Built upon Frank's work is the world-systems school originated by Immanuel Wallerstein.[13] Shifting the ground of inquiry even farther away from individual nations and their particular social formations, this school studies the historical emergence of one capitalist world system, "a unit with a single division of labor and multiple cultural systems" (Wallerstein 1974:390). Wallerstein's interest in individual units is limited to showing how they became incorporated into this system and the subsequent effect upon their social, political, and economic systems. Several scholars have attempted to use mathematical models to describe this process and to measure "degrees of dependency."[14]

Though it is an economic determinist paradigm like Frank's, Wallerstein's approach uses a less static zero-sum model. He posits a tiny, select third category of countries, "the semi-periphery," sandwiched between the core and periphery. Its members play a strategic role in preventing all-out conflict between the two poles. There are three strategies by which peripheral nations can attempt to achieve semi-peripheral status: aggressive state action when global and domestic opportunities exist; invitation from multinational corporations; and self-reliance (Wallerstein 1979:76–81).

Writers of the above schools, mostly concerned with explaining the global expansion of capitalism, one-sidedly focus on external reliance and assume that patterns of domestic economic and political structures are a byproduct of this reliance. The handful of works about Taiwan in this vein[15] make the same error: because the island relies on trade and investment, its political leaders, allied with big business, must exploit workers and peasants. Taiwan is in the semi-periphery because the U.S. government and American and Japanese TNCs invited it in to exploit its cheap labor.

Cardoso also employs the concept of dependency, but as a "methodology for the analysis of concrete situations of underdevelopment" (Palma 1978:881), not as a "theory" with testable propositions and predictions.[16] In his definition, "from the economic point of view a system is dependent when the accumulation and expansion of capital cannot find its essential dynamic component inside the system" (Cardoso and Faletto 1979:xx). But to explain this situation of dependency and the possible directions toward which it might evolve requires examining not only economic variables (primarily externally derived ones such as trade, investment, and technology), but, more important, the internal social and political relations enforcing the economic structure and offering potential transformation of it—"an interpretation emphasizing the political character of the process of economic transformation" (Cardoso and Faletto 1979:172).

Rather than starting from the assumption of a mechanical, unidirectional causal relationship between external forces and internal structures, Cardoso examines how the relationship between the two is expressed in the social structure of the underdeveloped country. Further, this is not a static or fixed structure, but a relationship with potential for change. Because Cardoso examines internal and external forces in dynamic interaction, he can explain those few cases where the outcome leads to development—what he calls "associated-dependent development" (Cardoso 1973)—as well as the more frequent cases of continued failure to develop.

Peter Evans (1979) successfully employed this methodology in his case study of Brazil. He described the emergence of an elite triple alliance ("*tri-pé*") of the state, multinational corporations (MNCs), and local capital over time, its different interactions in various industrial sectors (textiles, pharmaceuticals, and petrochemicals), and the consequences for national integration.[17] This form of dependent development results in certain adverse consequences. There are several forms of disarticulation: 1) MNCs use capital-intensive technology, inappropriate for the social structure, which exacerbates unemployment problems; 2) there is a lack of linkages between MNCs and local firms; 3) there are trade imbalances and foreign debt; and 4) people develop a taste for consumption goods from the core, which harms local industry. The other main genre of grim aftereffects is exclusion: worsening income distribution as the masses are excluded from the fruits of their labor, and demobilization of the masses from political participation and installation of repressive military regimes.

Cardoso and Faletto call their methodology "historical-structural" because, by focusing on historical "moments of significant structural change" (1979:xiv), they can determine how economic relationships and the social structure that underlies them arise as a result of human activity, and how they can be transformed through social action. Rejecting the notion, fundamental to many dependency theorists, that once in place these structures are stable and permanent, capable only of "generating more underdevelopment and dependency" (1979:x), they look at specific situations of dependency and assert that the structures themselves generate possibilities for transformation. Cardoso and Faletto do not predict necessary outcomes; they analyze facts and suggest possible alternative lines of development. Their analysis is comprehensive because it examines the continuous interaction among economic, social, political, and ideological variables, at both societal and international levels. This contrasts with much of American social science, which is split into narrow disciplines that pay scant attention to the insights or methods of the others (also a shortcoming of the economistic studies cited above).

I began this chapter by demonstrating how much Taiwan's economy and society have developed and, after finding fault with past explanations for this, now write approvingly of a method of analysis originally formulated to explain the shortcomings of such development in Latin America. This leads logically to two very fair challenges: Is this method even applicable to the Taiwan case? And how is it an improvement over previous explanations?

Although initially derived from studies of the Latin American experience, the historical-structural method can be disengaged from that region and used as an approach to analyze development or underdevelopment elsewhere. The historical-structural method starts by analyzing a situation of dependency but does not thereby rule out the possibility of development. Taiwan's starting place was in most ways very similar to that of the Latin American countries whose experiences formed the empirical foundation for the dependency school. Taiwan went through a classic dependence or colonial phase, when a foreign power skewed the economic structure, as well as the social and political systems, to the needs of the metropole. Integration into the global economy was done by foreign actors, not an indigenous group.

Taiwan then entered a stage during which its capitalist economy had to rely on external factors for capital, capital goods, technology, and trade in order to expand. It depended almost exclusively on the United States for these, and this relationship brought about certain domestic social and political adjustments.[18] The domestic economy lacked natural resources, foreign exchange, and capital; could not produce most of its own inputs; and was poorly integrated. The autonomous state played the role dominant classes played in Latin America. When foreign investors began to arrive, they established industries in enclaves without domestic links, thereby tying segments of the economy and work force into global structures divorced from the local scene.

Yet well before the mid-1980s, things had changed dramatically. Capital for investment was primarily from domestic savings, and the state's coffers were flush with foreign reserves. While the island relied heavily on imported capital goods and technology, these were for a higher stage of industrial production, and Taiwan was exporting its own capital goods, technology, and whole plants to less developed countries. Taiwan-based transnational corporations were making direct foreign investments in the United States, Europe, and the Third World. Trade was still concentrated on two countries, the United States and Japan, but markets and sources for the trade-dependent economy had been diversified. The domestic production structure, including foreign-owned enterprises, had become increasingly integrated vertically and horizontally. The social dislocations commonly associated with dependency, such as an impoverished rural sector and glaring inequality, had been largely eliminated. New social forces had emerged and the state's relations with society as well as its own makeup had changed considerably.

The Cardoso and Faletto method is applicable precisely because, taking all relevant factors into consideration, it can address the question of how it was that Taiwan's specific situation of dependency yielded development, not underdevelopment. It is an improvement over previous economistic or dependency explanations because it is intentionally designed to ferret out all of the factors that were clearly involved in effecting this transformation, many of which are overlooked in other methodologies. It can incorporate and link the findings of economists, historians, anthropologists, political scientists, and sociologists, locate them in a global context, and answer critical questions that narrower approaches ignore. One does not plug data into preassembled boxes, but uses them as a guide to ask certain types of questions. While Cardoso and Faletto note this method's Marxist origins, it is neither dogmatic nor a call to arms, and, in fact, it owes more to Max Weber than to Karl Marx—facts upsetting to more committed colleagues.[19]

This book uses the Cardoso and Faletto methodology in the following way. I break Taiwan's history down into periods distinguished by major transformations of economic structure: from a self-strengthening Chinese society to a Japanese colony; a chaotic interregnum as a new structure emerged; then import substitution, export orientation, and export-oriented import substitution, all under Chinese Nationalist leadership. Each chapter examines the international context, domestic economic and social structure, form of political domination and integration, and linkages among them. I explain the evolution of these structures, the origin of development strategies, and then reasons for their transformation. I argue, in the final chapter, that the Chung-li Incident signalled the start of a new era when the state will be much more accountable and vulnerable to society if Taiwan is to survive economically and politically as a de facto independent nation.

A Note on Terminology

Because of the centrality of the concepts of "state" and "society" in this book, I should make clear how I use these and other terms.

I adopt Marx and Engels' (1970:57) definition of civil society as "embrac[ing] the whole material intercourse of individuals within a definite stage of the development of productive forces. It embraces the whole commercial and industrial life of a given stage." This book begins when Taiwan's social formation was precapitalist, that is, prior to the emergence of a capitalist class or bourgeoisie that privately owned the means of production and a working class or proletariat that sold its labor power to the capitalists. One objective of this study is to describe the unique way in which these classes took shape and to explain how that influenced social and political change.

I adopt Skocpol's (1979:29) definition of the state as "a set of administrative, policing and military organizations headed, and more or less well coordinated by, an executive authority" that controls a specific territory. In a class society, the state "at the highest level of abstraction . . . refers to the basic alliance, the basic 'pact of domination,' that exists among social classes or fractions of dominant classes and the norms which guarantee their dominance over the subordinate strata" (Cardoso 1979:38). It is thus more than what we mean by "government"—particular incumbents of organizations who exercise authority—as it includes the social context in which it operates.

In a society divided by classes, the state by its actions and policies inevitably serves the interests of particular classes or class fractions. But I reject the simplistic notion of the state as the instrument by which one class dominates another; some policies work against the interests of classes that other policies favored. While social groups may try to penetrate and control it, I agree with Skocpol (1979:29) that "the state properly conceived is no mere arena in which socioeconomic struggles are fought out." That is, the state, as a set of organizations, has its own interests beyond those of particular social forces and, in the first instance, looks after its own preservation. To the extent that it can preserve itself and implement policies that in the short run might harm the interests of particular social groups, even the most powerful ones, it enjoys relative autonomy from constraints imposed by various domestic or foreign forces. In some cases, a tightly organized, well-disciplined political party representing a class or several classes (fractions) may create and dominate the state.

In the developing world, states commonly emerge through a struggle for independence. The state structure that is established, and the background and loyalties of the cadres who populate it, reflect the relative power of various social forces (peasants, workers, capitalists, military, landlords, minority ethnic or religious groups, foreigners). The new state has a more or less aboveboard agenda for the political system, economy, society, defense, culture, and international relations. This may be elaborated in an official ideology. Priority goes to the state's ability to extract resources in order to consolidate power and preserve itself domestically and internationally, and also to the maintenance of order and economic production. In implementing the agenda the state faces a plethora of constraints: opposition from social groups; conflicts within and between state organizations; struggles between professional bureaucrats and politicians; lack of state cadres or civilians with requisite talent or training for the tasks at hand; lack of domestic or foreign sources of resources, capital, and technology; obstructionist expatriate foreigners or their domestic representatives; external enemies; external allies offering assistance but with onerous strings that force a compromise of plans.

Relations between the state and society range between extremes: from a state that is little more than a puppet of powerful domestic or foreign forces to a cohesive state with complete autonomy from domestic or foreign interests. Coercive, administrative, and extractive state organizations attempt to assert and maintain state power over society or, at least, subordinate strata. Their actions may be carried out by formal groups, such as the judicial and police systems, legislative bodies, economic planning agencies, and tax authorities, or by informal ones, such as secret security and internal spy networks, extortionists, red-tape bureaucracies, and patron-client ties. Which bodies are most active varies among types of systems and cultural proclivities.

In some systems, social forces have freedom to organize to press their interests against the state. They may organize political parties, put up candidates for elections, lobby powerholders, influence official appointments, or mount propaganda campaigns. In other systems, social forces enjoy no such rights. The state prevents free association, speech, lobbying, publishing, etc. and either atomizes individuals or strictly regulates social intercourse, appointing its own trusted individuals to head social groupings, or infiltrating them with secret agents. In such systems, it becomes very difficult for society to constrain state actions. It can try to resist violently, passively, or by emigrating, or it can accept the reality of the situation and make the best of things for the time being. This may result in sullen acquiescence or, if the structure permits, eschewing political activities for other approved endeavors.

In this book, we confront a unique case where a fully elaborated state, controlled by a Leninist party, imposed itself over a society in which it had no power base. In the extended process of political consolidation and economic growth, state-society relations assumed a shape that facilitated explosive development of productive forces and rapid social change but political stagnation, until pressures from society and within the state itself, in concert with a changing international environment, stimulated political democratization.

2

Taiwan
Prior
to
Japanese
Colonization

In the early 1970s when I was teaching at Tunghai University, I prided myself on knowing every back alley in nearby Taichung, a city of some 500,000 people. But in 1982, alighting from the Taipei-to-Taichung bus, I had no idea where I was. In the old days, the sleek, air-condition-ed Golden Dragon Express would let me off after a four-hour ride at the front gate of the university, conveniently located on the two-lane main thoroughfare. Or I would go on to the Taichung Highway Bus Station and take the Provincial Highway Bureau bus up the seemingly endless hill to Tunghai.

But this 1982 bus—a private "wild chicken" vehicle put on to handle the weekend traffic—had let me off somewhere else, far from the shops and markets I had haunted. Everything about the two-plus-hour drive had been unfamiliar. The bus had sped down the new Sun Yat-sen Expressway—which looks like Route 101 in California—pass-ing no recognizable landmarks except for the exit to the new Taipei International Airport, which isn't even in Taipei anymore, but in T'ao-yuan.

In Taichung, after several false starts I sighted a familiar landmark—the Highway Bus Station. Along with the train station and the parade ground it was undergoing a total facelift. I was late for my luncheon date with a professor at Tunghai, so instead of taking the city bus

(Tunghai is now just another local stop on the municipal line) I decided to splurge and go by taxi.

Taxis are still driven with abandon, but now, instead of a white-knuckled ride in a broken-down Yue Loong, dodging bicycles, Vespas, taxis, buses, and water buffaloes on the winding climb, I was trapped in a bordello-on-wheels: plush red plastic interior, blinking seductive lights, Teng Li-chün crooning on the stereo tape deck, and a Cantonese hack beating out all the privately owned Ford Cortinas and BMWs at seventy miles per hour on the Taichung Harbor Road—another express-way and now the main route out to Tunghai. What was once an expanse of rice paddies and distinctive farmhouses is now a sea of apartment complexes and industrial parks. Taichung Valley is awash in smog. Tunghai's main gate has been pushed back to make room for the six-lane highway and you must take a subterranean tunnel to cross the road. But what is there to cross for? The familiar row of noodle stands and snooker parlors has vanished. Lao Wang is closing up and A-fen moved her sundry shop and shaved-ice emporium up to the trendy Tunghai Villa above campus, where undergraduates enjoy the benefits of un-chaperoned coed living.

I will not go into how much the campus has changed. At least the magnificent I. M. Pei–designed chapel remains, still soaring heaven-ward.

If I could get lost in Taichung and feel like a stranger at Tunghai, things had changed in some very fundamental ways. And they had changed very quickly. But while much of Taiwan, surface and sub-stance, has changed dramatically, many essential features have not. "Taiwan" refers to one major island and several smaller offshore islands (the largest of which are the Pescadores) located approximately 100 miles across the Taiwan Straits from the southeastern coastal Chi-nese provinces of Fukien (Fujian) and Kwangtung (Guangdong). The Tropic of Cancer cuts across its southern portion. Total land mass of 13,840 square miles makes it the size of the Netherlands.

Nearly two-thirds of the island is mountainous, providing spectacu-lar scenery but severely limiting the amount of arable land. The popula-tion is thus concentrated on the west coast, where the largest expanse of flatland lies. About one-fourth of the land is cultivable. Although the land's natural fertility has been depleted after several hundred years of intensive use, Taiwan's semitropical climate and generally abundant rainfall permit multiple cropping throughout the year on chemically fertilized soil.

Taiwan is also poor in natural resources, especially petroleum, although it does have moderate deposits of coal and natural gas. There are extensive forests and some other mineral deposits.

Taiwan's Incorporation by China

Because Taiwan is an island, its original settlers had to have made a concerted effort at no small risk to venture there. Lying off the China coast in the middle of what would become major shipping lanes, it was perhaps inevitable that Taiwan would have some sort of economic and strategic relationship with China. As international maritime activity developed, traders and warships naturally called there.

But the original settlers of Taiwan were not Han Chinese. They were a diverse collection of Malayo-Polynesian people now referred to generally as aborigines. They engaged in horticulture, hunting, and gathering, inhabiting both the lowlands and mountainous regions of the island. Many were headhunters.[1]

The first Han Chinese to stop in Taiwan were traders and pirates—the same thing, in effect, as a maritime ban in the sixteenth century made all overseas trade tantamount to smuggling. Most of those reaching Taiwan were from the vibrant and cosmopolitan ports of Ch'üanchou and Chang-chou in Fukien, links in the Japan-Southeast Asia trade route. They used Taiwan for rest and recreation.

When the Ming government replaced the maritime ban with a system of licensing trading ships in 1567, Chinese merchants bartered jewelry and cloth with the aborigines for coveted deer products. A small Chinese colony to service the trade was established by 1600. Around this time, non-Chinese began arriving in the waters off Taiwan as well. Portuguese sailing by called it "Ilha Formosa" (Beautiful Island). Japanese forays were terminated in 1653 by that country's national isolation policy, which lasted two hundred years.

The Dutch East India Company, headquartered in Batavia (present-day Jakarta), established a base named Fort Orange in 1624 near the site of today's Tainan. The Dutch occupation of Taiwan was part of Holland's expanding global mercantile activities. The Fort Orange settlement (later called Zeelandia) provided a jumping off point for trade with China and Japan and served as a base to compete in commerce, war, and missionary work with the rival Spanish and Portuguese. Reacting to the Dutch challenge, the Spanish sent an expeditionary force from their base in the Philippines to establish small settlements in northern Taiwan beginning in 1626. The Dutch drove them out in 1642, and they had little effect on Taiwan's subsequent history.

The Dutch exported Taiwan's deerskins and sugar and transshipped goods between China, Japan, Batavia, and Europe. Because half of the Dutch residents were soldiers, the authorities aggressively recruited mainland Chinese, mostly males, to come as traders, farmers, and general laborers. The Dutch offered them incentives such as oxen and cash and provided funds, seeds, tools, irrigation works, and protection from aborigines (Hsu 1980a:18). Many of the peasants came only for the growing season and then went back to the mainland. The Chinese population, concentrated in the Tainan area, reached approximately 50,000 by 1662, the end of the Dutch era (Hsu 1980a:17).

Although they successfully stimulated economic activity, the Dutch also taxed it heavily. This exacerbated resentment at general exploitation and spawned a Chinese rebellion in 1652, which the Dutch crushed ruthlessly with aborigine assistance.

Throughout this period, Taiwan remained marginal to the larger drama of Chinese history, and the Imperial Court made no effort to lay claim to the island. This situation changed radically, however, in the middle of the seventeenth century when the Ming dynasty collapsed in the face of widespread peasant rebellions and the expansion of non-Han Manchus into China proper from the Northeast. A leading Ming loyalist, Cheng Ch'eng-kung, son of a Japanese mother and a famous Fukienese pirate who had surrendered in 1628 and helped crush other pirates, resisted the Manchu advance into South China. After suffering defeat at the Ming capital, Nanking, he retreated to Amoy (Xiamen) in 1660 and decided to establish a base across the Straits on Taiwan. His fleet landed on the island in 1661 and he expelled the Dutch early in 1662. This feat earned him a hallowed spot as a model Chinese nationalist.[2] His use of Taiwan as a base from which to launch an attack to recover the mainland made him an invaluable symbol for the Chinese Nationalists three centuries later.

Cheng Ch'eng-kung died soon after taking Taiwan and was succeeded by his son, Cheng Ching. The Cheng period saw the implantation of Chinese-style administration on Taiwan. The Zeelandia site (renamed An-p'ing) became the capital. Taiwan was divided into one prefecture and two districts. The Chengs appointed officials and established education and civil service systems to train and recruit new bureaucrats. But their rule was generally quite harsh, relying on what amounted to martial law and levying heavy taxes on the populace.

The Cheng authorities exerted great efforts to develop the island's economy. In spite of Manchu policies prohibiting emigration and moving Fukienese away from the coast to prevent them from supporting the renegade Chengs, large numbers of Chinese moved to Taiwan. By the end of the Cheng period (1683), there were an estimated 100,000 Chinese there (Hsu 1980a:23). The Chengs promoted land reclamation by both civilians and soldiers. An extensive system of military colonization helped open the southwestern plain to cultivation. Taiwan's trading tradition continued, with the island's residents exporting mainly rice and sugar to Japan, Southeast Asia, and, clandestinely, China. The Manchu prohibition of maritime trade and evacuation of the coastal regions were a boon to the development of Taiwan as a trading center away from mainland control.

By the time of their collapse and defeat by the Manchus' Ch'ing dynasty in 1683, the Chengs had established the institutional, social, and cultural foundations of Chinese civilization on the frontier island. Over the next two centuries, the increasingly sinicized Manchus continued the process. They made Taiwan a prefecture (*fu*) of Fukien province. The dynasty's overriding concern was to maintain security, and to that end it also made Taiwan a military district (*chen*) of Fukien and built a network of military garrisons to enforce pacification. Despite the ban on emigration, people kept coming to the place where "gold covered your ankles." Although the ban was loosened at times to allow wives and children to join husbands, the sex ratio of the population remained lopsided.

The Ch'ing government's role in the administration and extraction of surplus from Taiwan was minimal. The quality of officials sent from Peking was notoriously poor, and many spent very little time actually on the chaotic and disease-ridden island. Partially as a result of the absence of effective government control and partly from the rambunctious nature of these pioneers of China's Wild East, Taiwan was wracked by social unrest well into the nineteenth century. It was known as a place where there was "a minor revolt every three years and a major one every five years."[3]

Responding to the lack of effective authority, the settlers banded together. They joined on the basis of same surnames, ancestral place, dialect, or belief in a common deity. Voluntary associations, some of which were secret societies, took charge of water control and mutual aid, as well as participating vigorously in armed battles (Hsu 1980b).

With so much disorder and ineffective government, there were many opportunities for local strongmen to arise.[4] A premier example is the Lin family of Wu-feng in central Taiwan. Local strongmen with private militias, the Lins at times helped the Ch'ing quell rebellions on the mainland and served the authorities on Taiwan as well. For this they were amply rewarded and eventually coopted into the establishment, becoming one of Taiwan's leading gentry families by the late 1800s.

Into the nineteeth century, as families formed and permanent settlements grew, life in Taiwan increasingly resembled that on the mainland. Most of the settlers engaged in agriculture, but there were numbers of traders and fishermen. The major crops—rice and sugar—and deerskins were actively exported to the mainland in exchange for silk, textiles, and opium. Ports such as Lu-kang and commercial centers such as Chang-hua developed. Schools were established and a literati class began to appear.[5] The land tenure pattern in much of Taiwan was the complex "one field, two owners" (i-t'ien liang-chu) system also seen in Fukien.[6] In principle, all land belonged to the emperor. Some settlers gained title to land through deals with aborigines, but the more characteristic and legitimate method was to obtain a patent from the authorities. The petitioner received a deed of perpetual "ownership" if he could bring the land under cultivation within a specified period of time. Typically, the licensee would recruit peasants from elsewhere on Taiwan or from China proper to do this work in exchange for annual rent payments (ta-tsu), fixed at about 10 percent of the value of production. The recruits in turn received ownership rights to the land surface while the original landholder (ta-tsu-hu) kept the subsoil and paid the government land tax. To complicate matters further, the recruits (hsiao-tsu-hu) would then take on tenants who paid rent (hsiao-tsu) in kind to them.[7]

Many of the numerous migrants of the eighteenth century started as tenants at the bottom of this system and acquired their own land in time. Wickberg (1970:80) estimates that "perhaps as much as 75 percent of the land was tenant-cultivated" in northern Taiwan, somewhat less elsewhere. Taiwan's tenancy rate was high compared with the mainland (Wickberg 1981:214). Most of the original landholders were absent from the land, residing in Taiwan's urban areas or on the mainland (Shih 1980:195).

Imperialism and Self-Strengthening on Taiwan

In the mid-nineteenth century, the global context changed radically for China with repercussions in Taiwan as well. In the 1830s, aggressive Western traders began to enter the China market, ending the monopoly of Britain's East India Company. Opium importing brought them enormous profits. Chinese government efforts to stop the trade resulted in the Opium War with Britain, handily won by the latter in 1842.

During the war, British ships shelled several ports on Taiwan as a sideshow to the main action. The subsequent Treaty of Nanking in 1842 opened a new era in China's foreign relations, forcing it to accept the Western imperialists' concept of how the world should be run. Under duress, China opened five new ports ("treaty ports") to foreign trade and residence in addition to Canton, the only port that foreign traders could use up to that time. China also had to grant extraterritoriality to foreigners, accept tariff limitations, and open the interior to Christian missionaries. This unequal treaty system expanded over the next decades and the privileges granted in the first instance to Britain were extended to the other foreign powers as well, as they too industrialized and embarked on global adventures. An implicit cooperative policy among the competing Western powers and Japan during the mid-nineteenth century ensured that each nation shared in these privileges while restraining them from obtaining territorial concessions (Gordon 1970:94).

It was against this background of Chinese domestic turmoil and official impotence, imperialist demands, and commercial and political rivalry among the powers that, by the terms of the 1862 Treaty of Tientsin, treaty ports were opened in Taiwan: Hu-wei (Tamsui), 1862; Keelung, 1863; and An-p'ing and Ch'i-hou (Kaohsiung), 1864. Before long, European and American consular officials, trading houses, and missionaries set up operations. The British were most active, establishing strong links between Taiwan and their colony of Hong Kong. The British-dominated Chinese Imperial Maritime Customs opened an office to handle the increased volume of trade. The ports of Tamsui and Kaohsiung were the main centers of activity. As might be expected, there were numerous confrontations between foreigners and Chinese. American, British, Japanese, and French punitive expeditions were sent to Taiwan to redress one grievance or another from the 1860s into the 1880s. A major source of friction was the unfortunate habit of the aborigines of beheading survivors of ships wrecked in the treacherous waters off Taiwan. The Chinese government was forced to apologize, pay indemnities, and suffer punitive attacks numerous times on account of this.

For the next four decades, Taiwan's agriculture-based economy continued to grow, with expanding foreign trade becoming the engine of growth. Rice remained the major food crop, most of which was consumed locally, with the remainder being shipped to the mainland. The dominant export items were sugar, tea, and, to a much lesser degree, camphor. These three accounted for 80–90 percent of the value of Taiwan's exports (Ho 1978:14). From 1872, Taiwan had a favorable balance of trade (Myers 1972a:378).

Stimulated by this trade, Taiwan began to develop an integrated economy. Peasants cultivated cash crops that were sold to brokers, then processed by local and foreign-owned establishments on Taiwan and exported by foreign or Chinese-owned trading firms. Thus, early on, Taiwan's economy developed along the lines of its comparative advantage in certain goods as determined mainly by external markets. Increases in production occurred primarily through extension of areas under cultivation, as there was little change in agricultural methods or technology during the Ch'ing (Ho 1978:17). Other than the processing of agricultural goods, manufacturing remained undeveloped. Taiwan's trade structure resembled the classic colonial pattern: exporting primary products and importing manufactured goods, in this case mostly consumer goods like opium and textiles.

The increasing importance of commercial activities affected the structure of Taiwan's society in several ways. As the population filled out the island and engaged in exchange relations, much of the violent subethnic rivalry subsided. Large landowning families diversified their commercial interests into activities such as trade, retailing, and camphor processing (Meskill 1979:238–39). A new stratum of compradors emerged to deal with the foreign traders.

As more wealth was accumulated, the island's elites became increasingly sinified. From their origins as bandits, strongmen, and peasants, they became wealthy landowners and merchants. Some had their sons trained in classical learning to enable them to take the civil service exams and thereby enter the state bureaucracy, the most cherished status in traditional Chinese society. Others used less noble means of achieving this same highly prized objective: they bought degrees and titles that gave them comparable gentry status. Still others received titles for military exploits. Having achieved this status, they then began to adopt the refined life style typical of gentry families in China, especially cultural pursuits and public service.[8] Families of this status intermarried, reproducing themselves as a distinct social stratum on Taiwan. They also maintained close ties with government officials.

Most of the residents were peasants (owners and tenants), but through the cultivation and marketing of cash crops they too became increasingly linked into commercial networks that extended beyond the island to the rest of the world. Given China's relatively fluid class system, peasants also had the chance of accumulating the land and wealth required for eventual entry into the scholar-official-gentry class.[9]

Although formally part of China since 1683, Taiwan had been largely neglected by the government in Peking, and its people had run their own affairs. But foreign aggression against Taiwan as well as demands that the Ch'ing bear responsibility for the actions of the island's inhabitants forced Peking to assert its sovereignty. In the process, the court became increasingly aware of the strategic value of the island as the front line of defense of the motherland. To bolster Taiwan, the moribund dynasty instituted many of the same "self-strengthening" (*tzu-ch'iang*) policies that it was implementing on the mainland. These included modernizing the military forces (especially the navy), beefing up defenses, establishing defense industries, teaching Western science and technology, and stimulating economic development. The proximate stimulus for implementing self-strengthening on Taiwan was the imminent danger in 1874 of Japanese occupation and threatened annexation as reparations for aborigine savaging of shipwrecked Ryukyu fishermen in 1871.

Undoubtedly the most effective of the series of officials charged with this task was General Liu Ming-ch'uan (1836–96), who served on Taiwan from 1884 to 1891.[10] Liu instituted major reforms in Taiwan's administration, infrastructure, and economy. Taiwan was upgraded to provincial status in 1887 and the administrative districts were redrawn with the governor relocated to the northern city of Taipei. A census turned up 2.5 million residents (Shih 1980:133). Liu ordered a land survey and revised the ownership system so that the *hsiao-tsu-hu* were made responsible for paying land taxes, which were then collected with renewed vigor. Other taxes were levied to increase the government's share of the burgeoning trade in sugar and camphor. This led to tensions with the foreigners, who were active in this commerce as well.

Liu's major efforts were oriented toward defense, which also had economic repercussions. He reinforced Taiwan's land and sea defenses and employed foreign advisers to train his troops. He built an arsenal and imported modern firepower and ships. Liu made major contributions to the modernization of Taiwan's infrastructure, as under his tenure a railroad was built, a telegraph link was instituted with the mainland, harbor construction was undertaken, a public postal service was established, electric lighting was installed in Taipei, and a modern school was built.

He encouraged land reclamation, especially in the mountainous areas to exploit the camphor and lumber there. This involved pacifying, educating, and sinicizing the aborigines as well as building roads. New Chinese settlers were recruited, the prohibition against emigration having been officially lifted in 1875. In direct economic construction, Liu funded coal mining and hired foreign experts to manage the operation. He also promoted the sulphur industry and sericulture.

When not threatening their vested interests, Liu's policies received support from at least a section of Taiwan's elites (Speidel 1974). The Lin families of Wu-feng and Pan-ch'iao were especially active in contributing funds and personnel. As Taiwan's gentry class was still rather new and not entrenched, it did not resist the technological changes as had its counterparts on the mainland. But Peking itself obstructed some of Liu's bolder efforts, such as joint ventures with foreigners to develop coal and petroleum mining (Kuo 1973:231–32).

Liu's successors lacked his vision and competence. As a result, many of his projects were left uncompleted. In 1895 Taiwan was ceded to Japan and entered a track of world history different from China.

Taiwan on the Eve of Japanese Rule

What can we say about Taiwan's socioeconomic situation on the eve of transfer to Japanese rule?

Taiwan had an agricultural economy based on small peasant owner or tenant cultivators, very similar to that in Fukien or Kwangtung where most of the population originated. A landlord-gentry class provided local social and political leadership whether or not Peking sent competent officials. Taiwan had long participated in external commodity trade with the mainland and with nations of the West and Asia. Mainland Chinese and foreign merchants created and dominated the primary goods export sector. As a result of the trade, the economy and society especially in the north were becoming increasingly commercialized, probably more so than the rest of China. External demand accounted for much of the steady economic growth. It would be far-fetched to claim, however, that Taiwan was developing a capitalist mode of production any more than China as a whole was. Among the Taiwanese, commodity production was being extended but no distinct (or even nascent) capitalist or worker classes were being formed. A handful of officials had promoted economic development, primarily for defense purposes, but the majority of officials and social elites, as well as their dominant ideology, remained hostile to private business activities.

Were capitalism to come about, it would have to be introduced from the outside and involve a fundamental revision of economic, social, political, and ideological structures.

3

Taiwan Under Japanese Rule

Unlike the experience of Latin America, Africa, and much of Asia, it was not the advanced industrial powers of the West that brought capitalism to Taiwan as a part of their global rivalry. Rather, the Japanese, themselves the victims of Western imperialism, performed the service of getting capitalist development underway in Taiwan as part of their own program of achieving national sovereignty and industrialization. They initiated the process of primitive accumulation, introduced capitalist relations of production, and subordinated Taiwan's economy to Japanese capital.

The Japanese, in contrast to the Chinese response to the mid-nineteenth-century encroachments and demands of Western imperialism, vigorously attempted to regain their sovereignty through a fundamental revamping of their social, economic, political, and ideological systems. This involved first the selection of a model: moribund and victimized China, historically Japan's mentor for everything civilized, now provided a negative example of the consequences of failing to achieve "national wealth and military strength" (*fukoku kyōhei*). The strong and aggressive Western countries still threatening Japan served as positive models of what had to be done to survive in the new era.

The men who overthrew the Tokugawa shogunate in 1868 and nominally restored power to the Meiji emperor centralized power in the new government, abolished the feudal political and social system, and took the initiative in developing the economy. Lacking materials, capital, and technology to say nothing of a capitalist class, the state itself spearheaded the industrialization effort. It started up a broad range of industrial projects, many of which it later sold at a fraction of cost to prospective capitalists, while continuing to subsidize and protect them. It also established a modern financial system and built up the nation's physical and social infrastructure.

Economic development was not merely an end in itself. It was one part, albeit the central one, of the overarching goal of *fukoku kyōhei*. Japan's leaders were determined to demonstrate the nation's strength and parity with the Western powers in order to abolish extraterritoriality and regain tariff autonomy, two humiliating legacies of the initial contact with the West. The march to this goal took the Japanese beyond their own borders and into active participation in the imperialist contest for control of East Asia.

In Lenin's (1939) classic statement, imperialism was first an economic phenomenon: International monopoly-capital combines representing the marriage of industrial and financial capital carved up the world among themselves in the search for markets, investments, and materials. State power entered the picture only later, to divide up the world's territories.

But in Japan's case, the two phases occurred simultaneously. While Japan indeed needed raw materials and, later, markets, clearly the initial impetus behind its imperialist activities was political: to establish a cordon sanitaire (which included Korea and China) and to convince the Westerners to grant Japan big-power status and restore full sovereignty to it.

Taiwan had the dubious honor of becoming Japan's first colony. Japanese moves to occupy it dated back to 1874, but the actual winning of the island came about indirectly. In 1894, China attempted to reassert its traditional suzerainty over Korea in the face of a revolt there, only to find itself challenged by a large Japanese military force also in Korea to push Japan's interests on the peninsula. China had made major investments in military modernization, as had Japan, and both sides were eager to show off what they had accomplished. The Japanese, relying on their navy, delivered a most unfilial defeat to their former mentors. The Treaty of Shimonoseki, signed in April 1895, compelled China among other things to cede Taiwan and the Pescadores to Japan. The fact that Russia, France, and Germany forced Japan to relinquish other booty originally awarded in the treaty (the "Tripartite Intervention") further motivated the Japanese to accomplish great things on the territory they did get, to prove their mettle.

Japan's colonial policy for Taiwan did not emerge full-blown. In fact, it got off to a rather chaotic start, and some Japanese called on the goverment to get rid of the island and go on to other business. Japan's colonial policy was the product of the needs of the developing home islands and expanding empire, which in turn were intertwined with its evolving relationship with the Powers and China. The colonial occupation can be broken down into three periods: 1) 1895–1919, the harsh period of consolidation of political control and reshaping the economy to make it suit the needs of Japan; 2) 1919–1936, a relatively liberal interlude characterized by civil administration and demands for home rule reflecting changes in Taiwan's society; and 3) 1937–1945, renewed military rule and forced assimilation as Japan prepared for, waged, and lost global war.[1]

Consolidation of Control, 1895–1919

The mutually restraining cooperative policy among the imperialists collapsed in 1895 when the upstart Japanese insisted on the cession of Taiwan in the treaty ending the Sino-Japanese War and the other powers did not interfere. The Tripartite Intervention blocked Japan's attempt to take the Liaotung Peninsula as well, but did not force it to relinquish Taiwan. On the contrary, the Powers took this as the harbinger of a new era in East Asian politics—the Chinese tributary system and the British commercial empire soon gave way before a naked imperialist scramble for territorial concessions and spheres of influence.

Japan was an aggressive participant in these activities and did not see Taiwan as the last piece of Asian territory it would possess. In subsequent years it joined the Allied Expeditionary Force against the antiforeign Boxer Rebellion in China (1900), formed an alliance with Britain (1902), decisively defeated Russia in war (1905), annexed Korea (1910), and signed treaties with other powers acknowledging its imperialist claims. Japan achieved its goal of at least formal acceptance as an equal by the Powers. They abolished extraterritoriality in Japan in 1899, and Japan regained tariff autonomy in 1910. The diversion of the Western Powers' attention back to Europe during World War I gave Japan breathing space to pursue its ambitions against China. It assumed Germany's position in Shantung in 1914 and in the following year issued the Twenty-one Demands to China in an attempt to reduce that hapless nation to the status of a Japanese protectorate.

Domestically, Japan's industry continued its rapid growth. The victory over Russia provided a tremendous stimulus to the economy, as did the global boom following the end of the First World War. Japan stood to profit immediately as the actual combatants still had to recover from devastation. Politically, the Meiji oligarchs had passed from the scene and a new generation of leaders worked to implement a stable constitutional government.

But back in 1895, Japan was preoccupied with establishing control over Taiwan to show the Western Powers that it deserved to be counted an equal. This had to be accomplished rapidly to prevent Western meddling or any indication of Japanese inefficacy. Because they had had no prior presence on the island, there was no indigenous or expatriate constituency that could be mobilized for support. Instead, they had to rely on their army to take things in hand.

Japan had to expend unexpectedly great effort to subdue resistance by the islanders. After Peking ceded the island, the last Chinese governor, T'ang Ching-sung, had hurriedly established a Taiwan Republic and solicited aid from the Western imperialists.[2] But the effort collapsed from lack of domestic or international support and T'ang fled to the mainland. Taiwan had no other cohesive or legitimate organ of state power to stand up to the Japanese, but several Taiwanese did mobilize private defense forces to resist the Japanese southward advance. The Ch'ing government, having formally ceded the territory, offered no assistance. Although the occupation of Taipei, facilitated by the actions of the adventurer Ku Hsien-yung, was bloodless, it took the Japanese five months of fighting—until late October—before they could declare that the island as a whole was secure. Even then, sporadic armed resistance continued for many years.

The Japanese established a structure of control to suppress further outbreaks and to ensure their unchallenged hegemony. The supreme authority was the Government-General (*Sōtokufu*). The first nine governors-general, up to 1919, were active military officers, reflecting the emphasis on control. The governor-general had extensive political, bureaucratic, military, and legislative powers over the colony. Diet Bill No. 63 granted him the authority to rule almost by fiat.

Japanese held the top posts at all levels of government. The only exceptions were a handful of Japan-educated Taiwanese who were appointed village headmen later in the occupation.[3] Taiwan basic-level society was further divided into *kō* (units of ten households) and *ho* (ten kō). This was a beefing up of the traditional Chinese *pao-chia* system of mutual responsibility for criminal activity and public service that was nominally already in effect. The elected leaders of the *hokō* were Taiwanese, but they were closely supervised by Japanese police. Only one-sixth of Taiwan's police force were local people, and no Taiwanese was appointed above the rank of captain (Chen 1970). By extending effective control throughout the island and penetrating down to the village, the Japanese removed many of the elements that had traditionally fostered the rise of local strongmen beyond state control, which had bedeviled the Ch'ing.

The other main Japanese priority was to develop Taiwan's economy to support Japan's drive to wealth and power. As was the case with Japan's own economy after the rise of the Meiji oligarchs, the basic tasks associated with capital accumulation fell to the state by default. The Japanese did not intend, however, to industrialize Taiwan as they had their motherland, but rather to develop its agriculture to supply foodstuffs and raw materials to the industrializing home islands. There was thus to be a functional and geographical division of labor within the integrated economy of the expanding empire.

A coherent strategy for the economic development of Taiwan did not crystallize until the term of the fourth governor-general, Kodama Gentarō, and his civil administrator, Gotō Shimpei, 1898–1906. Kodama, the military man, stressed the development of Taiwan's resources to improve Japan's standing vis-à-vis the West. He and Gotō recruited a cadre of technocrats and moved vigorously to integrate and subordinate Taiwan's economy with Japan's and to develop the island's latent productivity along the desired lines. The system of weights and measures and the currency were standardized; foreign trading houses were expelled; and trade was reoriented from China to Japan by means of tariffs.

Using deficit financing, the government made major investments in the infrastructure, rehabilitating and expanding Liu Ming-ch'uan's railway, building roads, extending telegraph lines, and dredging the harbors at Kaohsiung and Keelung. Monopolies were established over camphor, salt, tobacco, opium, and liquor.

Within the dominant agricultural sector, the Japanese selected rice and sugar to lead the development. In addition to improving the transportation and communication infrastructure, the Sōtokufu aided the construction of irrigation works. More important, it took a direct role in overseeing the transformation of Taiwan's agricultural sector to achieve significant production increases. A land survey was completed in 1904 and the following year the Sōtokufu instituted a land reform. It forced the *ta-tsu-hu* to give up claims to rent in exchange for government bonds and affirmed the *hsiao-tsu-hu* as actual landowners, making them responsible for payment of the land tax. It thereby introduced the legal protection of private property. To meet the regular payments that were now demanded of them, the *hsiao-tsu-hu* had to increase the productivity of the land to ensure a surplus. The Sōtokufu took over other farmland as well as forest and mountain regions for later development by Japanese capital.

The Sōtokufu introduced technological change in the form of new high-yield seeds, fertilizers, and advanced techniques, backed by an extension system that operated in conjunction with the *hokō* network and the farmers' associations that all peasants were compelled to join (Ho 1978:63). Rural credit cooperatives made working capital available to peasants. In the years to 1920, agriculture grew at a rate of 2–2.5 percent a year (Ho 1978:28).

The Japanese made certain that they controlled the surplus. In this period, 20 percent of Taiwan's rice and 90 percent of its sugar were exported, nearly all to Japan (Ho 1978:31). Japanese control of the sugar crop extended beyond the harvested cane. The Sōtokufu solicited Japanese capitalists to invest in sugar refineries in Taiwan. It offered them a package of guaranteed profits, low-priced land, military protection, regulation of capacity, exclusive refining rights, and protective tariffs (Chang and Myers 1963:444–45). With the boom brought on by victory over Russia, Japan's newly powerful financial-industrial-trade conglomerates (*zaibatsu*), in league with bureaucrats, began to invest in a variety of enterprises in Taiwan.

In these early years, then, the Japanese skewed Taiwan's economic structure so that it became a producer mainly of rice and sugar (refined in Taiwan in Japanese-owned mills), the bulk of which was destined for export to Japan in exchange for manufactured goods. These dynamic policies had rapid returns: New sources of revenue such as the land tax, excise taxes, and monopolies put money into the Sōtokufu's coffers, and by 1905 the colony was self-supporting (Chang and Myers 1963:448).

Gotō Shimpei had a vision for Taiwan's society as well as its economy—to improve the social environment so as to induce economic progress. To this end, he invested in the social infrastructure, mainly through improving public health and sanitation, education, security, and public services.

While implementing a land reform, the Japanese did not seek to alter fundamentally the relations of production in the countryside. The *tatsu-hu*, already divorced from the land, were formally eliminated as a class while the de facto landlords, the *hsiao-tsu-hu,* were now legally reinforced. There was no redistribution of land. The majority of peasants continued as cultivators on family farms, which they owned or rented in whole or in part. In a significant departure from European colonial practice, the Japanese did not drive the peasants off their land or establish plantations. In fact, they used the police and administrative means to preserve the rural social structure. They divided the island into fifty sugar districts, each with a Japanese-owned mill at its core that purchased cane from Taiwanese peasants at a previously announced price. The peasants had to sell to the mill in their district and were reduced to a near serf-like relation to it (Williams 1980:234). The farmers' associations functioned as instruments of control as well as a channel for new technology and capital. In this way, the peasants' activities became increasingly integrated into the cycle of capitalist reproduction with its origin and endpoint in Japan.

In the nonrural sector, Japanese policy was to develop a dual society, then gradually introduce Japanese language and customs until integration could be achieved in the distant future. The cornerstone of this policy was the educational system, based on the successful Meiji model.[4] A network of compulsory six-year elementary schools was to be set up to impart basic literacy and skills to Taiwanese boys and girls and to indoctrinate them in loyalty to Japan and the emperor, while weaning them away from China. Gentry and merchant children were targeted for the first schools. A corollary of the educational policy was the elimination of the traditional teaching and administrative functions of the remaining Chinese literati. By restricting the traditional Chinese schools and employing their own expatriate administrators, the Japanese achieved this goal. They also used positive methods to flatter the literati to win their allegiance while removing their prestige (Tsurumi 1977:38–39). In 1906, about 5 percent of the Taiwanese school-aged population was enrolled in common schools, though actual attendance was even less (Tsurumi 1977:19). By 1920 this approached 39 percent for boys (Tsurumi 1977:63). Japanese students on the island had their own tracking system and schools.

As in the Meiji system, beyond the elementary or common schools (*kogakkō*) was a handful of normal schools to train common-school teachers and one medical school that permitted further upward mobility to a tiny minority of ambitious Taiwanese. The children of the elites were especially recruited for better education, including being allowed entrance to the Japanese schools, as a way of setting an example for the rest of society, even though the authorities made it clear that education should not be seen as a channel for social advancement for all Taiwanese. All but a few Taiwanese were to take up careers in agriculture or commerce like their fathers or become unskilled laborers. This was the Japanese reaction to what had happened in India, where, they felt, education had made the natives too uppity. Frustrated with the odds against admission to higher schools on Taiwan, increasing numbers of Taiwanese who could afford it were sending their children to Japan to study. Once there, they were free to study any subject they wished, limited only by scholastic aptitude and language fluency (Tsurumi 1977:65–66).

Eager to win allegiance from influential Taiwanese, the authorities used monopoly licenses and other economic privileges as well as appointment to basic-level administrative posts to this end. But while allowing Taiwanese to participate in commercial activities, the Japanese used legal and economic means to prevent all but a handful of top collaborators from entering the modern industrial sector. Capitalist institutions such as a development bank (The Bank of Taiwan, 1899), legal protection of private property, limited liability companies, and so on were introduced to benefit Japanese investors and workers; the Taiwanese in general were related to the periphery of the capitalist mode in their own society.

As a result of Japan's social, political, and economic policies, Taiwanese society began to undergo some slight changes in this period, mainly in the urban areas. As noted above, peasants became more tied to the land and large landowners now received legal protection. A small stratum of common-school teachers, government clerks, and doctors emerged through the pyramidal education system. Many were the children of the former elite. An even smaller number of active collaborators achieved a certain amount of prominence.

There were five major families who benefited from collaboration. Two, the Lins of Pan-ch'iao (near Taipei) and the Lins of Wu-feng (near Taichung) were wealthy landowning clans prior to the Japanese takeover who were targeted by the Sōtokufu for cooptation. Their business activities diversified into finance, trade, and sugar refining. A different track brought wealth and honors to three other men: Ku Hsien-jung of Lukang, Yen Yun-nian of Keelung, and Ch'en Chung-ho of Kaohsiung. They assisted the Japanese in their occupation of Taiwan and subsequent imperialist ventures. They were rewarded with monopoly privileges and went on to invest in various undertakings in sugar milling, land development, retailing, and mining. All accumulated land.

After 1910, some elements of the urban population, namely businessmen and educated youths, especially those who had studied in Japan or China, began to oppose the dual social structure forced on them and agitated for assimilation. Aided by a noted Japanese liberal, Itagaki Taisuke, in December 1914 they formed the Taiwan Assimilation Society, seeking equality with the Japanese. The society was opposed by the expatriate Japanese elite and suppressed a month later (Lamley 1970–71).

By 1919, the Japanese had firmly consolidated their political control, sparked economic (mainly agricultural) growth, and begun to introduce capitalist relations of production and remove impediments to capitalist development. They developed human resources while freezing the social structure for all but a handful of the colonized Taiwanese. But some fundamental changes soon began to take hold as a result of the interaction of events outside Taiwan and actions taken by the Taiwanese themselves.

Assimilation and Home Rule, 1919–1936

The end of World War I ushered in a period of expansion in the global economy. Japan had profited greatly from the war, supplying munitions and consumer goods to the combatants. It had markedly improved its standing vis-à-vis the industrialized Western nations, which it emulated and feared. Taiwan's economy, tightly integrated into Japan's, benefited in direct proportion, and both continued to grow through the 1920s.[5] Exports of rice and sugar—their productivity increased via new technological inputs—continued to lead Taiwan's economy. The penetration by Japanese capital and Taiwan's further integration into the cycle of Japanese capitalist reproduction were spearheaded by private capital as the Sōtokufu, having prepared the necessary social and economic conditions, withdrew from direct participation. The *zaibatsu,* flushed with capital, increased and diversified their investments in Taiwan, and several Taiwan-based Japanese capitalists emerged.

In Japan's home islands, American President Woodrow Wilson's liberal ideals of self-determination and internationalization, combined with Japan's increased self-confidence, ushered in a period of domestic political liberalization and party politics called Taishō Democracy after the emperor who assumed the throne in 1911. But other events in Japan and abroad prompted a countertrend: The turmoil of party politics, close and often corrupt relations between the burgeoning *zaibatsu* and government bureaucrats, and the success of the Bolshevik Revolution in nearby Russia provoked a conservative backlash from the right and the military. From the end of the 1920s, a newly unified and determined Republic of China under Chiang Kai-shek represented a potential impediment to Japanese expansionist ambitions, further strengthening the hand of Japan's militarists. The Great Depression gave impetus to the anticapitalist strain in their appeal.

Colonial policy reflected these contradictory trends. Early in 1919, emboldened by Wilsonian principles, disgruntled Koreans rebelled against Japanese colonial rule. They were suppressed with such force that international censure compelled the Japanese to relax their control somewhat. Subsequent reforms were extended to Taiwan as well.

In the fall of 1919, Taiwan received its first civilian governor-general, Baron Den Kenjirō (1919–1923). From 1920, Japanese law was to be applied as much as possible in Taiwan, although the governor-general still retained the power to determine the limits of its applicability. In 1921, the governor-general included nine eminent Taiwanese on his Consultative Council (*hyōgikai*). Though its functions were only advisory and it was convened only at the governor-general's invitation, this body did afford members of the Taiwanese community access to the top administrative circles. Advisory councils had been established in 1920 at local levels too. In 1923, the rules for establishing companies were liberalized, facilitating entry of Taiwanese entrepreneurs into the modern sector, though still subordinate to Japanese capital. Up to that time, modern joint-stock companies were required by law to have Japanese partners (Chang 1955).

Den's major mission, however, was to speed up the process of assimilating the Taiwanese. Whereas a few years earlier the Japanese had set this goal for the distant future and disbanded the Assimilation Society, in the new liberal environment the policy was reversed. Assimilation was to be pushed throughout society, but naturally the focus was to be on children in the schools. New measures extended postprimary vocational training to Taiwanese and integrated all postprimary schools. Several thousand ambitious youths continued to seek higher education in Japan, where there were no racial quotas and there was a larger number and variety of schools to choose from. Furthermore, Taiwanese had more options as to courses of study in Japan, and many chose law, business, and politics, off-limits to them at home (Tsurumi 1977:126).

Thrown together with Japanese, Chinese, and Korean youths, exposed to currents of thought in liberal Japan not accessible to them through Taiwan's controlled press, and encouraged by liberal and anticolonial Japanese, Taiwanese youths abroad achieved new political consciousness. Toward the end of civilian rule on Taiwan, returned students and other members of the intellectual elite formed several organizations to press for integration, local autonomy, and elections. The mainstream reflected the influence of Japanese and Wilsonian liberalism and employed nonviolent tactics, operating within the bounds of Japanese law.[6] Dominated by social forces created by the Japanese system—students, doctors, merchants—these organizations represented a new stage of opposition to Japan after the brutal failure of spontaneous and uncoordinated armed resistance in the first period.

One figure dominated the movement during these years: Lin Hsient'ang, of the illustrious Wu-feng clan. A landlord, businessman, and social activist, Lin was influenced by Chinese politicians Liang Ch'ich'ao and Tai Chi-t'ao, whom he had met with in Japan, Taiwan, and Peking. Both told him that China would not be able to support Taiwanese aspirations for self-determination and urged him to follow a path of reform within the colonial framework.

Through a succession of organizations, Lin and his compatriots in Taiwan and Japan pressed for the repeal of Diet Bill No. 63 and for home rule. Others, following a leftist line, organized workers and peasants who were agitating on their own against Japanese industrial and rural policies.

Japanese tactics in reaction to these struggles ranged from suppression of organizations mobilizing workers and peasants to planning a new program in 1935 for Taiwan's autonomy, including elections. But a military man assumed the governor-general's post the following year, and such political movements were terminated as the war atmosphere intensified.

Taiwanese students in China continued to organize, however, and their groups tended to be more radical. An example is the tiny Taiwan Communist party, founded in Shanghai in 1928 and crushed in Taiwan in 1931. It called for mass-based class struggle and overthrow of Japanese rule.[7]

Stimulated by and taking advantage of the liberal environment of the times, Taiwanese intellectual elites had pressed for more equal treatment within the framework of Japanese rule. Not surprisingly, the governors-general and Japanese expatriates resolutely opposed them. While failing to achieve their ultimate goals, the Taiwanese did force some reform of the system. More important, they experienced a political awakening, an understanding of Taiwan's social structure, and a strong desire for political equality.

War and Forced Assimilation, 1937–1945

While Taiwanese social forces were struggling for political representation, events were occurring in Japan that would bring the movement to a halt. When the Great Depression spread to Japan in 1930, the militarists began to increase their political power at the expense of political parties. Japan's extreme vulnerability to global economic conditions stimulated a search for a way to overcome this weakness. Control over sources of raw materials and markets was one way.

By 1930 Japan had already amassed a huge economic stake in Manchuria, in trade and direct investments. This appeared to be threatened both by the aggressive drive northward by the Chinese Nationalists, who were attempting to unify their country, and by the constant presence of Soviet Russia. To protect Japanese interests, the army, on its own, fabricated an "incident" in the fall of 1931 and began to occupy Manchuria; by the following March, the "independent" state of Manchukuo was born. Condemned as aggressors by the League of Nations, the Japanese responded by withdrawing from that body. At home, the military and the radical right came into power. On the continent, the Japanese consolidated their Manchurian foothold and continued to expand.

By 1937 Japan was at war with China, and the next year the Japanese launched total war on the mainland. In September 1940, Japan signed the Tripartite Pact with Nazi Germany and Fascist Italy; in 1941 it began invading Southeast Asia. As Japan's forces expanded throughout Asia, challenged America, and then found themselves overextended, Taiwan's function in the empire shifted. It was now to serve as the stepping stone to the South Seas. This meant that while continuing to produce rice and sugar, Taiwan would introduce some heavy industry that could process raw materials coming from Southeast Asia for stock-piling and shipment to serve the imperial war machine. Taiwan was also to increase its self-sufficiency in consumer goods. As the tide of war turned against Japan and the sea lanes were cut off, Taiwan had no choice but to rely on itself.

To accomplish this, the major *zaibatsu* and expatriate firms worked closely with the Taiwan Development Company, a national policy company established in 1936 to exploit resources in Taiwan, facilitate Japanese immigration to the island, and establish economic links between Taiwan, South China, and Southeast Asia (Naito 1937:222–23). Industrial chemicals, ceramics, aluminum, machine tools, and textiles were some of the industries introduced at this time. As part of this industrial mobilization, Taiwanese-owned modern enterprises were merged into Japanese firms. Economic control was thus concentrated almost entirely in Japanese hands. Through these and other wartime controls, the Japanese ensured their own direct control over production and surplus extraction in industry as well as the critical agricultural sector.

In addition to its mobilization of Taiwan's economy for war, Japan militarized the island's political and social spheres. After 1936 all governors-general were military men. Police organs were expanded and strengthened. Dissent and social activism were suppressed. To compel the Taiwanese to be loyal to the cause, the Japanese implemented a new policy of forced assimilation, *kōminka*, literally, "to make into the emperor's people." Both in the newly militarized schools and in society at large, Japanese language and customs—including clothing and Shinto religion—were pushed vigorously. Taiwanese were also pressed into service at the front as soldiers and laborers, and then for defense of the island against an expected American invasion. The invasion did not come, but Taiwan did sustain severe bombing from late 1944. Military and industrial targets were heavily damaged.

The Japanese Legacy

Over the course of five decades, the Japanese brought about fundamental changes in Taiwan's politics, economy, and society. The authoritarian, development-oriented Sōtokufu, using coercive measures in the first instance, took the lead in creating what today would be called a good investment climate on the island: enforcing law and order; unifying weights, measures, and currency; guaranteeing private property rights; building a modern infrastructure; mobilizing natural resources; increasing agricultural productivity; making investment capital available; and developing human capital, including the provision of public education and employment for women. In the process, the Japanese removed bureaucratic, legal, and social impediments to the development of capitalism and demonstrated to the Taiwanese the potential of capitalist industrialization.

The Japanese implanted a structure for dependent capitalism: The economy was skewed to concentrate on the production of two primary goods, the bulk of which was exported to one market—Japan—by Japanese trading houses. In exchange, the island imported manufactured consumer and producer goods from one source—Japan. As in most European colonies, the economic structure was disarticulated as production was geared to external demand and the daily necessities of life other than foodstuffs could not be produced domestically. The capitalist production and financial sector was a near monopoly of home-based and expatriate Japanese whose overwhelming economic dominance was buttressed by legal statutes obstructing Taiwanese participation in any but a subordinate way. By the end of World War II, the Taiwanese industrial bourgeoisie was almost nonexistent. Though Japanese policies spawned new social forces, the masses as a whole were excluded from political participation.

But the Japanese legacy differed from the more typical dependent structure in important ways significant for the future. The infrastructure and factories built by the Japanese were dispersed throughout the island, thus avoiding the common phenomenon of a tiny modern channel in a sea of traditional society. Such a distortion was further prevented by the major investment in education and technological upgrading, which brought at least a minimal level of literacy, skills, and appreciation of modern business practices to the majority of the population island wide. While demand was externally generated and industry introduced only in the closing years of the occupation, the basic demands of Taiwan's people for food and consumer goods were not neglected. Although Japanese owned great stretches of land,[8] the Taiwanese peasants were not driven off their land and onto plantations, the general rule in other colonies. They retained their private holdings and learned to appreciate and apply scientific inputs to improve productivity. Land ownership patterns were marked by continuity. While consumption was held down, the overall quality of life as measured by a better standard of living, security, health, and education improved markedly.

Drawing lessons from Japan's own successful, state-guided developmental experience, the colonial administrators were sensitive to the changing global economic and political environment in which trade-oriented Japan and Taiwan existed. Their approach was dynamic—to anticipate directions of change and devise economic policies to take advantage of them. Taiwan was undeniably restructured by its dependent relation with Japan; it was not underdeveloped.

4

Chaotic
Interregnum

Retrocession and Retrogression, 1945–1947

Japan's unconditional surrender in August 1945 did not make the Taiwanese people sovereign masters of their own soil. Before Japanese occupation, Taiwan had been a province of imperial China; in 1945, by a plan drawn up by Allied leaders, it was retroceded to China, now the Republic of China (ROC). Once more the island became war booty, and once more an external power sent in personnel to manage the island's affairs to suit that power's needs.

But China had lurched from crisis to crisis while Taiwan experienced fifty years of stable economic and social development under repressive Japanese imperial rule. The vastly different experiences of the Chinese on the mainland and those on Taiwan would have tragic consequences when they collided. It is necessary to review briefly what had transpired on the mainland during Taiwan's decades as a Japanese colony.

The Ch'ing dynasty had continued to decline after 1895 under the combined weight of imperialist encroachment, domestic disintegration, and incompetent, reactionary leadership. Some Ch'ing officials made half-hearted attempts at reform, but it was too late. Chinese in ever greater numbers engaged in revolutionary activities to demolish the dynastic system and establish a modern republic. The most influential revolutionary was Sun Yat-sen (1866–1925), a Cantonese Christian medical doctor educated in China, Hong Kong, and the United States.

The Ch'ing fell in October 1911, as much due to internal decay as to an orchestrated revolutionary onslaught. The new Republic of China, though nominally a single nation ruled from Peking, soon disintegrated into a congeries of warring regional kingdoms dominated by warlords.

Inspired by the example of the Soviet Communist party and advised by its agents in China, Sun Yat-sen reorganized his National People's party (Kuomintang, KMT, or Nationalist party) along Leninist democratic centralist lines. He inaugurated a united front with the Chinese Communist party, which had been established in 1921. Leading Communists joined the KMT. The Soviet Union assisted him further in building a party army, and Sun sent his loyal lieutenant, Chiang Kai-shek (1887–1975), to the Soviet Union for training. Upon his return in 1924, Chiang headed the new Whampoa Military Academy near Canton.

Sun further developed his ideological program, *San Min Chu-i*, the Three Principles of the People. These principles are *min-tsu* (nationalism), originally anti-Manchuism, then anti-imperialism and self-determination for the Chinese nation; *min-ch'üan* (people's rights or democracy), administration of, by, and for the people through their direct powers of election, recall, initiative, and referendum, plus a five-function government; and *min-sheng* (people's livelihood), a vague concept akin to socialism in its advocacy of regulation of capital and equalization of land tenure (Sun was deeply influenced by Henry George), but minus class struggle and with a major role for free enterprise.

Sun developed cancer in the course of this work and died on March 12, 1925, leaving the deathbed charge, "The revolution is unfinished. All my comrades must strive on." Sun Yat-sen became deified as the National Father of the Republic of China, and his ideology was canonized.

In 1926, Commander-in-Chief Generalissimo Chiang Kai-shek led the army that he had built from Canton on a Northern Expedition to rid China of warlordism and imperialism and realize Sun's dream of a unified nation. Helped by Communist mobilization of workers and peasants, the campaign was enormously successful from the outset, but Chiang turned away from mass mobilization and anti-imperialism and instead unleashed a bloody slaughter of Communists in the KMT when the army reached Shanghai in April 1927. Chiang's forces took Peking in June 1928. He made Nanking the capital (it had been the capital of the Ming, China's last Han-nationality dynasty) and renamed Peking, the former Ch'ing capital, Pei-p'ing (Northern Peace). Thus began the Nanking decade.[1] Chiang held a variety of posts in the Nanking government, including president, premier, and president of the National Military Council. In 1938 he became the *tsung-ts'ai* or director-general of the KMT.

The new Government of the Republic of China (GRC) began recovering autonomy and building political and economic institutions inspired by Sun's teachings. But the Nanking government never effectively controlled much more of China than the Yangtze River delta and some other large cities. The "republic" was a loose collection of competing warlords, and the KMT deteriorated into a melange of warring factions manipulated by an increasingly conservative Chiang. He was also obsessed with eradicating the remaining Communists. Sun Yat-sen's recipe for constitutional democracy was put on the back burner and his strategies for economic development and social welfare neglected almost entirely in practice if not in rhetoric.

Whether or not Chiang intended to implement the Three Principles became a moot point when the Japanese moved south in 1937, launching all-out war. The Nationalists retreated inland, eventually establishing their wartime capital in the hilly backwater town of Chungking, Szechuan.

Holed up in the hinterland until 1945 and buoyed by vast amounts of American aid after the United States entered the war in 1941, the Nationalist party-state degenerated. The Americans became increasingly involved in Chinese internal affairs and the fate of ally Chiang and his political apparatus.[2]

As one of the war's Big Four leaders, the Generalissimo attended the Cairo Conference, a meeting which sealed the postwar fate of Taiwan. In the Cairo Declaration of December 1, 1943, Roosevelt, Churchill, and Chiang agreed that Korea would become free and independent but Taiwan, the Pescadores, and Manchuria would be turned over to China. The Potsdam Declaration of July 1945 reaffirmed this.

Soon after Cairo, Chiang established a Taiwan Investigation Commission under General Ch'en Yi, a former Fukien warlord who had visited Taiwan under Japanese rule and appreciated its wealth. This commission made plans for the takeover of the island.

Taiwan's formal retrocession to China on October 25, 1945 inaugurated a period of rapid underdevelopment. Economically, politically, and culturally it was suddenly yanked out of the Japanese orbit and appended to China in another colonial relationship. The corrupt and vindictive new rulers restructured the island province to fulfill the needs of their mainland regime, insensitive to the history or aspirations for equality of the disoriented Taiwanese people. All aspects of life came under mainlander-KMT control.

The overarching need of the Nationalists was to fuel their war machine once the struggle against the Communists revived in 1946. After decades of intermittent warfare, the mainland's economy was in disarray. Taiwan's bountiful rice and sugar could fill an immediate need. The usable machines and stockpiled raw materials could help revive production. Before long, Taiwan's resources were siphoned off to the mainland by private carpetbaggers and government agencies charged with confiscating enemy assets. Factories were dismantled and shipped to China along with raw materials, thus devastating the part of Taiwan's economic base that had escaped American bombs. How much actually contributed to the war effort and how much went to the warehouses of the corrupt bureaucrat-capitalists around Chiang's brother-in-law T. V. Soong remains unanswered.

With civil war on the mainland, the regime stepped up its nationwide political repression. The Taiwanese had eagerly welcomed the Nationalists in 1945 and looked forward to participating as full citizens of the Republic of China. But their liberators suppressed them, treating them suspiciously as collaborators with China's mortal enemy and arrogantly as a colonized people. In a symbolic move, Administrator-General and Garrison Commander Ch'en Yi moved into the Sōtokufu building and staffed his government with other mainlanders (called *ah-shan* or mountain people by the Taiwanese) and token Taiwanese who had spent the war years in China (*pan-shan* or half-mountains). Other Taiwanese were relegated to the lowliest positions. Ch'en and his coterie treated the local People's Political Council, elected in 1946, contemptuously and announced that the new ROC Constitution would not go into effect on Taiwan at the same time as the rest of the nation.

Along with economic and political retrogression, the carpetbagging Chinese brought lawlessness, corruption, plunder, inflation, disease, and an environment of general disorder. The Japanese physical and social infrastructure sustained a severe blow. Long quiescent, the Taiwanese penchant for violence exploded. On the evening of February 27, 1947, after Monopoly Bureau agents beat a woman selling cigarettes on the black market and shot a protesting bystander, a Taipei crowd attacked a police station, set fire to a police vehicle, and went on a rampage when the police refused to turn over the policeman who had fired the gun. On February 28, larger crowds turned their anger against all mainlanders and their Taiwanese cronies. The violence spread in ensuing days. As Taiwanese took over the administration in a number of localities, a conservatively oriented Settlement Committee tried to negotiate an end to the turmoil. Ch'en Yi acceded to its "Thirty-two Demands" for reform and promised not to bring in additional troops.[3]

Nevertheless, on May 8, upward of 10,000 troops from the mainland came ashore at Keelung and another 3,000 landed at Kaohsiung, with reinforcements coming later. The next day the Nationalists opened war on the Taiwanese, unleashing a fortnight of terror and looting. While on one level the killing seemed indiscriminate, a pattern is discernible: the Nationalists intended to liquidate the Taiwanese intellectual and social elite. They went after the Settlement Committee members, teachers, students, newspaper editors, lawyers, and anyone considered critical of the government. Figures for the total number of victims island-wide range from 10,000 to 20,000 (Kerr 1965:310).

The Nationalists blamed the Communists and fellow travelers, Japanese-era gentry, Taiwanese demobilized from the Japanese armed forces, hoodlums, and disgruntled bureaucrats for what is generally agreed to have been a spontaneous and leaderless uprising. They did not apologize for the savagery used to quell it. In fact, they rewarded one of the most vicious officials, P'eng Meng-chi, the "Butcher of Kaohsiung," later the minister of national defense and ambassador to several countries. Nevertheless, they did replace Ch'en Yi with Wei Tao-ming, a civilian who had served as the ROC ambassador in Washington and therefore could appear more progressive to the regime's American backers. Ch'en Yi was transferred to the position of governor of Chekiang province. The Nationalists also upgraded Taiwan from a military territory to a province and called for immediate local elections. There were some administrative reforms, "the military was kept out of sight" (Department of State 1967:309), and several "half-mountains" were brought into the government to show there was no discrimination against Taiwanese.[4]

The "2–28 Incident," as the series of events came to be known, had a profound effect on the Taiwanese people. They had already seen the mainlanders plunder and wreck their economy and lower their material and cultural standard of living, which under the Japanese surpassed that of nearly all of the rest of China. Now, they saw the government headed by Chiang Kai-shek break a pledge and send troops to Taiwan to support the rotten administration it had plagued them with in the first place. In the popular view, then, Chiang and all mainlanders were associated inextricably with Ch'en Yi and company. The masses lost faith in the regime.

But more important, seeing their elite and its successors systematically hunted down and murdered by the mainlanders traumatized the Taiwanese to the point that the phrase "politics is dangerous" became a watchword etched into their collective unconscious. Political activity became associated with a violent end. As they had been after the brutal Japanese military takeover fifty years earlier, the reconquered Taiwanese again became leaderless, atomized, quiescent, and apolitical. It was learned behavior, not a cultural trait.

Debacle and Retreat, 1947–1950

The 2–28 Incident should be kept in proper perspective. For the Chinese Nationalists, Taiwan was merely a sideshow in their grander efforts to recover and reunify all of China after World War II. People in other occupied areas were also the victims of corrupt, vindictive, and rapacious KMT liberators. The events just described were hardly unique in the China of that day.

Confident of their military superiority, backed up by the United States, the Nationalists revived the civil war against the Communists and scored early victories. But the tide began to turn as the Communists started a counteroffensive in central China. This gathered momentum into 1948 and the United States authorized special additional grants to help the Nationalists.

Destruction from the fighting and the siphoning off of resources for war had a disastrous effect on China's economy. Inflation took off. As the KMT's position weakened it issued more currency to make up for its budget deficits, with the not surprising consequence of aggravating the inflation even more. Prices of goods increased exponentially within the space of a day.

The government took several desperate steps in August 1948 to gain control of the economic situation. First, it inaugurated a new currency, the gold yuan, at the value of one gold yuan to three million old yuan (*fapi*). It banned unauthorized wage and price increases and instituted the compulsory purchase of gold, silver, and foreign exchange. Chiang Kai-shek, newly elected as the nation's president in April, sent his eldest son Ching-kuo (b. 1906) to Shanghai to try to set an example by successfully implementing the reforms in China's most volatile city. Although Chiang Ching-kuo's brutal methods cowed Shanghai's speculators and merchants into temporary submission, the program was not implemented to the same degree elsewhere in China. Internal and external economic pressures, aggravated by news of military defeats, pushed matters to a head. By October, goods were in short supply, the wealthy were moving their capital out of the city, and people stepped up their hoarding. The government gave up in early November and prices took off to stratospheric levels. Exacerbating the economic debacle, the People's Liberation Army (PLA) launched an all-out military offensive at about the same time.

Taiwan did not escape the effects of these events. Ch'en Yi's looting and the use of the Bank of Taiwan to issue the island's currency to cover deficit financing for the government and its enterprises had created an environment conducive to inflation. The reforms of August 1948 compounded by a sudden rush of capital fleeing the mainland sent prices on the island up 1,145 percent in 1948 (Lin 1973:30).

Chiang Kai-shek retired from the presidency in January 1949 after a disastrous defeat at the Battle of the Huai-hai. His successor was Vice-President Li Tsung-jen, but from his position as *tsung-ts'ai* and supreme commander, Chiang continued to run things. As the Communists pushed southward, the GRC withdrew from Nanking to Canton (April), Chungking (October), and Ch'eng-tu (November). The People's Liberation Army took Shanghai in May, effectively severing Taiwan's main link with the mainland. Chiang resumed active control of the party in June, but the situation was obviously hopeless. The office of *tsung-ts'ai* was moved to Taipei in August. The Communists advanced into Szechuan, Li Tsung-jen went to the United States, and on December 9, 1949 the KMT government moved its temporary capital one more time: to Taipei, Taiwan.

Despite a visit by Madame Chiang to the United States and a propaganda crusade by missionary and right-wing supporters of the regime there, the American government, disgusted with their incompetence and insatiable appetite for funds that simply vanished, decided that the Nationalists were finished and that Taiwan would soon fall as well. It ceased additional assistance—which had exceeded US $2 billion since V-J Day (Department of State 1967:xv)—and decided to stand back until the dust had settled.

Chiang Kai-shek did not come to Taiwan without having made prior arrangements. In December 1948, sensing that he might need a secure bastion for a last stand, he had sent a trusted general, Ch'en Ch'eng (1897–1965) to be Taiwan's new governor and had assigned Chiang Ching-kuo to head the provincial party organization.

Ch'en Ch'eng's efforts went toward stabilizing the local economy. He began a land reform in April by imposing an upward limit of 37.5 percent of the volume of the crop as rent on tenanted land; set up the Taiwan Production Board to coordinate the economy in May; and issued a new currency, the New Taiwan dollar (NT$ or *T'ai-pi*) in June (Lin 1973:31–32, 52).

Chiang Ching-kuo's major responsibility was to stablize the island politically. He prosecuted the task ruthlessly, resulting in the incarceration or murder of thousands of Taiwanese and mainland refugees then on the island (Kerr 1965:368).

In addition to the mandate to eliminate opposition, Chiang Kai-shek imparted to his Soviet-trained son the task of revamping the complex internal security (*t'e-wu*) apparatus to get rid of the overlapping, often incompetent faction-based spy organs.[5] In August 1949, Ching-kuo became the primer inter pares of the Political Action Committee (*cheng-chih hsing-tung wei-yuan-hui*), a new super-spy organ charged with coordinating and overseeing security work throughout the party, army, state, and society.[6] The concentration of power represented by his eventual control of this committee paved the way for Ching-kuo to construct his own power base. In the army, he became director of the General Political Department of the Ministry of Defense in 1950, giving him the power to check on the loyalty and indoctrination of military officers. In the party he became a member of the Central Reform Committee (1950–52) and Central Standing Committee (1952). He subsequently gained power over youth, by organizing the China Youth Anti-Communist National Salvation Corps. His rise in the government followed.[7]

Chiang Ching-kuo's political stabilization task was made easier by the proclamation of a general state of siege on Taiwan on May 19. This included the imposition of martial law (*chieh-yen*), thereby greatly expanding the scope of power of the Taiwan Garrison Command and suspending the protection of individual rights guaranteed in the 1946 Constitution.[8]

As 1950 began, the outlook for the Nationalists on Taiwan was still bleak. The Communists were landing on Hainan, China's other large, but much less developed or defensible, island. In a short time somewhere between one and two million civilian and military refugees from the mainland descended on Taiwan, which in 1945 had had a population of only six million. Supplies were short and inflation was still out of control.

Chiang Kai-shek resumed the presidency in March. He moved Ch'en Ch'eng up to the premiership and appointed the American-educated former mayor of Shanghai, K. C. Wu (Wu Kuo-chen), to be the new governor. Wu was charged with spearheading administrative reforms, mainly as a ploy to solicit more American aid. The reforms included the implementation of local self-government on Taiwan and readjustment of the island's administrative districts. But as power became increasingly centralized at the national level, Governor Wu was rendered virtually impotent.[9]

Then, on June 25, in a bizarre plot twist, North Korea's Kim Il-sung entered the story as the Nationalists' deus ex machina by invading South Korea. Two days later, President Harry Truman reversed the American hands-off policy toward the KMT and sent the Seventh Fleet into the Taiwan Straits to protect the Nationalists from imminent Communist invasion and to draw the line against communism in East Asia. Economic and military aid were to be resumed as well.

5

Rehabilitation and Import-Substitution Industrialization, 1950-1959

Global Geopolitics and Political Reform

The mysterious forces of history had given the Chinese Nationalists and the people of Taiwan a second chance to work out their relationship. The setting—global and domestic—in 1950 was quite different from that in act one, 1945.

In that first encounter, the Nationalists had had no social base or administrative infrastructure on the island. Coming out of eight years of war, the Nationalists were on the victorious side, one of the Allied Powers, and could count on U.S. backing, even though the Americans were concentrating most of their vast resources on the rehabilitation of Europe. The KMT had its political headquarters in Nanking, a large cadre of officials, a formidable military machine, and a continent of untapped resources. All of this made them cocky about recovering territories formerly under enemy occupation. It mattered little to them that they had almost no understanding of Taiwan's social structure or cultural heritage, or that they were insensitive to its people's long-pent-up aspirations. Their arrogance, compounded by the debilitating corruption of their regime, obsession with security, vindictiveness toward those who had lived under the Japanese, and eagerness to make up for the years of relative deprivation in the hinterland, poisoned their approach to Taiwan.

In 1945, for their part, the people of Taiwan were war-weary but optimistic. They were eager to be rid of the repressive colonial regime that had accorded them inferior status, and to become full citizens of Asia's first republic. They welcomed and trusted the Nationalists. Unlike in other former colonies, there had been no independence struggle in Taiwan and there was no battle-hardened core of leaders ready to take over. The elite of the island, most of whom had collaborated with the Japanese, approached the new era in a spirit of cooperation.

Five years later, in 1950, the Nationalists had established something of a bureaucratic foothold on Taiwan, using a handful of local collaborators but mostly appointed officials from the mainland. But rejected by the majority of their own people and abandoned in disgust by their former allies, they had nowhere but Taiwan to flee to, and their war machine was in shambles. They had no funds or access to adequate resources and were being trampled by runaway inflation. Their earlier arrogance, corruption, and violence had thoroughly alienated the people of Taiwan.

Some Taiwanese sought the island's independence or even a return of Japanese rule. The people expected of the Nationalists little more than a continuation of the disaster perpetrated on them for half a decade, until the Communists came and something new began. Taiwan's elite had been destroyed and most families had lost a relative to the mainlanders' death squads, or knew someone who had. Production was at a standstill and the murderous inflation made economic activity—other than smuggling and speculation—a grim prospect. There was no guarantee of the protection of private property. The relentless repression and reign of terror inhibited people's efforts to express their interests. There was no law. The people of Taiwan had basically no alternatives but to wait and see what new tribulations they would have to endure.

But to the Chinese Nationalists, two extreme options presented themselves at this juncture. They could continue business as usual, turning in a gyre until things fell apart. Or they could reform themselves, establish a new relation with Taiwanese society, and make a united stand against the Communists.

They chose the latter. Desperate and humiliated, the remnant Nationalist leadership, especially President Chiang himself, realized that to resist the Communists effectively and even to preserve the KMT's tenuous position on Taiwan, the party had to be fundamentally cleansed and the people of Taiwan given an incentive to support it. Chiang drew on a long legacy of party reform, going back to Sun Yat-sen, aimed at making the KMT a more effective revolutionary weapon (Shieh 1970:208–209). Chiang was also sensitive to his place in history and correctly saw a final chance to accomplish something positive for the Chinese people inspired by the teaching of Sun Yat-sen.

But the decision from within Taiwan to rectify the leadership cannot be separated from the international context of 1950. Most important was the cold war. The loss of China, compounded by the bloodletting in Korea, had galvanized the United States and its allies into adopting a policy of containing the further spread of international communism. The witchhunt in the United States to affix blame for the loss of China brought the KMT's American friends—military, political, mission-ary—into prominence.

America, the world's most powerful nation, located the fate of KMT Taiwan squarely within the larger context of the global anti-Communist crusade.[1] Taiwan became "Free China," the name used during the war for mainland areas not occupied by the Japanese, and now used to indicate regions not in Communist hands. American military might shielded the island from Communist invasion. American financial and commodity assistance insulated the island's economy from external forces. Afforded security and breathing space, the KMT could under-take a major reform and adopt a fresh strategy in its approach to relations with state and society in its new habitat. As an added incen-tive, American aid was tied to reforms.

In many ways, the modus operandi that emerged in 1950 resembled the American occupation in Japan, then successfully drawing to a close. To be sure, the Nationalists were not America's vanquished enemy, but they were nonetheless a defeated force in a hostile environ-ment in disarray and devoid of confidence. As in Japan, the Americans sent in a battery of civil and military advisers to assist in the necessary rebuilding of the decimated structure along new lines.[2] As in Japan, the locals governed, but the Americans constituted enough of a shadow government to influence a wide range of political and economic deci-sions made by the Chinese.

It was a dialectical relationship that succeeded because enough Chi-nese—backed by the Generalissimo—realized clearly the urgent need for reform and were committed to it, and the Americans provided the wherewithal, and sometimes the pretext, to set it in motion. Control-ling the Nationalists' life-support systems gave the Americans great power to influence the direction of change, while the fact that the Nationalists were not an enemy but a sovereign state in the United

Nations as well as an ally, and really did face an implacable and threatening force, limited how far the United States could push the regime in the direction of reform without risking destabilizing it and smashing the whole house of cards.

Much of the KMT's reform was accomplished by self-selection: those who came with the Generalissimo to an uncertain future on Taiwan were generally loyal and willing to make sacrifices, whereas the most egregiously corrupt and harmful persons by and large did not go to Taiwan at all. They scattered, with their assets, to Hong Kong, Southeast Asia, and, to a large extent, the United States. Chiang's notorious brothers-in-law, H. H. Kung and T. V. Soong, retired to New York. Ideologue and intelligence czar Ch'en Li-fu became a chicken farmer in New Jersey. An exception was Ch'en Yi, who was brought back to Taiwan under arrest for allegedly making a deal with the Communists. In a symbolic act functionally equivalent to the Allies' hanging of Tojo, Ch'en was shot in Taipei to atone for his crimes against the people of Taiwan. For those of doubtful allegiance who came willingly to Taiwan, Chiang Ching-kuo's ascendancy in the security apparatus provided extralegal means for getting rid of a range of his father's opponents. Chiang Kai-shek broke the factions that had rent his mainland regime and took personal charge of party and state affairs (Barnett 1954:2).

More formally, in August 1950, the elder Chiang, as *tsung-ts'ai* of the party, dissolved its Central Executive Committee and established a Central Reform Committee in its place, charged with implementing the "Reform Program of the KMT."[3] The KMT admitted past errors and moved to purge bad elements, recruit new members (including Taiwanese), and strengthen discipline and indoctrination to reinvigorate the party. The KMT's Seventh National Congress elected a new Central Committee in October 1952, signalling the conclusion of the reform.

State Structure and Party-State Relations

In coming to Taiwan, the Nationalists brought along their formal national-level party and government structures and superimposed these on the party and governmental structures of one province, the land mass of which was .37 percent of China's total, the population 1 percent. As with the Communist mainland, there are parallel party and state structures at all levels—national, provincial, county, municipal, and district—to ensure firm party control.[4] Major governmental policy decisions are generated or approved by relevant party organizations.

At the very top of the KMT is the National Congress, with a Central Committee (flanked by the Central Advisory Committee) and its powerful Standing Committee that handles work when the Congress is not in session. Formally, at least, the KMT is still Leninist in structure and in its democratic-centralist principles of organization. Its rank and file are members of party cells that exist in schools, the military, residential street offices, enterprises, social organizations, and overseas Chinese communities. Their main function is to ensure that party policies are implemented and to resist challenges to KMT domination. Four hundred service centers around the island provide a variety of social services as well as a means of keeping informed of local affairs. "Security offices" (an-ch'üan-shih) in private enterprises, schools, and civic bodies perform a control function. At the local level, party cadres are also charged with selecting candidates for elections and using whatever means are necessary to see them through to victory. This function gained in importance with the implementation of local self-government. It often meant coopting local elites and manipulating extant factional conflicts (Jacobs 1980).

The chief of state is the president. Since 1948, with the enactment of Temporary Provisions during the Period of National Crisis, the president has been granted a wide range of emergency powers. He is elected by the National Assembly for a six-year term. Originally a president could only serve twice, but this rule was amended due to the Emergency. The National Assembly itself is elected by the people directly for a six-year term. Its other powers include electing the vice-president and amending the constitution. The first session of the National Assembly was convened in March 1948 in Nanking with 2,961 delegates. It elected Chiang Kai-shek president and Li Tsung-jen vice-president. Subsequent sessions have been held in Taipei.[5]

There are five branches of the national government:

1) the Executive Yuan or Cabinet, with a range of ministries and commissions, which is appointed by the president and whose own president is the premier. The division of labor between president and premier is vague, and either one could be the effective ruler. All provincial governments and special municipalities administered directly by the central government come under this yuan's direct control, and it appoints their leaders.

2) The Legislative Yuan, elected by the people based on region and profession. It is responsible for legislation, approving the budget, interpellation of government officials, etc. The first election for three-year terms under the new constitution was held in May 1948: of the

759 elected legislators, 684 attended the first session in Nanking (*China Handbook* 1956–57:117).

3) The Judicial Yuan, whose justices are appointed by the president.

4) The Examination Yuan for examinations for the civil service and professional licenses, whose members are appointed by the president.

5) The Control Yuan, the chief watchdog agency, whose members are elected by provincial and municipal councils. Before the situation got out of control in 1949, 180 members of a projected 223 had been elected (ibid.: 188).

When the electoral bodies were established, KMT dominance was overwhelming. There are two other parties, which field a few candidates, and independents run as well. After removal to Taiwan, the KMT suspended general elections until the regime returns to the mainland, so the party has maintained its dominance by freezing the membership of these organs. Perhaps as important, the original mainlanders still occupy the majority of seats. At the "national" level, the distinction between party and state, including their budgets, was blurred until the rise of an opposition movement in the 1970s.

Beneath and subordinate to the national level, but governing the same piece of real estate (with the exception of a few offshore islands that are part of Fukien province), is the Taiwan Provincial Government (TPG). Its seat is in Wu-feng, Taichung county, 100 miles south of Taipei. The Executive Yuan granted Taiwan self-government (*tzu-chih*) or home rule, the same demand of the Taiwanese under the Japanese, in 1950. A fifty-five-person Provisional Provincial Assembly was elected by county and municipal assemblies at the end of 1951. Subsequent assemblies were elected by direct vote of the electorate. The main duties of the Provincial Assembly, established in 1959, are approval of the provincial budget, interpellation of provincial officials, and an assortment of mostly advisory powers. Its sessions are carefully monitored by officials sent from the national party and state organs. KMT members are expected to submit to party discipline and vote as a bloc.[6] The governor of Taiwan is appointed by the president.

Beneath the provincial level are elected county (*hsien*) and municipal assemblies and governments, which have a great degree of say over local affairs. Magistrates and mayors are elected except for the mayor of any city run directly by the national government. An administrative reshuffle in 1950 divided Taiwan into sixteen counties and five municipalities. Though continuing its dominance of government at all levels, with the introduction of direct suffrage and self-government, the

KMT's proportion of local elected representatives fell below that at the national level. To compete effectively, the party had to field Taiwanese candidates, so it actively recruited natives into its ranks.

Government and party cadres and military officers with no property or connections in Taiwan comprised a large part of the mainlanders who sought refuge on the island. They had to be rewarded for their fealty with some sort of secure income-generating position, so they were farmed out to the various bureaucracies, which rapidly became bloated and overstaffed. Chances for Taiwanese to advance to leadership positions above the local level of government or party were remote. A promising military career was unthinkable. While this mainlander monopoly sparked resentment among Taiwanese, the mainland cohort did include an abundance of well-trained, extremely talented, and committed men who found their way to the top, especially in the bureaucracies charged with management of the economy.

Although Chiang Kai-shek, Ch'en Ch'eng, and other leaders had military backgrounds, they established a civilian government and the party retained control of the gun. Nonetheless, an extensive network of overt and covert quasi-military security agencies plays an important role in maintaining KMT rule and suppressing dissent. It comprises the following bodies at least:[7]

—National Security Conference: coordinating body directly under the president of the ROC. (President Chiang Ching-kuo's second son Hsiao-wu became its executive secretary around 1980, a career pattern similar to his father's). *Free China Journal* (March 10, 1985:1) calls the NSC "the highest government decision-making body."

—National Security Bureau: officially under the National Security Conference and directly responsible to the president, it also ideally coordinates, supervises, and plans the work of the intelligence and control system, although each agency's head has alternative routes to the president. Its budget appears to come under the Ministry of National Defense, and its chiefs have all come from the military. Its leaders are not accountable to the Legislative Yuan.

—Investigation Bureau: under the Ministry of Legal Affairs, it is equivalent to the American Federal Bureau of Investigation. It handles mainly domestic security.

—Intelligence Bureau: under the Ministry of Defense, it takes responsibility for collecting foreign intelligence and doing counterintelligence work.

—General Political Warfare Department: Also under the Ministry of

Defense, it was set up by Chiang Ching-kuo and was important in his rise and the maintenance of his power. Its Political Warfare College trains political commissars for the armed forces, but they actually play a major role in general social control. The department has special influence over the media and education.

—Taiwan Garrison Command: A military agency under the TPG, it is the body most civilians come into contact with under the status of martial law and suppression of rebellion. It enjoys a reputation for arbitrariness and ruthlessness. It opens mail, censors and shuts down publications, and generally intimidates dissenters.

—Military Police: responsible for military discipline and traffic control.

—Police: under the Ministry of the Interior, responsible for social order.

—KMT: has its own security network and agents in government and social units. It also runs the Anti-Communist National Salvation Youth Corps, which administers a gamut of activities from military training to dance parties.

In addition to its role in domestic security, the National Security Bureau maintains agents abroad who keep records on students and businessmen as well as Chinese who have taken foreign citizenship. Unlike the Chinese Communist Party, which renounced its authority over them, the KMT still claims jurisdiction over all Chinese everywhere, no matter what their citizenship. Students abroad are encouraged and sometimes pressured to file reports on their fellow students, for which they receive financial remuneration. A number of professional students from Taiwan populate foreign campuses.

The leadership revamped the armed forces by mass retirements, universal conscription of males, improved training with U.S. assistance, and indoctrination and close supervision through a system of political commissars administered by Chiang Ching-kuo. Although Taiwanese youths naturally comprised the bulk of the conscripts, mainlanders dominated higher positions. By the end of the decade, the total regular forces numbered around 600,000 (Clough 1978:104).[8]

After retiring tens of thousands of old soldiers, the Nationalists did not just cast them out upon society. In 1955, the government established the Vocational Assistance Commission for Retired Servicemen (VACRS) under provincial governor C. K. Yen (later under Chiang Ching-kuo), charged with training and resettling demobilized old soldiers and caring for those who were ill. American technical and financial aid, including a grant of $42 million in 1955 (Jacoby 1966:188), facilitated the operation. Able-bodied retirees found themselves engaged in major infrastructure construction—creating highways through rugged mountain terrain, opening up virgin farmland, building factories, and so on. VACRS burgeoned into a huge operation owning a collection of productive enterprises of its own in addition to undertaking contract work.

From a very tenuous military situation in 1949, the KMT-mainlander regime became increasingly secure on the island. The U.S. Seventh Fleet physically sealed off Taiwan from the mainland. The establishment of the U.S. Military Assistance Advisory Group (MAAG) in May 1951 and a massive infusion of military aid were a further boost to morale.[9] Perhaps the greatest confidence boosters were the December 1954 Mutual Defense Treaty and a subsequent congressional resolution authorizing President Dwight Eisenhower to assist Taiwan militarily against renewed Communist aggression. America's willingness to protect Free China, to the point of committing troops, clarified the U.S. posture after years of uncertainty. The Nationalists had a future.

Revolution from Above

Taiwan offers a textbook case of elite-led revolutionary social transformation.[10] With their enormous party and state bureaucracies, military machine, security network, industrial assets confiscated from the Japanese, and the Americans insulating them from external enemies, the Nationalists had control over the situation in Taiwan to a degree they never approached on the mainland. What is more, there was no viable opposition to them. Between 1947 and 1949, Taiwan's old intellectual and political elites had been liquidated. There was no indigenous capitalist or financial class to challenge the regime economically. Taiwan had no warlords. Peasants were not mobilized or agitating for land reform. There was no organized political movement nor an armed force to threaten KMT-mainlander hegemony. Because, on the one hand, the regime faced no more internal opposition and, on the other, as an external occupying force it had no base within Taiwanese society, it had free rein for activity.

After 1950 the regime adopted a corporatist approach[11] to Taiwan's society quite different from the strategy it had used so unsuccessfully on the mainland. There it had perceived political and social power as something that had to be eliminated by force or compromised with tactically. It fed parasitically off wealth generated by others. On Taiwan, the KMT moved to create a base in society where none existed, coopt potential allies, and create wealth. The mainlander elite set out to reshape Taiwanese society step by step, with minimal further violence. The objective, of course, was self-preservation, but the means and side effects were generally positive.

The vast majority of Taiwanese in 1950 were peasants, so an important step in building a base was land reform, whether or not it was necessary. Although a key part of Sun Yat-sen's ideology and long a plank in the KMT's platform, land reform was never implemented systematically or effectively on the mainland. Realizing that skillful use of the land question had helped the CCP mobilize tens of millions of peasants to overthrow them, the Nationalists took this object lesson to heart and placed priority on land reform in Taiwan to nip the problem in the bud (Chen 1961). In addition to removing the economic and political base of the indigenous elite, the KMT's objective was conservative—to prevent peasant upheaval rather than to be charitable to the rural folk.[12]

As the mainlanders did not themselves own land and the KMT was not allied with Taiwanese landlords (the largest of whom had been active Japanese collaborators), there were few obstacles to undertaking the reform. Also, fresh from a successful reform in Japan, the Americans strongly urged land reform on the Nationalists and supplied experts, advice, and funds to see it through, all funneled through the Joint Commission on Rural Reconstruction (JCRR).[13]

The land reform proceeded in three stages.[14] First, in April 1949, farm rents were limited to a maximum of 37.5 percent of the total annual main-crop yield as approved by specially appointed Rent Campaign Committees. In stage two, lasting from 1948 to 1951, public farm land, which had formerly belonged to the Japanese government or individuals and had been confiscated by the Nationalists, was leased or sold to tenant farmers. By 1953, 63,000 chia had been sold.*

The third stage, "land to the tiller," was more complex and required detailed preparation. First, the land was classified by owners and graded for quality. The Land to the Tiller Act of 1953 set an upper limit of three chia of seventh- to twelfth-grade paddy field for landlords to retain; all land over three chia was subject to compulsory pur-

---

*One chia = .97 hectares = 2.4 acres.

chase by the government for resale to the present cultivators. Landlords were compensated 70 percent with land bonds in kind (rice for paddy land, sweet potatoes for dry land) and 30 percent with shares of stock in four government enterprises earmarked to be transferred to private ownership—Taiwan Cement, Taiwan Paper and Pulp, Taiwan Agriculture and Forestry, and Taiwan Industry and Mining.

In all, about one-quarter of Taiwan's cultivated land was affected (Ho 1978:163). Land cultivated by owner-cultivators increased from 50.5 percent of the total in 1949 to 75.4 percent in 1953. Tenant-cultivated land fell from 41.8 percent to 16.3 percent over the same period (Tang 1954:14, 18). Owner-farmers increased from 33 percent of the total in 1948 to 57 percent in 1953; part owners declined from 24 percent to 22 percent. Tenant farmers fell from 36 percent to 15 percent (Lin 1973:203). Small landowning families became the dominant force in Taiwan's countryside. The land reform, in the aggregate, had a major positive effect on income distribution in rural areas.[15]

The smaller landlords were the big losers. Prior to the reform, land values had plummeted so the valuation was set at a price much lower than its real value (Lin 1973:53). Landlords regarded the government enterprise bonds skeptically and sold them off below par value to speculators, missing out on the later boom. (Yang 1970:157) By contrast, through investment in industry and finance, the largest landowners made out quite well.

The land reform is touted as having been bloodless (especially in comparison to that of the Communists) but this must be qualified. According to interviews with children of former landlords, the brutality and violence of 1947 and 1949, though primarily an urban phenomenon, had touched almost every family on the island. When the authorities announced a land reform, therefore, the targets knew that the KMT would not shirk from employing force again if it saw fit, so the landlords acquiesced. Furthermore, they were scattered, disorganized, and unarmed.

In the countryside, the government did not stop with land reform. It organized peasants and rural residents into 340 KMT-controlled farmers' associations, which offer credit, introduce technology, supply inputs, and serve as marketing cooperatives (Yang 1970:407–11).

With substantial American assistance through JCRR, the government aggressively pushed the development of agriculture, mainly through repair and upgrading of the Japanese-built infrastructure (especially irrigation works) and the introduction of new techniques and cash crops. While sugar and rice were still the main crops and among Taiwan's few exports at the time, the rural sector broke from the sort of monocultural colonial legacy that has stifled so many other developing countries. After recovery from the destruction of World War II and its aftermath, agricultural production grew at an average rate of 3.9 percent for the years 1953–59.

At the same time, the state squeezed agriculture to feed the huge urban population, to supply materials and funds for industrialization, and to sell its products abroad to earn hard currency. In addition to a land tax in kind and compulsory sale of rice at below-market prices, the main means for extracting surplus was the rice-fertilizer barter system. All chemical fertilizer came from the state (via either imports or domestic production by the state-owned Taiwan Fertilizer Corporation) and was provided to peasants in exchange for rice at rates very unfavorable to the peasants. Thus, while investing in agriculture to increase production, the state controlled peasants politically by the Farmers' Associations and economically by the rice-fertilizer barter.

Economic Recovery and Import Substitution

With the backing and advice of the Agency for International Development (AID), the government established institutions for guided capitalist development, although their primary purpose at the time was to stabilize the chaotic situation and revive production. The chastened political leaders, notably Chiang Kai-shek and Premier, later Vice-President, Ch'en Ch'eng, attributing their debacle in large part to the collapse of the economy, gave greater scope over Taiwan's economy to Western-trained experts and intervened less than they had on the mainland.

Within the economic bureaucracy there was a division between those who favored continued state dominance of the economy based on its ownership of dozens of confiscated Japanese enterprises in several sectors[16] and those who advocated more range for a private sector. Both sides could claim legitimacy through Sun Yat-sen's vague instructions on the restriction or regulation of capital (*chieh-chih tzu-pen*).[17] Sun had written that the state should own enterprises in key sectors related to national defense, natural monopolies, or where capital requirements were so stiff that no private entrepreneurs could afford the risk. Everything else could be left to private capital. In the early 1950s, to revive production, the more socialist-oriented cadres prevailed; in the latter part of the decade, combining their own inclinations with U.S. pressure, the free enterprisers came to the fore.

The Taiwan Production Board (TPB), established in May 1949, was the first organ to stabilize the economy. It was chaired by the provincial governor. With the addition of an Industrial and Financial Committee in early 1950, its activities expanded beyond coordinating production, supply, and trade. In 1953 it was absorbed into the Economic Stabilization Board (ESB), established in 1951 on American advice. The ESB itself was reorganized from the Financial and Economic Working Group of the Executive Yuan. The ESB, chaired by the governor and later by the premier, had committees for monetary banking and trade policies, utilization of U.S. aid, budget and taxation, agriculture, and price stability, as well as an Industrial Development Commission (IDC). The IDC was responsible for overseeing the formulation and implementation of the economic plans that began the same year. Moving the chief economic agency from provincial to national level increased its power and merged the identity of the central government with the island. The state thus had bureaucratic agencies to guide all aspects of the economy in addition to its own unassailable position as the dominant capitalist.

One man dominated and forged the broad lines of Taiwan's economic path in the 1950s. K. Y. Yin (1903–1963) was trained as an electrical engineer and worked for Westinghouse. After his return to Taiwan, he held a number of posts more or less concurrently: permanent member, then deputy chair, of TPB; general manager of the Central Trust of China; member and later secretary general of ESB and convener of IDC; minister of economic affairs; chair of the Foreign Exchange and Trade Control Commission; vice-chair of the Council on U.S. Aid; and chairman of the board of the Bank of Taiwan. Former secretary to T. V. Soong, outspoken, and authoritarian, Yin had a number of enemies who tried to destroy him, but to this day he is worshipped by officials he trained and businessmen he assisted. Since his death, no one man has wielded so much power over the economy. He also established a pattern of engineers, not professional economists, running the key economic planning agencies.

But the Chinese government did not have final say over its economy, as the Americans, through AID, had de facto veto power through their control of the Nationalists' economic lifeline. Americans sat in on ESB meetings, and many Chinese government agencies had to hold their meetings in English for the benefit of American advisers. The key organ charged with administering American assistance was the Council on U.S. Aid (CUSA), composed of relevant cabinet members and chaired by the premier. Enjoying a degree of financial independence and not being nested in any particular ministry, CUSA maintained an autonomy comparable bodies in other recipient nations lacked. It was thus relatively free of the manipulation, corruption, and red tape that plague aid programs elsewhere. Americans who dealt with CUSA were unanimous in their praise for the agency and its members. The Chinese members, fluent in English and American-oriented, carried the ideology and methods learned from the CUSA experience into their leadership of Taiwan's economy over subsequent decades.

When the American aid program resumed in Taiwan late in 1950, its primary objective was to help the Nationalists achieve political and economic stability.[18] To this end, of the $1.5 billion in nonmilitary aid obligated to Taiwan between 1951 and 1965, 54 percent came under the rubric defense support, earmarked by Congress "to enable the recipient country to maintain an agreed level of military strength without retrogressing economically" (Jacoby 1966:39). Another 8.5 percent of aid was direct forces support, used to maintain ROC "military forces necessary to carry out mutual Chinese-U.S. objectives" (ibid:42). In addition to these categories of aid, America also provided surplus agricultural commodities under Public Law (PL) 480. These accounted for 25 percent of aid obligations. Combined with concerted Chinese efforts to control prices, foreign exchange allotments, the money supply, and fiscal practices, American aid helped to stabilize the economy, including inflation, while permitting the Nationalists to maintain their gargantuan military machine, which was consuming an average of 85 percent of the national government's expenditures (ibid:118).

Aid in the first few desperate years was nearly all of the nonproject type, mainly commodity imports. These helped supply basic necessities to the people and ease inflationary pressure. By the middle of the decade, basic stability had been achieved and the economy had recovered to the level of prewar production peaks. The character of aid shifted from plugging holes in the dike to fostering economic development, even though it was still justified to Congress as military support. The proportion of project aid increased. This meant that the recipient had to apply for assistance for a specific project, giving the donor more control over the disbursal of monies. The Chinese government also moved in the direction of building up Taiwan per se, and in 1953 it produced a Four-Year Economic Plan to this end.

The ESB's First Plan was "a rather crude effort" (Li 1976:93) encompassing only industry and agriculture. The Second Plan (1957–1960) added separate communications projects and special projects such as the Shihmen Reservoir, tidal land reclamation, vocational assistance for retired servicemen, and public housing. It specified measures for achieving the targets (Li 1976:93). The essence of the plan was really a linking together of applications for AID monies.

The 1950s also saw the emergence of the first postwar generation of industrial capitalists. Almost no leading mainland capitalists followed Chiang Kai-shek to his island redoubt; they went to more secure climes, such as Hong Kong or the United States. The few businessmen who did go were loath to commit capital as they were convinced that their stay on Taiwan would be short. The environment was so unsettled and inflationary that it was faster and made more business sense to make a killing through speculation than sinking funds into risky manufacturing ventures. It fell to the state to foster the emergence of a bourgeoisie, the same situation Japan's Meiji oligarchs faced.

The KMT dominated most industry, but partly under U.S. pressure and partly due to the insistence of K. Y. Yin and the pro-private-sector bureaucrats, it devised measures to promote capitalists in certain key sectors such as cotton textiles and flour milling.

The first men to benefit were mainlanders from Shanghai and Shantung province. They applied to the government for an allotment of AID-financed imported cotton or wheat. In the textile sector, Yin employed an "entrustment" scheme whereby the state supplied raw cotton, paid wages to workers, and purchased the yarn. CUSA's Textile Subcommittee also controlled cloth weaving. The "entrepreneur" had no risk and stood to make a fortune in a market where demand far outstripped supply. This indeed happened, and the overpriced, poor quality textile goods stirred resentment among captive consumers against these government-backed manufacturers. Major corporations such as Tai-yuen Textile, Far Eastern Textile, and Chung-hsing Textile got their start in this environment. They expanded into man-made fibers with additional state and U.S. assistance later in the decade.

Although officially anyone could apply for AID allotments, in practice mainlanders had an inside track, being familiar with procedures and having friends or relatives in the bureaucracy. American officials complained about this to the Chinese.[19] Only a few Taiwanese, such as Wu San-lien, a journalist who had spent several years serving the KMT on the mainland, benefited. The Tainan Textile Corporation, which he fronted for a group of Taiwanese businessmen from Tainan, became a major manufacturer and later a diversified conglomerate.

Some other Taiwanese did become capitalists in the mid-1950s, also via Chinese government and U.S. help. One type is represented by Y. C. Wang, a lumber-yard owner who agreed to manufacture polyvinyl chloride (pvc) in a plant established by AID. Wang built Formosa Plastics and spinoff companies into Taiwan's most successful and best integrated conglomerate.[20]

Other Taiwanese industrialists got a boost from the land reform. They accumulated shares in the four state enterprises used to compensate landlords for compulsorily purchased land. In 1954 the state began to transfer these firms to private ownership amidst a flurry of stock price manipulation. The main beneficiaries were the biggest landlords, the Japanese-era collaborators. The five families concentrated on the Taiwan Cement Corporation. Lin Po-shou of the Pan-ch'iao clan became the first posttransfer chairman, succeeded by C. F. Koo, son of Ku Hsien-jung. The company enjoyed state protection and contracts. A seat on its board became a coveted status symbol for later generations of Taiwanese capitalists.

In 1951, leading businessmen set up an umbrella organization, the China National Association of Industry and Commerce. Cabinet officials charged with economic affairs maintained close links with it. It functioned as a channel by which government policies were relayed to businessmen, unlike Japan's Keidanren, which is an association for the private sector to represent its interests to the bureaucracy.[21]

AID also supported the growth of a private sector through its Small Industry Loan Fund and Model Factory Program. Venture capital was not forthcoming through the state-owned banks that businessmen refer to disparagingly as pawnshops. Aspiring industrial or commercial entrepreneurs with no collateral had to turn to friends, relatives, and loan clubs for funds.

Once it was clear that there was expanding scope for private enterprise (including for Taiwanese), that the government was committed to industrialization, and that Taiwan had a future, there was an explosive release of the latent productive forces on the island. Numerous entrepreneurs, without a yarn allocation, bought looms to get in on the textile boom. To protect infant industries, the state employed a battery of measures such as multiple exchange rates, tariffs, and import restrictions. This import-substitution strategy paid off quickly.

The island's economy underwent a fundamental reorientation: from a typical colonial-style orientation of primary products traded for manufactured goods with Japan and then China, the volume of trade (not counting imported AID commodities) declined dramatically. This was mainly because those traditional markets had been lost and with the rapid population increase the domestic market consumed nearly all of what could be produced. By the middle of the decade, however, as industrial production expanded, the domestic market for textiles, wood products, and rubber goods became saturated (Lin 1973:68–70). Price wars ensued, and as production declined the demand for the few locally made capital goods did too. Import-substitution industrialization was having deleterious spread effects. Foreign exchange controls acted as a disincentive to export. Businessmen called for cartelization and government assistance.

By the end of the 1950s industrial production had doubled and its contribution to net domestic product increased while that of agriculture declined. A shift in employment out of the primary sector and into manufacturing could also be discerned. A further trend was the increased value of industrial production from the private sector (50/50 by 1958) and its faster growth rate when compared to public enterprises. This reflected a determined effort by AID to build up the private sector by granting seed money, loans, and advisers, and continued divestiture by the state.

The 1950s as a Starting Point

In the critical 1950s, the KMT regime, guided and supported by the United States, institutionalized the structure within which Taiwan's economy, society, and politics would evolve. In 1949 and 1950, the defeated and cornered Nationalists desperately needed a wealthy and powerful savior; the Americans sought front-line allies in the crusade against communism. The United States incorporated the eager Nationalists into the pax Americana to play a political, not economic role.

The emigré regime, with its full-blown and overstaffed bureaucracy, backed by overt and covert military force, faced few obstacles to consolidating its position on Taiwan and integrating the nation. It built on the Japanese authoritarian legacy, literally ensconcing itself in buildings the Sōtokufu had erected. The KMT had already liquidated

Taiwanese community leaders; with U.S. backing, it continued its revolution from above and outside by removing the big landlord class. It penetrated society to the residential neighborhood, village, school, and larger work unit. It encountered no enclaves of disobedient foreigners. The United States needed a stable ally, which constrained its ability to soften the KMT dictatorship.

In the economy as well, the state dominated. It owned all large industrial concerns and banks. It stimulated agricultural production while ensuring its own control of the surplus. Without Taiwan's former abundant exportable agricultural surplus and export markets, and hampered by a lack of foreign exchange, the state turned Taiwan's economy to import substitution in light industry to conserve funds, absorb labor, supply the domestic market, and accumulate capital rapidly. It selected cronies to become industrialists and made certain they depended on the state for capital, foreign exchange, equipment, raw materials, energy, and docile labor. The state did not obstruct small businesses, but neither did it facilitate their establishment or operation.

The main leverage held by Americans, and consequently the regime's prime constraint, was U.S. assistance. Economic transformation, whereby the state retrenched somewhat from production and helped a few private entrepreneurs, can be traced to American insistence and the threat of withholding aid. But the pace was slow.

The state also controlled relations with the outside world. It allocated financial aid and commodities. It closely regulated trade. There was virtually no direct foreign investment. The state thus mediated external linkages—most of which were with other nations' officials—and did not permit an untrammeled private foreign presence or a segment of Taiwan's society to represent alien interests.

Within the elite, however, factions took positions on the scope for a private sector, the role for market forces, and the suitable degree for the emigré regime to become rooted in Taiwan. American preferences influenced which positions won out, with important repercussions later on.

The emigré regime could not oppress the Taiwanese without limits. It needed their allegiance to fill the ranks of the armed forces and to revive production to improve supplies. It facilitated this by granting home rule at the local level and not stifling upward mobility through business. These sufficed to motivate the Taiwanese to channel their talents along the desired lines.

6

Export
Orientation
and
Political
Quiet,
1960-1973

In the mid-1960s, as a seasonal extra at a major department store in Cincinnati, I frequently found myself assigned to the Bargain Basement. A noticeable proportion of the merchandise down there carried a "Made in Taiwan" label. These rather shoddy goods were replacing those often ridiculed "Made in Japan" vendibles that had moved upstairs to the better departments. By the 1980s, the Taiwan-made merchandise, manufactured under some of the toniest designer clothing labels or high-quality electronics brand names, had also migrated upstairs, and the budget items came from—the People's Republic of China.

In these days of protectionist tariffs and Orderly Marketing Arrangements (OMA), we take for granted Taiwan's status as a single-minded exporter of manufactured commodities whose flood of goods harms American enterprises and workers. In the popular view, just as Taiwan's Little League baseball players constitute a menace to American dominance of what is, after all, our national pastime, this is a threat that must be curbed.

But Taiwan's adoption of a strategy combining export orientation and direct foreign investment (DFI) to stimulate industrialization was not inherent in its import-substitution economic strategy, although it could claim some legitimacy from the inherited ideological legacy. Rather, the shift from import substitution to export orientation as a strategy for industrialization derived from political debate within the leadership, influenced by American pressure, after it was decided that the substitution of light consumer goods had exhausted its potential. This chapter examines the crucial economic and social transformation made in the 1960s and how it laid the groundwork for later popular political activity.

The Road Not Taken

When Latin American countries faced a similar crisis of exhaustion of the import-substitution strategy, they did so from a base considerably different from Taiwan's. This naturally influenced the direction they took and its consequences. Import substitution in Latin America involved substantial TNC participation. Foreign corporations invested in those countries, leaping tariff barriers to retain or establish a presence in the large domestic markets there. They denationalized a number of industrial sectors, forcing local capitalists out.[1] The states played a very minor direct role in the economy. Any new policies to resolve import substitution problems would thus have to consider the wishes and global strategies of the TNCs.

On Taiwan, the state dominated the heights of the economy and accounted for a sizeable and crucial portion of industrial production. The few foreign investments of note were linked to the state sector. Local capital and the state supplied the needs of the small and poor domestic market. Extensive import prohibitions, especially on nonessential consumer goods, severely curtailed a foreign presence.

The Latin American economies had for a long time been incorporated into the world capitalist system through DFI, trade, finance, and a foreign-oriented segment of the consuming elite. This constrained the state's ability to implement policies that encouraged self-reliance, regulation of foreign capital, and so on. By contrast, since the KMT retreat, Taiwan had been insulated from the world system, cocooned within a wide range of U.S.-supplied material, financial, and military buffers in addition to a state-promulgated, multifaceted package of import restrictions, multiple exchange rates, price controls, duties, and export disincentives. Lacking both foreign interests domestically and external economic pressures, the regime had more range to determine its relation with the outside, given American cooperation and assistance. Of course, the United States had veto power to restrict the KMT's universe of choices.

The Latin American states were in a weak position vis-à-vis their own civil societies and economies. Populist politics accompanied import substitution, and people organized to demand solutions to economic crises that were threatening the democratic states. The states did not control the economy, a fact that constrained their leverage over society and their bargaining power with outside actors. On Taiwan, the state was dominant economically and politically and internally cohesive. There was little chance of overt popular resistance to its policies.

In the 1960s, to solve the problems brought on by exhaustion of import substitution in consumer goods, Latin American policymakers opted to deepen and integrate vertically their industrial structures, that is, to move to domestic production of intermediate and capital goods. TNCs had the capital, technology, and material expertise for this, so they took the lead. The state and local capital also borrowed heavily from foreign banks to fund ambitious projects. To solicit investors and lenders, the state had to ensure a risk-free investment climate. Through stages, the countries of the region turned from democratic to military rule, excluding the masses from political participation. People with access to foreign capital, technology, or consumption goods formed an elite increasingly divorced from the masses. The state burgeoned, adopting a technocratic approach to economic development, supporting the elite, and ensuring a stable investment climate. This package has been dubbed "bureaucratic-authoritarianism." While a debate rages over whether bureaucratic-authoritarianism inheres in the adoption of a second-stage import-substitution strategy, no one denies the existence of authoritarianism in Latin America.[2]

The Economic Reforms of the 1960s

In Taiwan, some officials also advocated industrial deepening, building an integrated steel mill, and so on. But in the end, a different choice prevailed, fundamentally reforming the economy and its relationship to the rest of the world.

By the mid-1950s, the AID mission felt that Taiwan's economy had more than recovered prewar peaks and could embark on a path of sustained, rapid development.[3] Congress still considered assistance to Taiwan "defense support." Only in 1958, with the establishment of the Development Loan Fund, did it commence to provide aid with the express goal of stimulating development per se. In the same year, AID established an Office of Private Development. This shift in AID's own mission greatly influenced its policies for Taiwan.

Between 1958 and 1960, AID and the Chinese government worked out a package of reforms to speed development and push Taiwan toward "graduation" from foreign aid. In 1960, AID made clear its intention of phasing its Taiwan program out of existence, probably by 1968. The global political dividends of the Nationalists' success promised to be enormous.

In essence, the Nineteen-Point Program of Economic and Financial Reform liberalized controls on trade and industry, promoted exports, and created a business climate to stimulate private local and foreign investment. The reforms revised import duties, reduced tariffs on imported inputs, and provided rebates if the products were exported; unified the multiple exchange rates; liberalized controls on exchange and trade; encouraged savings and private investment; raised public utility rates; and held military expenditures (Jacoby 1966: 134–35; Lin 1973:ch. 5).

These reforms posed great potential danger to the KMT state. As a key official I interviewed recalled, reduction of controls could wreck hard-won price stability and bring back inflation, the cause, as the KMT saw it, of its loss of the mainland. Scarce foreign exchange might vanish. A rise in trade would increase vulnerability to the global economy. Foreign investment might resuscitate the hated treaty port system and extraterritoriality, when foreigners ran freely through the economy and society. Many officials still disliked businessmen, and these policies would further the state's retrenchment from the economy and grant ever greater rein to private capital. This would entail concentration of capital, something Sun Yat-sen opposed.

The autocratic K. Y. Yin pushed the reforms, backed by Chiang Kai-shek and Ch'en Ch'eng among other leaders. At least as important, the Americans threatened a reduction in aid should the government not adopt the package, but offered a $20–30 million carrot for prompt implementation (Jacoby 1966:134–35).[4] K. T. Li (Li Kwoh-ting), a British-trained scientist and Yin protégé and driving force behind the boom of the 1960s, claimed that Chiang Kai-shek supported the reforms because they would enable Taiwan to get off the dole and become self-reliant (*tzu-li keng-sheng*).[5] In other words, the KMT perceived being an aid recipient as dependence in the pejorative sense, while it viewed establishing an open economy, which meant assuming responsibility for making its own way in the world, in a positive light.

The Third Four-Year Economic Plan (1961–64), which predicted 8 percent per annum GNP growth, incorporated the Nineteen Points as well as the 1960 Statute for Encouragement of Investment, which offered incentives to stimulate private investment. The state took other measures to promote the private sector, such as establishing the Industrial Development and Investment Center and the China Development Corporation, which also had KMT capital in it.

The government made an important institutional reform as well. In September 1963, to prepare for AID's impending withdrawal (moved up to 1965), it merged CUSA into the new Council for International Economic Cooperation and Development (CIECD) under Premier Ch'en Ch'eng. He was succeeded by C. K. Yen (Yen Chia-kan).[6] CIECD, an organ of the Executive Yuan, represented a commitment to centralized planning and coordination as well as to Taiwan's new position in the world economy outside the U.S. economic womb, but still under its military shield. Constantly improving its statistical base and analytical skills, CIECD, whose leaders and members although holding high party posts were primarily engineers and scientists, not economists or politicians, took responsibility for the four-year plans and also promulgated a Ten-Year Plan for 1965–1974. Vice-Chair K. T. Li secured $180 million in low-interest loans from the United States and Japan to substitute for the loss of AID monies, a way of proving Taiwan's viability (Wen 1984:78). CIECD also continuously improved the investment climate as the situation demanded—what K. T. Li called "sweeping up leaves in the autumn wind."[7] The Statute for Encouragement of Investment, a barometer of such sweeping, was revised more than a dozen times by 1980. It was supplemented by frequently updated categories and criteria of strategic productive enterprises singled out for special encouragement. In addition, there were separate statutes covering investment by foreigners, Overseas Chinese, and technical cooperation.

Payoff

The new reform strategy needed a positive response from foreign and local capital to succeed. But why would a TNC consider investing in an overcrowded island with a small domestic market, limited industry, no resources, and a precarious political future? The Americans addressed these concerns prior to the end of the AID mission. AID contracted Stanford Research Institute (SRI) to prepare reports on the economic feasibility of certain industries of potential interest to foreign investors.

SRI selected certain petrochemical intermediates, plastic resins, synthetic fibers, transistor radios, electronic components, watches, and clocks. AID went on to publicize Taiwan as an investment site, and the U.S. government utilized several programs to facilitate and protect the flow of private capital to Taiwan and other less developed countries. These included the AID Investment Guarantee Program, Cooley Fund, China Trade Act, and Sino-American Industrial Guarantee Agreement.[8]

The breakthrough case came in 1964 when General Instruments took the plunge by setting up a bonded electronics factory near Taipei. Its rapid success demonstrated the potential of offshore assembly in Taiwan to other American firms. Seven more invested in 1964; seventeen in 1965.

Taiwan's allure as a site for DFI did not really emerge until global conditions matured in the mid-1960s. The relaxation of cold war tensions facilitated general expansion of world trade. Among the beneficiaries was Japan, by then well into its own "miracle." Low-priced Japanese textile, plastic, and electronic products had flooded American markets, sending American manufacturers scampering abroad in search of production sites with costs so low that they could compete with the Japanese in the U.S. market. Taiwan's new investment climate featured its comparative advantage in very cheap, abundant, disciplined, and educated labor. For example, in 1972, the wage for a skilled worker in Taiwan was $73 a month compared with $102 in South Korea, $183 in Singapore, $122 in Hong Kong, and $272 in Japan. For unskilled labor, the respective rates were $45, $68, $60, $82, and $120 (ADL 1973b:10–11). Taiwan's labor efficiency was ranked just below that of Japan and the United States (ADL 1973a:55).

Large Japanese corporations began to invest in Taiwan to lower labor costs to recapture U.S. market shares lost to offshore American manufacturers. Taiwan thus became vital to the global production structures of corporations from two different core economies.

The government took another important step to solicit DFI and further integrate Taiwan's economy with the global one. In 1965, it promulgated the Statute for the Establishment and Management of Export Processing Zones (EPZ). It selected a plot of reclaimed land in the harbor of Kaohsiung, a port city in the south of the island. Dedicated in December 1966, Kaohsiung EPZ (KEPZ) combined a modern harbor with an industrial park and centralized administration enjoying decision-making power beyond the red tape of the ministries. Investing firms—foreign and local—enjoyed tax incentives and avoided import duties on equipment and parts as long as they exported all that they manufactured or assembled.

The foreign investment response gathered steam. The Investment Commission of the Ministry of Economic Affairs (MOEA) approved 29 cases in 1961, 36 in 1962, 103 in 1966, 212 in 1967, 325 in 1968, and 201 in 1969 (TSDB 1981:236). Twenty-four were approved for KEPZ in 1966; 12 were open the next year. By 1970, 161 investments had been approved for KEPZ and 126 firms were operating.[9] Local capital, singly or in partnership with foreigners, invested actively as well.

In the EPZ and elsewhere, DFI concentrated in a few sectors, most notably in electronics and to a much lesser degree in plastics and garments. Government incentives were important in this, as was the nature of the investors' target markets, mainly the United States. In addition, as one TNC gained a competitive edge via investment in Taiwan, its competitors followed. Thus one could see virtually all of the large American television manufacturers set up on Taiwan one after the other. Soon their suppliers opened up there as well, to secure their market after the assemblers began to obtain parts locally instead of importing them.

American investors on Taiwan were generally large TNCs, which set up wholly owned subsidiaries to cut costs on goods targeted at the U.S market. They were willing to purchase locally made parts if they met specifications.

By contrast, Japanese investors, although including some large enterprises, tended to comprise small and medium companies. The big firms, often through joint ventures and licensing agreements, desired to penetrate Taiwan's domestic market in addition to exporting to the United States and other countries—usually anywhere but Japan. As Americans imposed quotas on Japanese imports, the Japanese assembled their parts in Taiwan for shipment to the United States before Taiwan fell under similar restrictions.

The smaller Japanese firms also frequently took local partners, preferring Taiwanese to mainlanders, as the former were more receptive and shared language and other cultural traits. Japanese sometimes aimed at local markets but more often sold to Japanese assemblers in Taiwan or back home. But large and small, they were all loath to purchase locally made goods and continued to import parts from Japan. They had invested abroad in response to the strategy of the Ministry of

International Trade and Investment (MITI) to address Japan's pressing problems of the early 1970s. Labor shortages, high wages, lack of land, pollution, and quotas led MITI to urge certain enterprises to invest abroad. Labor-intensive, technologically simple smaller firms migrated, so that the home islands could concentrate on high tech, i.e., capital- and knowledge-intensive, high quality, high value added goods.[10]

Taiwan thus became a repository for industrial sectors no longer viable for the United States or Japan. It entered the emerging international division of labor at the bottom end of the product life cycle.[11]

A third type of foreign investor was Overseas Chinese, generally from Hong Kong and Southeast Asia. Coming from countries less developed than Taiwan, they invested in textiles and other import-substituting light industries, which transferred little technology and competed with the exports of Taiwan's own capitalists. Their main contribution was political—demonstrating with their capital the conviction that the KMT was the legitimate ruling party of China.[12]

So far I have described the role of the state and foreign capital in the new, internationalizing investment climate, but perhaps the most indispensible contribution, like chilies in Szechuan cuisine, came from local capital. Despite hesitation in certain areas, entrepreneurs responded to the environment by seeking out and exploiting opportunities. They moved up a learning curve as they integrated their capital reproduction and expansion with the global economy. Direct exports, subcontracting and consignment work for foreign corporations, and joint ventures were the three primary types of linkages.

The first industries to export were those that already had experience in the local market and had enough capacity, namely, textiles and processed food. Initially, they utilized networks of Overseas Chinese traders in Southeast Asia to handle their goods. But breaking into markets devoid of such contacts and with unfamiliar tastes proved more difficult. For this, they turned to Japanese general trading companies (*sogo shōsha*) and American mass buyers. As a result, in textiles especially, a division of labor emerged between production (done by local industrialists) and global marketing (done by foreigners). Interviewees in both sectors consistently gave a figure of "at least 50 percent" of exports being turned over to foreigners.

In the apparel end of textiles, sales to mass marketers, such as K-Mart, and subcontracting for foreign brand names, such as Arrow and Jantzen, accounted for a substantial part of production. The foreign buyer would present specifications to several manufacturers he met through government and informal channels and select one based on quality and price. Fierce competition ensued for these contracts. A Canadian clothing buyer told me that as soon as word spread of his arrival in Taipei, company representatives flocked to his hotel room vying for business and undercutting each other. He never had to leave the hotel to complete his assignment.

Exports as a percentage of textile production expanded rapidly: 19.6 percent in 1961; 25.6 percent in 1966; 38.9 percent in 1969 (Ho 1978:201); and 80 percent in 1972 (Chou 1973:95). Taiwan's leading sector, locally owned, thus became export-dependent, with much of the actual marketing and know-how controlled by foreigners.

No sooner had the export drive begun than Taiwan faced quotas in its main market.[13] The United States began controlling cotton textile imports, imposing restrictions on major suppliers, first Japan and Hong Kong. Thus, as the export push began in the early 1960s, Taiwan knew it would have to take such restrictions into consideration. The government moved to hold cotton production steady, modernize the industry, upgrade the quality of cotton goods, and expand the synthetics sector. The United States stipulated quotas in terms of square yards of goods, not value, so the response of earning more value per yard made good business sense and stimulated industry upgrading. Cheating by over-shipment also raised incomes.

According to interviewees, the KMT state discriminated against Taiwanese in apportioning export quotas in response to American protectionism. Shanghainese enjoyed inside information and obtained rights to sell to the United States, which they then either utilized themselves or sold on an organized market.[14]

The textile industry already had a base on the island and entrepreneurs with mainland experience. It built an export sector on accumulated experience improved by foreign-introduced techniques and fashions.

The electronics industry represents a very different pattern, one shaped by global forces from its inception. Electronics had virtually no base on Taiwan, either built by the Japanese or in the form of transplanted mainland enterprises. Technical agreements between Japanese transistor-radio and television manufacturers and Taiwanese assemblers in 1962 signalled the start of this sector, one which SRI had recommended in its earlier reports. Local firms began by supplying such things as television cabinets, but gradually they learned how to make various components so that the government could start to set local content requirements.

Government efforts to solicit foreign investment, as well as increased U.S.-Japanese competition in the American market, brought in first General Instruments and then other companies. They set up bonded export factories throughout the island as well as plants in KEPZ. In 1966, the authorities decided to make Taiwan into an electronics industry center, continuing to solicit DFI and to revise laws to accord preferential treatment to investors in the electronics sector. CIECD established a Working Group for Planning and Development of the Electronics Industry. In 1967 and 1968 it held major exhibitions to introduce local manufacturers and foreign investors to each other. Its objective was to take what began as an enclave industry and use it to create in Taiwan an entirely new sector of parts-and-components makers and, eventually, assemblers of finished goods able to compete internationally.

The process was not smooth. Japanese investors were especially resistant to local procurement. In their view, their joint ventures, in which they commonly held a minority share, functioned as captive markets for Japanese-made parts assembled into goods for sale under Japanese brand names within Taiwan's tariff walls. Joint-venture contracts stipulated the purchase of Japanese parts and restricted the markets for finished goods. Japanese found numerous means to evade local-content requirements. The government took action on many complaints by local industrialists on tariffs and taxes, but it failed to redress fundamentally the local-content problem.

Nonetheless, a new cohort of entrepreneurs emerged, mostly Taiwanese of petit bourgeois background—not former collaborators—based on various forms of cooperation with foreign interests.[15] Best known is Lin Ting-sheng of Tatung, Taiwan's consumer electronics giant. Lin had a foundation in his father's Japanese-era construction firm. After Retrocession, he turned to consumer goods. His big boost came from an AID loan to assemble watt-hour meters from imported parts under license from Toshiba. A later technical agreement with Westinghouse gave a leg up to one of Tatung's leading products, electric fans. Utilizing foreign technical licensing but eschewing equity investment, Tatung went on to manufacture a variety of household appliances, machinery, and computers, developing its own brand name at home and through aggressive exports, and then its own DFI. It established its own technical institute. Lin himself became active in political affairs, as a Taipei municipal assemblyman (and speaker) and member of the KMT's Central Standing Committee, a connection that helped him over some troubled waters. His American-educated son became Tatung's president in 1972.

Ch'en Mao-pang of Sampo sold radios and phonograph records during the Japanese period. He read voraciously about electronics. After the war he moved into wholesaling parts, then producing them himself. In 1962 he created a new company to produce appliances out of imported parts under agreements with Sony and Sharp. In 1964 he merged his various companies into Sampo and started making his own components and consumer goods, mostly appliances such as televisions and refrigerators. Exports grew under the Sony and Sharp labels as well as for some U.S. brands. Ch'en briefly engaged in Taipei city politics in the mid-1950s, but he shifted direction to become the electronics industry's major spokesman as long-time president of the Taiwan Electric Appliance Manufacturers Association. He advocated government support and protection for the industry. In the late 1960s he began to stake out independence from the Japanese, developing his own Sampo brand in domestic and foreign markets.

Another electronics magnate is C. C. Hong (Hung Chien-ch'üan) of Matsushita Taiwan. He also sold radios in the Japanese era. After the Nationalists came, he imported electrical products from the mainland and soon captured 60 percent of the Taiwan market. He shifted to Japan when the mainland connection was lost, becoming general agent for Matsushita. In the early 1950s he began producing radios and parts under the National label and via a technical agreement. In 1962, when the government passed a new statute encouraging foreign investment, Hong and Matsushita formed a new company, Matsushita Electric (Taiwan). The Japanese held 60 percent of equity. Hong served as chairman, but the Japanese general manager and managing director clearly ran the show. Matsushita Taiwan became a major force in the domestic and export markets, producing mainly televisions, audio equipment, and home appliances. It ranked as Matsushita Japan's leading overseas venture. Hong built close technical and business ties with several hundred local suppliers, using a high proportion of locally made parts in his products.

The consumer electronics sector is a good example of a dynamic industry that the state helped initiate and guide, but otherwise did not invest in directly or tie to state enterprises. TNCs performed this function. This is a significant departure from the state-led pattern of the

1950s and represents a clear commitment to the American-promoted approach of granting increased scope for private capital, local and foreign.

Other sectors also grew in stages, based on an array of technical and equity linkages with TNCs. In the most often cited example, in 1963 the government permitted Singer Sewing Machine Company to set up a plant in Taiwan over the strenuous objections of the more than 250 small, locally owned assemblers and suppliers. The government argued that this would save foreign exchange and improve the quality of locally made parts. To ensure this, it imposed on Singer the conditions that it locally procure 83 percent of required parts one year after commencing operation and that it assist Taiwan's producers in meeting specifications. Singer ended up transferring technology, upgrading the entire industry, and boosting exports (Schive 1979).

As the various pieces fell into place in the 1960s, the economy took off. Agriculture's contribution to Net Domestic Product (NDP) (32.8 percent in 1960) declined dramatically to 14.1 percent in 1973, as industry's rose from 24.9 percent to 43.8 percent over the same period (ibid:34). Employment in agriculture fell from 56.1 percent of the total work force in 1960 to 37.2 percent in 1973, while industry's share rose from 11.3 percent to 23 percent over the same period (ibid:8–9). Trade once again assumed an important role in the economy (about 50 percent of the value of Gross Domestic Product [GDP] in 1970 and increasing since), but this time, the proportion of manufactured export goods relative to agricultural goods shifted in favor of the former. In 1960, exports of agricultural products, including processed goods, were worth $111 million, or 67.7 percent of that year's exports of $164 million, while industrial products were valued at $53 million, or 32.2 percent. By 1973, the proportions were 15.4 percent for agricultural and 84.6 percent for industrial products out of an export volume that reached $4.5 billion (ibid:189). Throughout this period, the average GNP growth rate was 10 percent in 1976 prices, not adjusted for gain or loss due to changes in terms of trade. It was 11.3 percent from 1967 to 1973, after KEPZ came on stream (ibid:23). At the same time, consumer prices grew at a rate of less than 4 percent per annum. The exchange rate between the NT and American dollar was frozen at 40:1. Gross savings as a percentage of GNP increased from 12.7 percent in 1960 to 34.6 percent in 1973 (ibid:49). Foreign sources of Gross Domestic Capital Formation (GDCF) decreased from 37.5 percent in 1960 to minus 18.2 percent in 1973 (ibid:48). A combination of ultraconservative policies to restrict the growth of the money suppy, limited foreign borrowing, and government budget surpluses contributed to preventing inflation.

While textiles remained the dominant sector, new export-oriented, foreign-invested industries such as electronics—parts to finished goods—grew exponentially. The electronics sector in particular assumed the shape of an internationalized version of Japan's industrial structure: a few very large assemblers in a sea of small suppliers. In Taiwan, the large assemblers were nearly all TNCs; the suppliers, TNCs and locals. Of the 1,255 factories operating in 1978, 1,091 were locally owned, but only 75 of them ranked among the 175 "large" plants.[16] Twenty-seven of the 36 American firms were "large," and they included giant TNCs such as RCA, Zenith, and General Instruments. Thirty of the 39 Japanese enterprises were "large." Only half of the Japanese-Chinese joint ventures were large-scale, however (CEPD 1980a:14). Unlike the subcontracting arrangement one sees in Japan, few Taiwanese suppliers enjoyed long-term fixed contracts with assemblers. Each contract involved new negotiations.

The electronics sector was export-oriented from the start. By 1969, exports accounted for 44 percent of the value of production; they reached 54.6 percent the following year and hit 80 percent by 1972 (ibid:22). The American market took 61.7 percent in 1974; the Japanese only 6.1 percent. Conversely, 55.6 percent of imports came from Japan that year, 29.5 percent from the United States (ibid:24). This reveals overconcentration of markets and suppliers and the central role of foreign-owned enterprises at its apex.

The KEPZ, burgeoning with electronics plants, proved so successful that in 1971 the government opened a new, larger zone at nearby Nantze, and a small one to the north at Taichung.

Other external factors stimulated the rapid growth of Taiwan's economy in addition to the Japanese-American rivalry. The U.S. government sent out tentative feelers to the People's Republic of China (PRC) in the mid-1960s, but before anything could develop from this, the Cultural Revolution erupted, sealing China off from the world and strengthening Taiwan's supporters abroad.

The escalating Vietnam War further poisoned relations between the United States and the People's Republic and firmed up America's commitment to contain communism. This brought billions of greenbacks to East Asia. As Japan had fattened off the Korean War, so Taiwan's economy received an incalculable boost from Vietnam's agony: American purchase of agricultural and industrial commodities, use of military facilities and depots for repair of equipment, designation of Taiwan as a destination for rest and recreation, contract work for and in Vietnam, etc., pumped vast amounts of foreign currency into the Taiwan economy.

Latin America also drove investment capital in Taiwan's direction. As countries there began to reconsider the place of TNCs in their economies, devising strategies to regulate them, Taiwan appeared on the scene, its accessible officials aggressively proferring allowance of 100 percent ownership, guarantees against nationalization, tax holidays, low wages, and no strikes.

While granting wide scope to the local and foreign private sector, reducing red tape, and liberalizing trade, but not relinquishing other instruments, the state ensured its continued determinant role in the economy. It maintained ownership of key upstream productive enterprises as well as of the banking sector. CIECD's plans, while indicative rather than commandist, did have teeth in them in the form of incentives for priority investments and red tape or sanctions for undesired activities, economic or political. While TNCs had leverage over local suppliers, the state could also get them to compete for investment approvals, in some cases imposing conditions, as in the Singer case. The state also channelled TNC investments into priority sectors such as electronics, intending for them to build the industry ex nihilo, and away from others such as textiles, to prevent denationalization. Keeping most TNCs in export industries made the domestic market off-limits. The Japanese, however, successfully circumvented this through joint ventures and licensing agreements.

Although encouraging trade, the government still maintained a long list of prohibited and controlled imports. Moreover, export incentives and other controls "created a kind of dual economy in which exports, but only exports, could be manufactured under virtually free trade conditions" (Little 1979:475). Taiwan did not develop a laissez-faire, free-market economy; the state retained multiple controls and only granted what seemed like free-market activities within strict bounds. There was a lot more going on than "getting the prices right."

Rapid Social Change

Capitalist social relations continued to evolve as the economy industrialized. One could feel a palpable energy in Taiwan at this time as people of all walks of life sought opportunities to get in on the boom. It was vibrant and anarchic, "Everyone wants to be chairman of his own company" serving as the motivating credo. As investors learned more about foreign goods and styles, their initial impulse was to imitate these items, down to the copyrighted and often hilariously misspelled logo. Chinese pedagogy is based on copying and memorization; in the culture, selection of a model for emulation demonstrates respect and flattery. This fundamental characteristic of Taiwan's bourgeoisie facilitated their adherence to foreign contractors' models and specifications without a sense of inferiority (though they sometimes shirked on quality or sold themselves under someone else's brand name). It also got them into a great deal of legal trouble.

Not only did more people enter the ranks of the bourgeoisie, but that class began to stratify as well. In the early 1970s, successful enterprises and individuals began to form business groups (*kuan-hsi ch'i-ye*) to invest in new companies or each others' firms. Investors saw this as a way to spread risk and integrate production. But laws restricting the amount of capital one firm could invest in another, tax incentives favoring new firms, capitalists' fears of growing too large and thereby attracting government attention and exactions, and moving capital about rapidly to evade creditors also stimulated this trend. A final reason for the appearance of such business groups lay in the paternalistic chairman's desire to let each of his sons be chairman of his own firm.

Textilers, as the first big capitalists, created many of the groups. Far Eastern Textile, a Shanghainese company with close government connections, vertically integrated its cotton and synthetic production to garments, then hived off a chain of department stores and a cement company. Another Shanghainese enterprise associated with the KMT leadership, Tai-yuen Textile, vertically integrated its textile operations under the chairman's wife, while the chairman himself, Yen Ch'ing-ling, established Taiwan's first automobile assembly plant via technical agreements with Willys and Nissan. The result, the Yue Loong, enjoyed protection and monopoly rights—and unremitting criticism from its purchasers—until the 1970s.

The politically connected Taiwanese firm Tainan Textile built an enormous group of more than twenty enterprises in cement, food, and plastics in addition to textile-oriented companies. The numerically smaller group based on Y. C. Wang's Formosa Plastics Company limited its sphere of investment, concentrating on integrating production of plastics and synthetics and dominating those sectors at the intermediate level.

As Taiwan's economy grew more complex, parvenu enterprises without political connections followed the expansion trend. By 1976, observors distinguished about 100 such groups, but they were but a shadow of their East Asian cousins, Japan's *zaibatsu* and Korea's *chaebol*, in terms of capital, scale, control of their own trade, and government connections.[17]

Taiwan's industry, both local and foreign owned, utilized labor-intensive technology, so employment opportunities expanded rapidly. Urban dwellers as well as peasants flocked to factories, which were dispersed in all of the major cities and in the countryside. Taiwan approached full employment in the late 1960s. From 1964 to 1973 the real wage rate increased 5.4 percent a year, well below the gains in productivity (Sun 1976:109).

A large proportion of workers (one-third of the total work force by the mid-1960s) comprised young peasant girls who worked for a few years, remitting money home, some of it for their dowry. When the time came for them to marry, they returned to the countryside and left the labor force.[18]

The state continued to repress the working class. It was helped in this by two characteristics of Taiwanese labor: first, workers generally did not picture themselves as lifetime industrial laborers; rather, a sizable number were using their job to accumulate enough capital to start their own enterprise. In the boom-town atmosphere, this was not a far-fetched aspiration. The other characteristic was the high turnover among female laborers. These two features worked against the formation of working-class consciousness, buttressing the effects of martial law prohibitions against strikes, party-manipulated unions, and security offices run by retired military officers in the factories. While low, wages rose faster than prices, and the steadily rising material standard of living in the consumer-oriented society and very real opportunities for rapid social mobility made a militant labor movement even less likely.[19]

For the peasantry, agricultural incomes stagnated as the state squeezed agriculture after the initial period of investments in the 1950s. The gap with nonfarming households widened from 39 percent in 1964 to 42 percent in 1968 (Hsiao 1981:63). Nonfarm sources of income "were responsible for all of the increase in real incomes" of the rural population during this period (Chinn 1979:293). Taiwan became increasingly a land of "part-time farmers" (Mao 1976:176–77;

Gates 1981). In addition to peasant-workers, there were numerous "peasant-capitalists" (Hu 1984:ch. 4).

A middle class comprising professionals and service personnel began to take shape. It bought into the system enthusiastically, eagerly buying from the cornucopia of consumer goods appearing in the stores, too busy to think about politics, fearful of risking the material gains it was making.

Tentative Political Stirrings

While new social groups were emerging and society as a whole was benefiting from economic growth, political development lagged far behind. The authorities had made it clear that they were completely behind the policy of rapid industrialization and trade and would grant virtual free rein to anyone to engage in business ventures. But there was no comparable simultaneous political relaxation. The result was another distinguishing characteristic of Taiwan's development: the bifurcation of the economy from the polity. The regime increasingly based its legitimacy on its ability to promote economic growth and, succeeding at it, created a commonality of interests with the new capitalist class, which tacitly agreed not to translate economic muscle into political activity. Though chafing at the mass of regulations, the bourgeoisie did not resort to politics to push for change—they feared instability above all. The state acted in their interests but usually without consulting them. The bourgeoisie supported repression of labor and squeezing of agriculture. The workers and peasants, eager themselves to invest in Taiwan's seemingly unstoppable growth, did not challenge this alliance; on the contrary, they aspired to join it. In the buoyant environment, Taiwanese-mainlander tensions relaxed as well. The mainlander political elite courted and allied with the emerging Taiwanese business elite to maintain the system that brought security and hope to both. Class began to supersede regional origin as the main cleavage in society (Gates 1981:269ff, Greenhalgh 1984:536–46).

Taiwan's students were generally apolitical and apathetic, concerned primarily with getting good enough grades to go abroad [20] or be snatched up by a corporation. The tight political control in schools at all levels was almost superfluous. There was a great deal of pressure on male university students to join the KMT, and they viewed party membership in a purely utilitarian way as a career boost. Not joining when rushed was a courageous act of political defiance. Youths who felt alienated did not turn to politics; instead they read the proliferating translations of Kafka and Camus.

What little political activity there was was restricted to local-level elections where an amalgam of factions, clans, ethnic groupings, local despots, and cronyism, successfully manipulated by the KMT, absorbed a great deal of energy. Non-KMT Taiwanese such as Kao Yü-shu (Henry Kao) successfully challenged party candidates for the mayoralty of several cities. To maintain party control of Taiwan's most populous city and the site of the largest concentration of mainlanders, the KMT declared Taipei a "Special Municipality" in 1967, thereby putting it under direct control of the Executive Yuan with an appointed mayor.[21]

At the national level, things remained virtually unchanged until the end of the decade. In 1960, the Nationalists responded harshly to a challenge by mainlander intellectual Lei Chen to their one-party dictatorship, clapping him in jail for ten years.[22] The next year they sentenced Taiwanese assemblyman Su Tung-chi to life in prison for allegedly plotting an armed rebellion. The rest of the decade was punctuated by the arrests of people on charges of advocating Taiwan's independence. The 1964 case of the internationally known legal scholar Dr. P'eng Ming-min was the most publicized.[23] But most of the political action directed at the ROC government took place in Japan and the United States, including the attempted assassination of Chiang Ching-kuo in the United States in 1970. Taiwanese formed numerous proindependence groups abroad, which split and reformed with regularity. Several notable figures in the movement, such as Liao Wen-yi (Thomas Liao), returned to Taiwan and made peace with the KMT.

The 1960s saw the continued rise of Chiang Ching-kuo, facilitated by the untimely death of his chief rival, Ch'en Ch'eng, in 1965 and the progressive physical weakness of his father, even though the elder Chiang was reelected president in 1972. Chiang Ching-kuo moved upward through the state hierarchy after firming up his influence in the military and security apparatuses. He became minister of national defense in 1965 and vice-premier in 1969.[24] He was also made head of CIECD and the coordinating agency, the Financial, Economic, and Monetary Conference. Under Chiang CIECD functioned as "an office of the general staff for economic development . . . responsible for long-term, medium-term and annual planning, coordination and follow-up in plan implementation and evaluation of performance" (Li 1976:92–93). These moves put Chiang Ching-kuo in charge of the key economic and financial agencies, and he brought along a cohort of younger technocrats to staff them. When he became premier, in 1972, he instituted a crackdown on rising corruption in the bureaucracy. He issued a set of stern dos and don'ts dubbed "The Ten Commandments" to state cadres.

In 1973, Chiang Ching-kuo replaced CIECD with the Economic Planning Council (EPC). Many experienced CIECD cadres went to other ministries, and EPC had a weak chairman. Its members comprised only officials concerned directly with the economy. It thus lost its significance and power as a supraministerial shadow cabinet. Its responsibilities included only economic planning and research. It had neither funds to implement plans nor power to evaluate them. The real policy-making power shifted to a new, five-man Finance and Economic Small Group of the Executive Yuan, headed by Central Bank Governor and Chiang family insider Yu Kuo-hwa. Yu reported directly to Chiang Ching-kuo (Wen 1984:23).

KMT and government posts experienced an infusion of younger, better-educated blood, including more Taiwanese at higher levels. It was estimated that 80 percent of the 1.25 million party members at the time were Taiwanese (Tien 1975:616). In December 1969, reversing its rigid position that elections for national office could not take place until after mainland recovery, the government held the first elections in two decades to fill the increasing vacancies in the National Assembly, Legislative Yuan, and Control Yuan. This also brought more Taiwanese into the national government, albeit in a still minuscule proportion that did not threaten KMT-mainlander dominance. The independent politician K'ang Ning-hsiang emerged as the spokesman for the non-KMT opposition through his election to the Legislative Yuan in 1969 and reelection in 1972. In 1972, Taiwan received its first Taiwanese governor, the civilian "half-mountain" Shieh Tung-min.[25]

These trends symbolized the regime's implicit acceptance of the fact that it would not be returning to the mainland. The successful PRC atomic bomb test in 1964 seriously challenged KMT boasts about retaking the mainland by force. The official strategy instead became to use 70 percent political and 30 percent military means for the mission. KMT resolutions significantly spoke less about mainland recovery and more about construction of Taiwan. The mainlanders had to begin to share power with the 85 percent of the population under their control who were native to the island. The diplomatic setbacks beginning in 1970 pressured the mainlanders into opening more opportunities in government to Taiwanese in the event that the island would have to go it alone. But at the same time, the KMT clamped down on the domestic dissent just then breaking the surface.

The first in a series of exogenous blows beyond Taiwan's control came in a dispute with Japan over the disposition of a group of islands (Tiao-yü-t'ai or Senkaku) occupied since the end of World War II by the United States. The issue became contentious after oil was discovered there. The United States inclined toward giving the islands to Japan. Students from Taiwan in the United States and elsewhere organized mass demonstrations early in 1971 to protest. The weak response by the Nationalists to the patriotic appeals of its citizens frustrated students outside and within Taiwan.[26] This lead to an uncharacteristic outburst of political activity on college campuses in spite of government objections. The activities took on an ugly anti-Japanese and anti-American tone.

At the same time, the People's Republic of China emerged from its self-imposed isolation and made tentative forays into the international arena. Western nations began to establish diplomatic relations with Peking, which, by the rules of the game agreed upon by the KMT and CCP,[27] necessitated breaking relations with Taipei. The secret visit to China by Henry Kissinger in July 1971 traumatized Taiwan, and then, making matters worse, the Republic of China "withdrew" from the United Nations in the fall of 1971 just before a vote by the General Assembly to give the China seat to the People's Republic.

When President Richard Nixon went to China and issued the Shanghai Communique with Chou En-lai in February 1982, Taiwan's fate was seemingly sealed, its people reminded of their vulnerability to outside superpowers. Premier Tanaka Kakuei also went to China that year, and Japan established relations with Peking. This provoked a bitter torrent of anti-Japanese invective from the "betrayed" Nationalists, who felt that they had treated Japan leniently after the war despite having borne the brunt of its aggression.

Taiwan's continued future as a de facto independent entity looked doubtful. Local businessmen began to move capital and assets abroad and emigration increased. Foreign trade and investment dipped. Students and young intellectuals, numerically few but influential by dint of their magazines (especially *Ta-Hsüeh* [The Intellectual])[28] and university positions, began publicly to question basic assumptions about KMT rule in Taiwan and the nature of society. They also pressed for reforms. These included democratic political participation, free speech, an end to martial law, protection of human rights, bringing younger men into government, and funding for social welfare. The movement revealed a lack of confidence in the regime's ability to control the island's destiny in global politics, much less to back up its claim to be the legitimate government for all China. It showed that people were concerned with national issues and wanted a voice in them. It also revealed that in stark contrast to Latin America, dissidents generally did not oppose economic dependency.

The response on campuses was electric. But the activists did not try to build a mass movement, and they lacked a coherent guiding ideology; they were mainly venting their frustration. By 1973, the KMT had rather handily coopted some reformers and forced others to retreat while not implementing the reforms.[29]

Economic development, a higher standard of living, nine years of compulsory education (from 1968), and an influx of foreign ideas and practices had created a more complex society in Taiwan. The KMT was clearly concerned about the possibility of future political activism by new social forces outside its control, especially in the face of an international political environment increasingly detrimental to the Nationalists.

At the same time, Taiwan's economy was falling victim once more to its own success. The vulnerabilities inherent in the export-oriented strategy all seemed to appear simultaneously: Taiwan's trading partners raised protectionist quotas against its exports; with full employment and a rising standard of living, wages and other costs rose; other less-developed countries with even lower labor costs and more abundant resources began to hone in on Taiwan's markets; and the infrastructure, most of which dated from the Japanese era, was stretched beyond capacity.

At this juncture, the state again turned to Americans for advice, this time commissioning Arthur D. Little, Incorporated (ADL) to suggest solutions. The consulting firm advised upgrading industry by investment in petrochemicals, electrical machinery and equipment, advanced electronics, precision machine tools, and computer terminals and peripherals. The export orientation would remain. The Sixth Four-Year Plan, formulated in 1972, reflected much of this.

Some of these sectors were suited for foreign investors, some for locals. Others, such as petrochemicals, involved such a high degree of risk as well as capital and technology, plus linkages to domestic downstream processors, that joint ventures were more suitable. It was a sign of how far development in Taiwan had progressed that such ventures were not considered farfetched. Other undertakings, such as the revamping of the infrastructure, were the state's responsibility, though for some projects it solicited foreign and local investors in a subordinate role. Plans were already well advanced when the Organization of Petroleum-Exporting Countries (OPEC) quadrupled oil prices after Yom Kippur in 1973.

Cementing the Foundations of Dependent Development in Taiwan

This chapter has shown how Taiwan's relationship with the international system underwent a fundamental change with far-reaching ramifications. The island's geopolitical significance and American-funded insulation declined as trade and DFI became the primary forms linking its economy and society to the outside. The shift grew out of an economic crisis—the exhaustion of first-stage import substitution industrialization—but occurred before this took on political dimensions. Taiwan still lacked the capital, foreign exchange, global credit, technology, internal market, or labor shortage to justify prestigious but costly second-stage import substitution. Analyzing the options, American advisers and powerful Chinese officials overrode other politicians' and capitalists' fears, choosing to liberalize and internationalize the economy instead of deepening it first.

The source of dynamism moved to external markets. The leading industry, textiles, turned outward, producing goods under contract for foreign buyers. The most dynamic sector, electronics, originated as a TNC enclave but rapidly established ties with local industry, spawning domestic suppliers and imitators. As technical and managerial expertise spread, a foundation capable of supporting second-stage import substitution took shape. In fact, as new contradictions in the economy appeared in the early 1970s, this became necessary.

Success of export-oriented industrialization entailed changes in state-society relations. Continued absolute state domination of production and stifling regulation of external linkages would constrain local capitalists and foreign investors or buyers. As Taiwan's international political status eroded, freeing up ties with a broad range of outside actors became imperative. The mainlander elite recognized further the necessity of giving Taiwanese a clear stake in the system. While not promoting them politically, it tied their futures to maintenance of the status quo. A coalition among the state, local capital, and TNCs took shape that stimulated economic growth in the expanding global economy and shored up Taiwan's identity in the threatening global political community. The state's role became more closely tied with fine tuning the investment climate as its domestic basis of legitimacy shifted from the sacred mission of mainland recovery to preserving wealth and stability on island China. Nonetheless, through its continued ownership of upstream enterprises and banks, its array of official and discretionary incentives and sanctions, its control of import and export licenses and foreign exchange, and its power to protect selected local industrial sectors, the state maintained a major role in guiding economic activity.

Ever-increasing opportunities for investment and employment, in large part generated by TNCs, dispersal of industry throughout the island, rapid absorption of peasants abandoning agriculture as their primary source of income, fluid mobility as long as one avoided politics, and lack of a social safety net, which forced people to make their own way and save a high percentage of their income against future needs, all contributed to maintaining stability and spreading wealth around. Society changed as new classes emerged, the material standard of living rose, education spread, and multiple foreign influences penetrated Taiwan. The state allowed these changes while maintaining its repression over political activity. But it could not stifle political demands much longer.

7

Industrial Upgrading and the Emergence of a Political Opposition, 1973-1984

The Resurgent Developmental State

The dislocations caused by the first oil crisis brought Taiwan's numerous vulnerabilities into sharp focus, and the rest of the decade was taken up with mitigating the hydra-headed menace. The mounting external economic, political, and military threats were beyond Taiwan's ability to control. In addition, for the first time, it appeared as if the meticulously crafted domestic arrangement was also unraveling. The fragile nature of Taiwan's economic foundation and special pact became obvious. The only actor capable of leading Taiwan through this minefield was the state. It adopted a strategy toward external and internal threats designed to ensure that in the short run, Taiwan could cope in its present form. For the longer run, it hoped to restructure the economy so as to anticipate and get a step ahead of events to gain some control of its own destiny.

To the mainlander-KMT regime, failure might mean the loss of its hegemony over Taiwan's society and eventually of the territory necessary to bolster its claim to be the legitimate Chinese government. To the people at large, failure might mean the end of their prosperous, capitalist, Western-oriented society and incorporation into the still unsettled People's Republic, one way or another.

The external economic threat was spearheaded by the jump in oil prices, but the attendant hike in the prices of other commodities, from food to capital equipment, necessary to Taiwan's survival, plus the subsequent recession in all of its increasingly protectionist markets hit Taiwan hard. The nadir came in 1974. In January, after many years of hard-won price stability, the government sought to cope with the imported inflation and sudden inflationary expectations by taking what it hoped would be a drastic but one-time measure: It raised deposit interest rates an average of 33.4 percent and loan rates 25.8 percent, oil prices 88.4 percent, and electricity rates 78.7 percent (Kuo 1983:211–14). It also increased taxes and stimulated the economy by going ahead with the ambitious infrastructural and industrial modernization scheme called the Ten Major Development Projects. For the year, wholesale prices went up 40.6 percent and consumer prices 47.5 percent, enough of a jolt that they fell back to minus 5.1 percent and 5.2 percent increases respectively in 1975 and decreased further until the second oil crisis of 1979–1980 (TSDB 1982:2). Despite grumbling from the public, the price hikes did not cause unrest, as the people recognized the necessity of drastic action and the harsh consequences of political demonstrations.

A labor shortage and a doubling of wages between 1976 and 1980 sent the price of Taiwan's exports up.[1] Compounding the problem of the subsequent rise in the price of Taiwan's exports, developed countries adopted neoprotectionist nontariff measures to restrict imports, especially of such Taiwan staples as textiles, footwear, mushrooms, and television sets.[2] In 1974 the island experienced its first trade deficit since 1970, amounting to $1.3 billion. According to official figures, the GNP grew only 1.1 percent that year. The extended global recession that followed the second oil crisis mired trade-dependent Taiwan in a seemingly endless period of stagflation. It did not recover until 1983.

The political and military threats came from across the Taiwan Straits. Under the radical "Gang of Four," the People's Republic began loudly clamoring for Taiwan's "liberation." It threatened American companies that if they tried to do business with Taiwan, they might as well write off the mainland forever, and it made an example of American Express by not accepting its travelers checks. Some companies, such as Pan Am and First National Bank of Chicago, withdrew their Taiwan operations. After the fall of the Gang in 1976, the Communists changed their approach to Taiwan, emphasizing "reunification" instead of "liberation" and promising a shopping list of concessions to the Nationalists if they would just open negotiations. But the Communists never renounced the right to use force; nor was the threat of a blockade counted out.

In spite of recurrent chills in U.S.-PRC relations, Taiwan knew that sooner or later the two would normalize relations as most of the world had done or was doing. American troop withdrawals from East Asia, including Taiwan,[3] cutbacks in U.S. arms sales to Taiwan,[4] the U.S. refusal to sell Taiwan the advanced equipment it desired (*FEER* October 27, 1978:17–20), and Communist victories in Indochina added to Taiwan's diplomatic isolation and fears of being swept up in a red tidal wave. At the very least, U.S.-PRC normalization would mean abrogation of the U.S.-ROC Mutual Defense Treaty, the bedrock of the island's security. U.S. military assistance had totalled more than $3.5 billion to the late 1970s (ibid:18).

The worst nightmare came true when the United States and the People's Republic of China established formal diplomatic relations as of January 1, 1979. The American embassy in Taipei was closed, although it was reincarnated as the nongovernmental American Institute in Taiwan, staffed by "retired" State Department officials. The Republic of China did the same with its embassy in Washington, establishing the Coordination Council for North American Affairs. The Mutual Defense Treaty expired on January 1, 1980. The Taiwan Relations Act, however, passed by Congress in March 1979 and signed by President Jimmy Carter on April 10, served as the basis for relations between the peoples of the United States and Taiwan. In 1980, the election of their stalwart supporter Ronald Reagan gladdened the Nationalists, but he too seemed intent on improving relations with the People's Republic, even if he was muddled as to the two-China issue. The so-called Second Shanghai Communique of August 1982, ostensibly clarifying U.S.-PRC relations and setting out an agenda for winding down U.S.-Taiwan military ties (especially weapons sales), frightened the KMT. But when President Reagan proceeded to ignore its provisions, KMT fears were allayed somewhat.

After 1979, the aggressive PRC opening to the outside world, its export drive into Taiwan's markets selling similar goods, its solicitation of DFI (especially from Overseas Chinese), its establishment of Special Economic Zones similar to Taiwan's EPZs, its membership in multilateral lending agencies, and its floating of bonds abroad posed threats of a previously unanticipated genre to the island's economy. In 1984, China's successful negotiation with Great Britain of an agreement to turn Hong Kong over to PRC sovereignty in 1997, with the explicit pledge not to change its former capitalist system for fifty years after reunification, was an obvious signal to the KMT to soften its rigid, no-talks stance and accept the inevitable embrace of the socialist motherland.

In the course of this decade-long downward spiral, the people of Taiwan experienced, quite naturally, a crisis of confidence in the ability of the Nationalist authorities to control the island's fate. Some Taiwanese suspected that desperate, homesick mainlanders were plotting to sell out the island to the Communists. Had there been much sentiment favoring Communist "liberation," this would have been a cause for jubilation; but after more than two decades of economic growth, social and political stability, and a vastly improved standard of living, reinforced by virulent anti-Communist propaganda, censorship of pro-PRC materials, and the Communists' repeated chaotic upheavals, even people who disliked the KMT saw the stake they had in the status quo. The declaration of an independent Taiwan, the de jure acknowledgment of the de facto situation, would have invited certain military action by the People's Republic and was thus not a viable option.

The external threats posed a much more serious challenge than any internal constraints facing the regime. After years of authoritarian control, the people looked to the KMT to get them out of their quandary. The severe political and economic challenges required increased state intervention after a long period of continuous retrenchment. The state devised a flexible, multifaceted strategy to reduce Taiwan's vulnerability to the instability of the global economy, primarily by vertically integrating and deepening industry and, to compensate for its diplomatic isolation, by substituting economic ties for political ones.

In industry, the first stage involved going ahead with the agenda derived from the ADL study of selectively building up heavy and capital-intensive industries and modernizing the infrastructure. Resembling their MITI counterparts, Taiwan's economic technocrats adopted a more aggressive stance toward restructuring the economy and inserting Taiwan into a new niche in the international division of labor.

Scrapping the Sixth Four-Year Plan, the EPC issued a Six-Year Plan for 1976 to 1981, emphasizing capital and technology-intensive industries, notably steel and petrochemicals. Domestic economic dislocations and lack of confidence pushed the state to the forefront as the only actor capable of bringing this to fruition. It linked several projects already underway as the Ten Major Development Projects and invested them with a great deal of its own capital and prestige. With a final price tag exceeding $8 billion (original estimates were $6.5 billion) (*Euromoney* May 1981:3), the projects comprised nearly 20 percent of the state's investment for 1975 and 1976 and helped the economy ride out the first oil crisis (Kuo 1983:216–17).

Whereas some of the Ten Projects were purely infrastructural (with a significant defense component), such as the North-South Expressway, airport, harbors, railway electrification, and East Coast railway, others, such as the integrated steel mill and Kaohsiung Shipyard, were intended to be joint state-private enterprises for profit. Long on the drawing board, the integrated steel mill had been repeatedly delayed for one reason or another.[5] When most of the private investors backed out, it became a virtual 100 percent government enterprise.[6] Using state-of-the-art technology, China Steel Corporation, under the dynamic stewardship of Chao Yao-tung, a former businessman who took the job with the understanding that he could operate the company free of the bureaucratic red tape that hamstrung other state firms, became one of the world's most profitable steel companies (*FEER* November 26, 1982:75). It was designed to supply domestic customers, but began exporting as well (*FCJ* July 29, 1984:4). In 1982, the outspoken and immodest Chao, capped with the nickname "Steelhead" after his success at China Steel, became minister of economic affairs.

Development of the petrochemical industry, strongly pushed by ADL and also one of the Ten Projects, was envisioned as a means to integrate vertically two of Taiwan's major industries—synthetic textiles and plastics—and thereby locate domestically as many stages of the production process as possible, further reducing vulnerability to price fluctuations in imported supplies.

As in Brazil,[7] the petrochemical sector brought the state, foreign, and local investors together as equity partners. In addition to capital, foreign partners supplied necessary technology and managerial expertise. Local partners, usually downstream and intermediate manufacturers, brought a captive market. The state, through monopoly control of oil imports, ownership of all naphtha crackers, and its own petrochemical plants, supplied raw materials, infrastructure, incentives, and overall coordination.

Most of the foreign partners were American petroleum and chemical giants, such as Mobil, Gulf, National Distillers and Chemical Corporation, and Union Carbide. The Japanese were consciously excluded. The construction of several petrochemical plants was underway when the first oil crisis hit. The second crisis nearly torpedoed the industry, as crude oil still had to be imported and the finished goods were nearly all exported at some stage or another of fabrication to markets in the throes of depression. In 1981, the petrochemical producers, squeezed in between the upstream state supplier and downstream customers, asked the government for regulation of imports, production, and prices. The state's reply was to encourage the downstream sector to increase value added and for intermediate producers to invest overseas close to sources of raw materials. One response: Formosa Plastics entered a joint venture as majority partner with the Louisiana Chemical and Plastics Corporation to build a 240,000-ton per year, $168 million pvc plant in Point Comfort, Texas (*Asian Wall Street Journal* [*AWSJ*] January 20, 1981:3; *Business Week* August 1, 1983:37). By 1983, the U.S. recovery and declining oil prices boosted the industry back to normal capacity.

The need for renewed vigorous state guidance of the economy resulted in another shakeup of the technocracy. Late in 1977, the government terminated EPC and the five-man small group and established the Council for Economic Planning and Development (CEPD), under loyalist Yu Kuo-hwa.[8] It recentralized power, taking responsibility for macroplanning, setting priorities, coordination, and evaluation. Its members are cabinet ministers, backed by a young and well-trained staff (Wen 1984:23). The MOEA's Industrial Development Bureau does detailed sectoral planning and execution.

The CEPD soon began shifting the emphasis in industrial restructuring, stressing technology-intensive, nonpolluting, nonenergy-guzzling industries, instead of heavy or capital-intensive ones. Its Ten-Year Plan for 1980–89 and Four-Year Plan for 1982–86 reflect this priority. CEPD devised a new incentive package to channel capital into strategic industries, such as computers, telecommunications, and robotics. It planned to let low value-added, labor-intensive industries such as textiles and footwear die out. Even more resembling the tactics of Japan's MITI, it tested its mettle with the private sector, pressuring five shaky synthetic-textile manufacturers to merge to create economies of scale, upgrade technology, and improve their global competitive position against threats from arch-rival Korea. The resulting Hualong Corporation represented a merger of well-connected Shanghainese and Taiwanese capital. The government sweetened the incentive to merge by converting the NT$ 750 million the five companies owed to its banks into shares of stock (Gold 1981:119–23).

CEPD's additional restructuring plans floated in 1983–84 included trade liberalization, offshore banking, and opening of the stock market (a haven for speculators, resisted by large companies) to foreign investors and venture-capital firms, although all were slow to materialize and were obviously the subject of bureaucratic contention.

The export-oriented electronics industry was the key to restructuring.[9] Primarily manufacturing or assembling televisions and other consumer goods, it was now deemed capable of upgrading into the information industry. One important objective was to enter a sector not yet subject to quotas or OMAs, something already very harmful to Taiwan's television exporters (*China Post* June 17, 1982:5).

CEPD's goal was to continue to utilize export demand to guide production but, rather than relying on the product life cycle or technology transferred from abroad, to nurture Taiwan's own research and development (R&D) capacity to develop new products, raise value added, and vertically integrate the electronics industry. The revised Statute for Encouragement of Investment, effective January 1, 1981, strengthened a provision, put in by technocratic genro K. T. Li, requiring industries receiving benefits under the statute to spend a standard amount of money on R&D.

To concentrate talent and resources, in 1980 the state established a new type of industrial zone, the Science-Based Industrial Park in Hsinchu, seventy kilometers south of Taipei. It offers the same incentives as the Statutes for Encouragement of Investment plus additional sweeteners. While still utilizing Taiwan's relatively low-cost labor force, its chief features are low-cost engineers, proximity to two leading technical universities, and the availability of the state-run Industrial Technology and Research Institute (ITRI) and its Electronics Research Service Organization (ERSO) division to develop and transfer technology. Further, the state is willing to take up to 49 percent of equity in ventures in the park, replicating the *tri-pé* model used in petrochemicals.

As of August 1984, the park had fifty-three approved investments, forty of which were already in operation. By mid-1983, local capital held nearly 70 percent of the investments (*Computer-Asia* July 1983:62). Important American firms such as Wang Laboratories and Qume set up in the park, but foreign companies without a prior presence in Taiwan or Chinese owners were slow to respond.

Of more significance is the presence of several computer companies owned by Chinese who had been trained and employed abroad and were recruited back to Taiwan by the government's aggressive global talent search. They represent the emergence of a new generation of Taiwan capitalists.

Some are the offspring of prominent older businessmen, such as Shantung magnate Miao Yü-hsiu's Berkeley-educated son Matthew (Feng-ch'iang), whose Mitac Computer Company enjoys his father's business group's backing and prestige. Mitac produces floppy disk drives, Winchester subsystems, Chinese terminals, and sixteen-bit personal computers. It leads in applying computer technology to Taiwan's industries.

Others had to find their own funds. An example is Bobo Wang, managing director of Microtek, who had worked for many years at Xerox and responded to the patriotic and financial attractions of having his own firm in his native land. Microtek's microprocessors are targeted primarily at design and test engineers.

Although not in the park, another member of this generation is Hong Ming-t'ai, son of C. C. Hong of Matsushita Taiwan. His Fulet Company manufactures top-of-the-line consumer electronics under the Proton label. If his father was unable to break from the Japanese himself, he has done it through his son. All three of the companies discussed here are promoting their own brand names and do their own R&D, while at the same time maintaining some connections with foreign corporations.

The state hopes that small, innovative companies headed by dynamic Chinese with experience abroad, buttressed by government technical and financial support, and, at least initially, with TNC linkages, can create a new niche for Taiwan goods in a global market before the Japanese get there. Although some of the firms are progressing well, there are also danger signals compounded by Taiwan's notoriety as the world's foremost violator of copyrights and trademarks.[10] In 1984, U.S. Customs agents seized Taiwan-made, ERSO-designed IBM-compatible personal computers as fake IBM pcs. ERSO and the Taiwanese firms, including high-flyer Multitech, claimed they were not counterfeits, just a coincidental replication of design of the Basic Input/Output System. ERSO redid the design and the Taiwanese products were imported successfully, but it may have been too late to penetrate the casualty-strewn U.S. pc market (*Business Week* September 24, 1984:110B–E).

While the electronics sector was being upgraded domestically, some firms went transnational to overcome tariff barriers in the Japanese fashion and to penetrate new markets. Besides companies setting up in the United States, including Silicon Valley, Tatung, the electronics giant, also began manufacturing video tape recorders, computer terminals, and microcomputers in Great Britain in a plant bought from the Decca Company in 1981 (*FEER* November 29, 1984:66–69).[11]

Beginning in 1980, the state also attempted to create a comparative advantage for Taiwan in automobiles, following the example of Japan and Korea. Ideally, this would stimulate the emergence of high-quality parts suppliers, as happened with sewing machines and electronics. The government negotiated with several Japanese makers to set up a *tri-pé*-style joint venture with China Steel and private interests. At the same time, General Motors pulled out of a defense-related joint venture with a state firm, KMT firm, and state bank to manufacture heavy-duty trucks (*FEER* August 13, 1982:112–13). In December 1982, the auto deal was penned with Toyota. Not surprisingly, Taiwan's other auto assemblers were quite apprehensive. China Steel's Chao Yao-tung, by then economics minister, opposed the truck deal but supported the auto plan, most likely because the former would be more subject to bureaucratic meddling while the latter better suited his private-enterprise proclivities. Opposition to the auto plant came from several quarters in the bureaucracy and business sector. After several delays, the scheme was scrapped in the summer of 1984, ostensibly due to disagreements over the preconditions that Toyota export half of the cars within eight years, accept a 90-percent local-content rate, and transfer technology to local partners (FCJ September 16, 1984:4; *FEER* September 27, 1984:165). In the midst of negotiations, Y. T. Chao was shifted from the MOEA to the chairmanship of CEPD, a move generally seen as a demotion.

These various ventures in petrochemicals, high tech electronics, and automobiles represent a strategy we may call by the cumbersome title, export-oriented vertical import-substitution industrialization. That is, import substitution will continue, in the form of vertically integrating and upgrading production, and a significant part of output will be exported. Success will require the cementing of a new developmental coalition among the state, high-tech TNCs, and a select group of local capitalists willing to commit themselves to a long-term investment. These latter will be a new generation of capitalists, better educated, more cosmopolitan and independent-minded than their predecessors. The coalition will also require technical talent. What this means is that the sector of Taiwan's society historically oriented toward emigration must be the backbone of the development strategy over the medium term. Many have already taken foreign citizenship. They are less likely to accept the conservative authoritarianism characteristic of KMT genro. But as those men die off, they are being replaced by a new cohort of foreign-educated, relatively liberal technocrats. The relations between the new generations of capitalists and politicians, most of whom grew up together in Taiwan, lived abroad, and have a great deal in common, are likely to be much smoother and coequal than those now phasing out. Taiwan's future rests in the hands of an elite many of whose members hold green cards.

Industrial integration was not the only means by which the state planned to increase Taiwan's ability to survive in the 1970s:

—To increase self-sufficiency in food, already at 82.7 percent (*FEER*, November 19, 1982:74–77), it moved to revive the declining agricultural sector. As early as September 1972, the state abolished the hated compulsory rice-fertilizer exchange system, lowered taxes, set guaranteed rice prices, made loan funds more available, and improved the marketing system in order to stimulate production. It revised regulations on selling land to promote land consolidation, a necessary prerequisite for mechanization, as farm sizes were too small (average one hectare) to make it feasible otherwise. This was seen as the key means to increase productivity and substitute for the rural labor force now in short supply due to urban migration.[12]

—To reduce dependence on imported energy, it turned to alternative sources (primarily coal and nuclear), engaged in oil exploration and investment abroad at energy source sites, strengthened relations with its main supplier, Saudi Arabia, [13] and encouraged the development of industries that were not big consumers of energy. Taiwan remained 73 percent dependent on oil (American Institute in Taiwan [AIT] 1981:3), and the first nuclear power stations did not come onstream until 1979. By the first half of 1984, though, "nuclear power accounted for more than 40 percent of all power generated" (*FCJ*, December 23, 1984:1).

—To improve defense capabilities, in addition to promoting heavy and high-tech industries and modernizing the transportation and communications infrastructure, which were part of the Ten Projects, the government stepped up domestic production of jet fighters, helicopters, guided missiles, artillery, and other weaponry, much of it under contract with American manufacturers (*NYT*, October 14, 1975:2; *FEER* October 27, 1978:18; *Daily Californian*, April 2, 1984:10). It also sought new sources of military goods, including the other pariah states, Israel (*NYT*, April 6, 1977:1; *FEER*, October 27, 1978:19) and South Africa (*FEER*, March 3, 1982:32–34).[14] Holland's decision in late 1980 to sell Taiwan two submarines and components for nuclear power plants over strenuous PRC objections was a tremendous coup for the regime (*FEER*, December 26, 1980:8–9). However, the fact that its extant weapons systems were nearly all American-made made it infeasible that it could really import massive amounts of goods from other suppliers. Despite the 1979 break in diplomatic relations and subsequent abrogation of the 1954 Mutual Defense Treaty, Section 3 of the Taiwan Relations Act commits the United States "to make available to Taiwan such defense articles and defense services in such quantity as may be necessary to enable Taiwan to maintain a sufficient self-defense capability." So Taiwan would still be able to purchase American military hardware as the United States saw fit. ROC defense spending exceeded half of the state's budget (*FEER*, October 27, 1978:19) and in 1980 was 25 percent above the 1979 mark (AIT, 1981:2), including $880 million in U.S. arms (*FEER*, January 27, 1983:28).[15]

—To reduce heavy trade dependence on the United States and Japan, the state led in diversifying partners. It opened new markets in Western Europe and liberalized imports from that region, and late in 1979 it abolished the ban on trade with Eastern Europe, except the Soviet Union (*AWSJ*, November 29, 1979:1). It solicited direct foreign investment from European countries and encouraged local corporations to invest abroad to guarantee supplies of raw materials and open new markets. It stepped up the activities of the China External Trade Development Council established in 1970 to promote the island's products through shows at home and around the world and to collect data on foreign markets. It also encouraged the formation of large general trading companies to wrest control of trade from Japanese general trading companies (*sogo shōsha*) and American buyers (*Business Asia*, November 17, 1978:364–65; *FEER*, January 5, 1979:52–53).

—To counter neoprotectionist quotas based on volume of goods, primarily textiles, the state encouraged exporters to produce more upscale, higher value items to earn more for each unit sold. This was another element in the strategy of upgrading the industrial structure.

—To win the loyalty of Overseas Chinese, as the People's Republic developed its own export sector, and, as the decade ended, even solicited direct foreign investment—targeting Overseas Chinese first—the

KMT stepped up its already aggressive wooing of that same constituency.

—To ensure access to foreign funds in the event of expulsion from multilateral lending agencies such as the World Bank, International Monetary Fund (IMF), or Asian Development Bank, it facilitated the opening of foreign commercial banks—mainly European and American—and encouraged local banks to open offices abroad.

—Finally, to entangle the island in as many foreign alliances as possible, despite its near total political isolation (by 1980, South Africa, Saudi Arabia, and South Korea were the only major nations to maintain full relations with it), the GRC adopted a much more flexible foreign policy and encouraged other nations to use trade offices as substitute diplomatic representatives, charged with issuing visas and other consular powers (*FEER*, December 26, 1980:8–9).

For all of the buffetting it sustained, Taiwan's economy survived the decade, continuing to grow at a clip faster than most of the rest of the world. With the global recovery of 1983, the economy resumed its high growth rates, although well below the pre–oil crisis boom. Except for cases such as computers, industrial restructuring made slow progress. It faced a variety of obstacles. Most important were doubts over the island's viability in the face of aggressive PRC efforts at reunification, compounded by Chiang Ching-kuo's refusal to select a clear successor. These dampened the willingness of local businessmen to invest in expensive new plants and equipment or commit capital with a slow return. As Taiwan's vitality and stability were in large part attributable to small investors, the state was loath to push them too hard to upgrade equipment, invest in R&D, build larger factories, or merge, thereby risking their resentment and the slowing down of investment altogether. Further, as the economics ministries remained mainlander preserves and the petit bourgeoisie Taiwanese, the state faced political constraints in its ability to implement policies threatening to this class.

The state still monopolized the banking system through its ownership of banks moved from the mainland and majority shares confiscated from Japanese partners in private local banks. Bankers are thus state employees and extremely cautious, preferring state enterprises and large private corporations with lots of collateral as customers. This forces smaller private firms to borrow from family and friends or from the unorganized kerb market at exorbitant rates (Caldwell 1976:736; *AWSJ*, December 4, 1979). To breathe life into the system, a 1975 Banking Law revision broadened the scope of banking practices. One result was the expansion of investment and trust companies, most of which are part of business groups, such as Cathay (*AWSJ*, January 1, 1980:1), that usually cannot merge productive and financial functions. They perform banking functions and, unlike state banks, make equity investments. A distressing percentage of their activities were purely speculative, and their wheeling and dealing in land fueled a building boom that sent Taipei property values up 150 percent between mid-1978 and the end of 1980 when the government moved in to deflate it.[16] In addition, there was a great deal of capital flight, much of it invested in California real estate, although hard figures are difficult to come by.[17]

Official encouragement of investment in the Caribbean Basin, stimulated by Ronald Reagan's Caribbean Basin Initiative, facilitated capital export and businessmen obtaining foreign residence papers, but in addition assisted sunset industries in prolonging their lives and avoiding U.S. quotas on Taiwan exports (*FCJ*, December 2, 1984:4). Here again, the Japanese model proved instructive.

The state's share in Gross Domestic Capital Formation increased noticeably from a low of 34.7 percent in 1973 to a high of 57.7 percent in 1975, remaining near 50 percent the rest of the decade (TSDB 1982:40). This was due to the state's role in the heavy industry sector as well as the Ten Projects. Completed in 1979, the Ten Projects were succeeded by a dozen new ones of a similar nature, designed to expand and upgrade the industrial structure, agriculture, and culture (*FCW*, June 21, 1981:1-2).

Trade continued to grow. By 1980, Taiwan was the world's sixteenth largest exporter (AIT 1981:1).[18] Trade was still 50 percent concentrated on the United States and Japan. To fend off protectionist moves against the island from its largest market, the government sent several "Buy American" missions to the United States beginning in 1978 for high-visibility purchases, generally of goods such as grain that it would have bought in any case. At the same time, frustrated by the refusal of Japan, its main supplier, to buy Taiwanese, the government imposed a temporary ban in 1982 on some 1,500 consumer goods from Japan (Arnold 1985:194-96).[19]

Taiwan's trading partners diversified somewhat, especially with new inroads to Europe. Taiwan-Europe trade volume rose from $2.1 billion in 1977 to $5 billion in 1980 (*FEER*, April 4, 1983:40). Exports to the European Economic Community (EEC) grew 30 percent a year from 1975 to 1980 (*Euromoney*, May 1981:17), led by the Nether-

lands, and by 1980 the EEC was Taiwan's second largest export market
(AIT 1981:12). By 1983, Taiwan had become the EEC's twenty-fifth
largest trading partner, up from thirty-first in 1978 (*FCJ,* December
16, 1984:4). This was in spite of the fact that Taiwan was not a member
of the General Agreement on Tariffs and Trade (GATT) and its exports
did not qualify for duty-free status under the Generalized System of
Preferences, while those of its arch-rivals did. Taiwan's businessmen
participated in East European trade fairs; two-way trade with that
region came to $60–70 million for 1980 (*WSJ,* March 24, 1981:5).

The Europeans' own need to find new markets to stimulate their
battered economies, Taiwan's aggressive, state-led wooing of Europe
for trade and investment partners, and Western disillusionment with
the market on the Chinese mainland all contributed to this growth. At
times the People's Republic did not try to prevent this activity; at other
times it raised objections but took no action.[20]

In the late 1970s, clandestine trade between Taiwan and the People's
Republic, mostly via Hong Kong, grew rapidly, encouraged by the
Communists as part of their push to open direct contacts with the
island's people. The trade was valued at an estimated $300 million in
1980 (*FEER,* June 5, 1981:53). Overall, Taiwan's trade grew at an
annual rate of 19.2 percent for the decade (Kuo 1983:315). Attempts to
promote big general trading companies and to wrest trade away from
foreign merchants foundered, however (*Economic News,* June 8–14,
1981:1–3).

Direct foreign investment bounced back vigorously after the Nixon
shock of 1971 and the oil crisis of 1974. Here, too, European investors
helped diversify sources of foreign capital. In the two years after
diplomatic relations were broken off between the United States and the
Republic of China, overall DFI increased 125.4 percent, spearheaded
as before by American investors (AIT 1981:3). Congress's passage of
the Taiwan Relations Act in March 1979, with its implicit American
commitment to protect Taiwan, no doubt contributed to foreign willingness to continue sinking money into the island. The People's Republic seemed to acquiesce in this, although there is no doubt that it
successfully lured a great deal of Overseas Chinese capital to the
mainland that would previously have gone to Taiwan.

In April and May 1980, Taiwan was expelled from the World Bank
and IMF, but at the same time there was an explosion of foreign bank
openings, with the Europeans leading the charge. The thirteen foreign
bank offices at the start of 1980 were joined by eight new ones by year's

end, five of which were European.[21]

To gain a foothold in the Taiwan market and qualify to open a branch, foreign banks lent generously to many local enterprises, a number of which could never qualify for loans from the state-owned banks. After being burned several times (for example, see *AWSJ Weekly*, December 6, 1982:9), foreign banks adopted a stance similar to that of the state banks and limited their lending to state enterprises and the largest local firms.

On the "diplomatic" front, through 1980, sixteen nations had established trade offices that functioned as pseudoconsulates. They included the Netherlands, Great Britain, France, West Germany, Spain, Greece, and Belgium. Taiwan maintained commercial relations with nearly 130 countries (*FEER*, May 22, 1981:32) and had technical missions—mostly agricultural—in more than 20 developing nations, especially in Africa and Latin America (*FCW*, January 10, 1982:4). "Economic complementarity" was the motivation behind uninterrupted "paradiplomatic" relations with Japan (Arnold 1985). Participation in the 1984 Los Angeles Olympics, although as Chinese-Taipei and not as the Republic of China, boosted public morale. A Taiwanese weightlifter even won a medal, stood on the winner's platform with a PRC medalist, and shook hands with him.

The strategy of substituting economic ties for diplomatic ones and utilizing them for security objectives paid off. In both the United States and Japan, businessmen with interests in Taiwan testified and lobbied on behalf of maintaining a variety of semi-official links with the island.[22]

The preceding examples illustrate the flexible ways in which the KMT state took the initiative at home and abroad in an increasingly unfavorable environment, to keep the economy growing and to maintain some sort of international identity.

Sudden Political Awakening

Social change advanced and by the middle of the 1970s brought on a surge of political activity. The occupational structure continued to shift from agriculture to industry, with increasing numbers of females entering the labor force, relatively and absolutely. The rural labor force and population became progressively older as rural youths migrated to the cities en masse.

The population became more concentrated in urban areas (41.9 percent in 1978). The birth rate declined only slightly in this period; in

1980 it was 2.34 percent. The rate of natural population increase that year was 1.9 percent (TSDB 1983:2). Population control had long been a controversial subject as it implied that the mainland would not be recovered and Taiwan's surplus would have nowhere to go. The issue of legalizing abortions—already numbering 200,000 to 400,000 annually—brought on a debate in 1984 (*FCJ*, April 29, 1984:3), as the population reached nineteen million.

Physical quality-of-life indicators—literacy, infant mortality, and life expectancy—continued to improve.[23] Quite importantly, income distribution still refused to follow the predicted pattern.[24] The income share of the top 20 percent decreased from 38.6 percent in 1972 to 36.8 percent in 1980, while the other quintiles improved their relative shares somewhat. As measured by income, well over 50 percent of the population was "middle class."[25] More tellingly, the GINI coefficient decreased from .318 in 1972 to .303 in 1980 and the ratio of income share of the top and bottom 20 percent decreased from 4.49 to 4.18. Recall that it was estimated to be as high as 11.56 as recently as 1961 (Kuo 1983:96–97).[26] The gap between farm and nonfarm family income did not close, as farm family income (only 25 percent derived from agricultural work) lagged at about two-thirds that of nonfarm families (*FEER*, November 19, 1982:74; Kuo 1983:104–105). Under conditions of full employment, combined with inflation, wages increased 20 percent a year between 1976 and 1980 (*FEER*, February 26, 1982:79).

An important element in social change was education. With the institution of nine years of free and compulsory education in 1968, the percentage of people age six and over with a secondary education increased from 18.9 percent in 1968 to 36.9 percent in 1980. In 1980 the literacy rate was nearly 90 percent (TSDB 1982:7). By 1980–81, nearly two-thirds of junior high graduates went on to senior high, and nearly 80 percent of those who finished senior high enrolled in postsecondary school (ibid.:257). There were more than 100 institutions of higher learning (ibid.:250). Taiwan replicated Japan's use of open examinations as the sole criterion for passing from one level to another, with the same consequences: an obsession with taking tests and a shadow educational system of cram schools, which students attended after regular school, exclusively to prepare for exams.[27]

The effect of education on social mobility in a rapidly industrializing society with a free labor market is obvious,[28] but more significant were the political consequences. By stressing a common Chinese heritage, enforcing the use of Mandarin in the schools and the progressive restriction of the Taiwanese dialect in the mass media, the government managed to decrease dramatically the linguistic and cultural differences between young people of mainlander and Taiwanese parentage, along with the justification for excluding Taiwanese from important government and party posts.

In addition to training in skills, Taiwan's education is highly ideological, with massive doses of Sun Yat-senism and official claims to be "free China," a democratic republic fundamentally different from its "totalitarian" Communist counterpart across the water. At the university level, students use English-language American textbooks and are exposed to numerous foreign instructors, many of whom are Christian missionaries.

Popular culture, enhanced by the rapid development of publishing and modern communications and the virtually complete penetration of all households by television, is also substantially dominated by foreign (i.e., American) fare. As a result, nearly everyone in this highly penetrated society is exposed frequently to American values of consumerism, individuality, human rights, electoral politics, and democracy. Nearly 1.5 million foreign and Overseas Chinese tourists annually flaunt these same values around the island. Taiwan's businessmen travelling abroad partake of the free economic and political atmosphere of the West and Japan on a regular basis. The availability since early 1979 of tourist passports has allowed large numbers of Taiwan's middle class citizens to savor these for themselves.

As described above, during Taiwan's first series of external shocks early in the 1970s, a group of liberal intellectuals—many of whom had studied abroad and, going against the "brain drain" tide, had returned to work on the island—pressed for political reforms. After the suppression of this movement, the domestic popular political scene was quiet for several years with the exception of the 1975 appearance and ban five issues later of an outspoken new journal, *Taiwan Political Review*, run by nonparty legislators Huang Hsin-chieh and K'ang Ning-hsiang.

Responding to social pressure and attempting to maintain control over the direction and speed of change, Chiang Ching-kuo emerged as the voice of moderation. After the death of his father in April 1975, from the premier's office and, more importantly, as the new chairman of the KMT Central Standing Committee, Chiang effectively became his own man. One of his first acts was to offer amnesty to a number of prisoners, including an estimated 130 political detainees, some incarcerated for more than a decade (Amnesty International 1976:558).

Skillfully using the mass media, Chiang created a radical new image of himself as a populist, neither the same man who had earlier been feared as head of the internal security apparatus nor of the same mold as his aloof and austere father. Each Sunday, the lead story on every television network news show displayed the premier, clad in turtleneck and windbreaker, going to visit the masses, sitting in their homes, dropping into their shops, eating noodles, and pressing the flesh.

Chiang also began a process of "Taiwanization." This refers not only to appointing natives to top party and state posts[29]—including Shieh Tung-min as vice-president in 1978 and Lee Teng-hui in 1984—but also to giving prominence to the children of mainlanders raised on Taiwan. Many of the latter are oriented primarily to the island, not the mainland, despite their public adherence to the "recover the mainland" slogan. Most were educated abroad and constitute a politically moderate force within the elite (Domes 1981:1024–25). Success in attracting them back required further political liberalization. Key portfolios such as economic affairs, finance, governor of the Central Bank, defense, and foreign affairs remained a mainlander preserve, however.[30]

At the same time, Chiang strengthened the position of his long-time comrade-in-arms, hardline security czar General Wang Sheng. In 1975 there was a determined crackdown on the alarming increase in crime. The following year saw several purported sedition cases, including an attempt on the life of then Governor Shieh Tung-min. In 1978, six young men received lengthy prison sentences for organizing a "People's Liberation Front" that took the unprecedented step, for Taiwan, of sending threatening letters to foreign businessmen demanding that they leave the country. Chiang thus gave contradictory signals, which kept the political malcontents guessing.

Activity shifted to the literary scene, where a remarkable group of Taiwanese writers published stories about the life of the common folk on the island.[31] This nativist (*hsiang-t'u*) literature flew in the face of mainstream literature, which comprised adventures about spies behind enemy lines, kung-fu epics, and melodramas of love in the upper classes, or else offered poems and stories imitative of Western modernist and existentialist writers. The new works took Taiwan as a social unit of its own, not merely a part of China, and unabashedly exuded local flavor.

Several developments in 1977 brought matters to a head on all fronts. In the spring, Hsu Hsin-liang, a former rising star in the KMT and activist in the 1971–73 reform movement, published a gossipy and critical memoir of his years in the Provincial Assembly, *Feng-yü chih sheng* (The Sound of the Storm), causing quite a storm of its own. Hsu did not flee from the publicity, as he was gearing up to run for the magistracy of T'ao-yuan County in that fall's regular quadrennial election for local officials. When the KMT did not nominate him, he violated discipline by running anyway and was expelled from the party.

During summer vacation, a number of college students were attracted to Hsu's cause and became actively involved in the American-style grass-roots campaign. U.S. President Jimmy Carter's aggressive advocacy of human rights emboldened them. Too young to have personally experienced the February 28 Incident and convinced that the KMT could never attempt a similar attack, they pressed on, baiting the party at every chance. *Hsüan-chü wan-sui* (Long Live Elections) (Lin and Chang 1977), the lively and detailed account of the campaign by two activists, confiscated at the printers by the Garrison Command, is a veritable handbook on how to run an electoral campaign in an authoritarian one-party society.

The literary and political strains soon merged, with unintentional KMT assistance. In the fall, the party committed a monumental blunder by delegating the extremely unpopular General Wang Sheng and several officially favored literati to criticize the Taiwanese writers as "worker-peasant-soldier" authors, implying they were both leftist and pro–Taiwan independence. This only increased the writers' self-consciousness as a distinct school. Their visibility and sales soared.

The spontaneous, anti-KMT Chung-li Incident, during voting that resulted in Hsu Hsin-liang's overwhelming victory, cemented the commitment of literary and political circles to challenge mainlander-KMT dominance of Taiwan's society. The unexpected spontaneous violence stymied the authorities. They let Hsu's victory stand but instigated a face-saving witchhunt against alleged perpetrators of the incident (Lin and Chang 1977).

The resemblance of this activity to China's May Fourth Movement is uncanny. On May 4, 1919, students of Peking University had marched to protest the sellout of the nation's sovereignty by the Powers and traitorous Chinese officials at Versailles. That demonstration had deep roots in social change underway in China after the fall of the last dynasty, and in frustration with ineffectual political leadership, lack of popular participation, and the influence of foreign ideologies. There followed several years of mass political activity and bold literary experimentation that both reflected and stimulated social change. Both the Nationalist and Communist parties grew out of this ferment.

Chung-li precipitated a comparable upsurge in political and literary activity.[32] There ensued a tug of war as the nonparty (*tangwai*) activists tested the permissible limits of democracy. Neither Chiang Ching-kuo, who in 1978 became president, nor the KMT ever explicitly defined the rules. This was a result of deliberate tactics to keep the dissidents offguard, as well as inner-party struggle over the correct response (Domes 1981; Winckler 1982). The *tangwai* utilized magazines as their main weapon between election campaigns. Denied permission to organize a party, they nonetheless established a network of liaison stations to coordinate political activities at local levels. They aimed to take their message to Taiwan's workers, peasants, and petit bourgeoisie, broadening their base away from the young urban intellectuals who had started the movement. *Tangwai* were garnering around 25 percent of the vote in various elections (*FEER*, December 17, 1983:32).[33] New, highly visible Taiwanese who were not "half-mountains" articulated the aspirations and interests of a sizable portion of the populace.

The movement's ideological background and platform were by no means unified,[34] although in this period the disparate elements cooperated tactically in the elections. The *China Tide* (*Hsia-ch'ao*) group was more oriented to intellectual and theoretical matters. This journal, lasting from July 1976 to January 1979, published histories of popular resistance movements in Taiwan and China, linking the two in obvious support of reunification. Its articles criticized foreign capital's role in Taiwan, exposed the harsh conditions of workers and peasants, called for more state expenditure on social welfare, and tied Taiwan's fate to that of the Third World generally.

Other activists, writing in a dizzying array of journals (a new one would spring up as an old one was shut down by the Garrison Command), were primarily oriented to elections, calling for "democracy" (never well defined) and exposing KMT malfeasance. The *tangwai* appeared headed for a major electoral triumph in national supplementary elections scheduled for December 1978, but President Carter's ill-timed announcement of U.S.-PRC normalization gave the KMT an excuse to cancel the elections.

The break with the United States had contradictory effects on Taiwan's polity: on the one hand, it helped to unify all ends of the spectrum in the face of impending disaster; on the other, several oppositionists perceived it as an opportunity to press harder for participation at the top in such a dangerous environment. The *tangwai* movement then split more openly into a moderate current around K'ang Ning-hsiang and his journal *The Eighties* and a more radical current centered around ex-political prisoner Shih Ming-teh, his American wife Linda Gail Arrigo, Yao Chia-wen, Hsu Hsin-liang, Chang Chün-hung, *hsiang-t'u* writers Yang Ch'ing-ch'u and Wang T'o, and feminists Ch'en Chü and Lü Hsiu-lien, and their magazine, *Formosa (Mei-li tao)*.[35]

The *Formosa* group opened regional offices around the island and began to function as a political party. Influenced by the Democracy Movement in the PRC and the Iranian revolution, its leaders misjudged the limits of KMT tolerance and held a mass rally in Kaohsiung on December 10, 1979, International Human Rights Day. Although the facts are still in dispute, the demonstration turned violent, the leadership cadre of *Formosa* was arrested, and after a public show trial they were sentenced to stiff jail terms.[36] Reverend Kao Chun-ming, the activist leader of the Presbyterian Church, was also put out of commission, jailed for sheltering Shih Ming-teh.

The fortunes of the moderate wing continued to ebb and flow. The postponed national elections were rescheduled for December 1980 and generally were judged to have been administered fairly, although the KMT imposed harsh controls on campaigning.[37] To win votes and retain its influential allies in the United States, the KMT was concerned to present a benign image of itself as a fair, electorally oriented party, something like the Republicans in the United States. Two-thirds of the electorate voted. The opposition scored some impressive victories, although the KMT won 80 percent of the ninety-seven contested seats for the Legislative Yuan and 83 percent of those for the National Assembly *(FEER, December 12, 1980:8-9; FCW, December 14, 1980:1-2)*. Most significant, the largest vote-getter in the contest for National Assembly was Chou Ch'ing-yü, wife of jailed lawyer-activist Yao Chia-wen. The voters obviously showed symbolic support for her husband.

The election increased the proportion of supplementary members in the Legislative Yuan, National Assembly, and Control Yuan to 23.3 percent, 6.2 percent, and 46.3 percent, respectively *(FCW, December 14, 1980:2)*. Although these figures were still small, many of the members elected on the mainland in 1947—and not required to stand for election since—were too decrepit to attend sessions in any case, so the infusion of younger, better educated, and articulate politicians could have a significant impact.

The subsequent triennial supplementary elections held in December 1983 delivered a slap at the *tangwai*. Their total vote fell from 30 percent to 22 percent (*FEER*, February 14, 1985:21). Internecine squabbling caused them to field too many candidates, thereby splitting the vote and handing the KMT a landslide victory. The *tangwai*'s moderate stalwart, K'ang Ning-hsiang, was a surprise casualty. The KMT strategy reflected a new approach to society and the electoral process. It limited its own candidates and nominated people with distinct voter appeal, such as businessmen, athletes, and intellectuals. It won sixty-two of seventy-one seats contested for the Legislative Yuan. Sixty-six of the victors were Taiwanese (*FEER*, December 15, 1983:15–17; *FCJ*, December 4, 1983:1; *Free China Review*, December 1983:36–45).

Taiwan in 1984

The end of the Orwellian year left Taiwan in a precarious transition stage on many fronts, facing an uncertain future. In the economy, the state had reassumed a major direct role in addition to its administrative guidance. Its ambitious plans to upgrade the industrial structure based on external demand ran into trouble due to the prolonged global depression, competition from the People's Republic and other less developed countries, and the reticence of local businessmen to make the necessary capital commitment in the face of political uncertainty.

In April 1985, facing a decline in export volume, a spreading scandal involving the once high-flying Cathay conglomerate and several government officials, and stalled investment,[38] Premier Yu Kuo-hwa established an Economic Revitalization Committee of cadres, scholars, and businessmen to seek solutions collectively. In its public pronouncements, the committee did not face up to the fundamental political causes of many of these crises, namely, the succession to Chiang Ching-kuo and Taiwan's continued independent existence, although the committee itself could perform a transition function (Kuo 1985). Y. C. Wang of Formosa Plastics headed the Industrial Subcommittee, bringing unprecedented public exposure to a businessman in a quasi-official capacity.[39]

Taiwan's society was assuming the contours of a middle-class consumer society, and the fault lines were taking on new forms. There was no extreme bifurcation between "transnational" and nontransnationally oriented classes common in other parts of the Third World.[40] Capitalist class differences were replacing those between mainlanders and Taiwanese as the main dividing line, but there was as yet no class-based political activity.[41] Social mobility stayed high and workers and part-time peasants aspired to middle-class status with a good chance of attaining it. Urged by social activists, the state began to pay more attention to the welfare aspect of its official ideology and to invest more in the well-being of the poor members of society. The generation under forty-five—mainlanders and Taiwanese—held a new, common, island-based identity which Taiwan's plummeting diplomatic fortunes reinforced. Even people who had sought refuge on the island in the 1940s and never considered their stay permanent had a change of heart. As they established contact with their relatives still on the mainland via Hong Kong, Japan, or the United States and learned what had happened to them in the intervening decades, they took new pride in what they had built on Taiwan and accepted it as home.

While still the major political force, and in firm control of the military and security apparatuses, the KMT's unquestioned dominance was weakening, especially at the local level. Once off-limits to any sort of challenge, the mainlanders found the legitimacy of their monopoly of state power questioned by a new cohort of well-educated, articulate, Mandarin-speaking Taiwanese (and younger "mainlanders"), both in and outside the party.[42] The KMT had coopted and incorporated emerging social forces for thirty years and was now, with the support of certain elements in the leadership, being reshaped by these internal reformers while at the same time it was forcefully prodded by external political forces. Its autonomy from society was reduced proportionately. It was too large to function as a vanguard elite and its membership was too independent-minded to submit to centralist discipline. The old division of labor, whereby KMT mainlanders ran national politics and enforced their will while Taiwanese made money in business and channelled their political ambitions into local contests, was breaking down.

The masses, still remembering the brutality of the early KMT days and now with a deep material stake in the status quo, favored stability and opposed the confrontational tactics of extremists. But they also clearly desired more meaningful participation in political decision-making. The KMT recognized this and also accepted the *tangwai* as a more or less permanent fixture on the political scene, though giving ground to them only reluctantly. It maintained martial law, while engaging in a sophistical propaganda campaign with the aim of convincing foreign critics that martial law in Taiwan was not martial law (*FCW*, August 21, 1983:4). Nonetheless, the U.S. 98th Congress expressed "the sense of the Congress concerning martial law in Taiwan" in May 1983, urging continued "democratic progress" and an end to martial law.

The KMT continued to keep the opposition off balance, though there began to be questions about just who was giving orders. On the significant date of February 28, 1980, as yet unapprehended killers brutally murdered the mother and twin daughters of *tangwai* legislator Lin Yi-hsiung, then incarcerated for the Kaohsiung Incident. In July 1981, in another unsolved case, Chen Wen-cheng, a Taiwanese professor at Carnegie-Mellon University who enjoyed U.S. permanent residence status, fell to his death from the fifth floor of the National Taiwan University Library after being questioned intensively about his involvement in Taiwan independence activities abroad (*FEER*, July 31, 1981:12–14).

In a countermove, in the fall of 1983, ultrahardliner General Wang Sheng, seen as pushing too hard to be anointed Chiang Ching-kuo's successor, found himself appointed ambassador to Paraguay, an effective sentence of exile (*WSJ*, October 3, 1983:28). Then in October 1984, journalist Henry Liu, who under the pen name Chiang Nan had written a gossipy critical biography of Chiang Ching-kuo, was gunned down in his Daly City, California, home. American police traced the shooting to the Taiwanese United Bamboo Gang, rumored to have connections with Chiang's son Hsiao-wu (*NYT*, December 5, 1984). Security agencies were in the midst of a popularly supported crackdown of the burgeoning and increasingly brazen underworld (*FCJ*, December 9, 1984:2). Solving the Liu murder evolved into an embarrassing exposure of the internal security network and its ties with the underworld as well as the KMT's massive spying and intimidation operations in the United States. Faced with congressional investigations and threatened cutbacks in arms sales, the KMT damage-control went so far as to bring about the arrest of several top security officials (*Newsweek*, January 28, 1985:38ff). In the spring of 1985, two United Bamboo Gang leaders, Chen Chi-li and Wu Tun, as well as military intelligence chief Wong Hsi-ling, received life sentences for the murder after very hasty trials and appeals.

In general, as the international environment continues to worsen for the Republic of China on Taiwan, the trend to democratization has to continue. The CCP's Nine Points for Reunification, the Sino-British

Agreement on Hong Kong, the PRC's radical structural reform and new probusiness image, stepped up trade between the People's Republic and Taiwan's arch-rival, South Korea (*FEER*, January 17, 1985:29), and increasing pressure by local capital to legalize trade with the mainland are pushing the KMT to the point where it must unite Taiwan's society and broaden the political base at the "national" level before it is abandoned. The party's admirable success at leading economic development and social change from a position of autonomy created the conditions for the withering away of its dictatorship. It has made marked strides toward political modernization, and the far-flung repressive apparatus has become anachronistic.

8

State
and
Society
in
the
Taiwan
Miracle

This book began by criticizing previous explanations of Taiwan's development as partial or misleading. To rectify this, I have utilized Cardoso and Faletto's comprehensive historical-structural methodology to retell the story of Taiwan's development. I also asserted that the 1977 Chung-li Incident was a watershed event for continued maintenance of the structure that had characterized Taiwan's postwar development to that time. In this concluding chapter, I will summarize the structure up to 1977, explain the significance of Chung-li, and in the process respond to the key questions I claimed other approaches left unanswered. Finally, I will comment on Taiwan as a model of development.

Clearly, any explanation of Taiwan's growth with stability must start with the Nationalist party-state. What leaps out from the preceding historical-structural analysis is the way in which Taiwan's political elite, with a great deal of autonomy from particular social interests, effectively led sustained economic development through several crises and maintained stability in the bargain. It did not just get the prices right, but it restructured society, channelled funds for investment, intervened directly in the economy, created a market system, devised indicative plans, determined the physical and psychological investment climate, and guided Taiwan's incorporation into the world capitalist system.

The KMT state's effectiveness derived from several factors. Perhaps most important was its relation to Taiwan's society. Cardoso's concept of "pact of domination" is irrelevant in the first stage, because the KMT began, in effect, as a colonial power occupying and restructuring a conquered and leaderless society. Comprising little more than a bureaucracy and army, the KMT had no social base on Taiwan with demands to constrain its actions. Taiwan was also devoid of foreign economic interests that might have hindered the KMT's efforts at control. The mainlander regime confiscated industrial and financial assets, carried out a land reform, and remolded social groups from an unassailable position of strength virtually without parallel in the Third World. Backed by a gargantuan, foreign-supported military machine, the organs of martial law, and a pervasive internal security system, the KMT stands as an almost overdetermined case of "revolution from above."[1]

Effectiveness also derived from the high degree of cohesiveness of the KMT on Taiwan. Negatively, this came from being a numerical minority, although armed to the teeth, in a hostile society, and from the threat it faced across the straits. The mainlander elite has never uncircled the wagons. Positively, though, its unity came from a strong leader, a commitment to prove it could succeed, its motivating ideology, and U.S. backing. Thus the factors that doomed it on the mainland—foreign military and economic occupation, a mass revolutionary movement, alliance with the most conservative social forces, rampant corruption, crippling factionalism, warlordism, demoralization, and a hesitant ally—did not confront it after 1950. Its autonomy, ruthlessness, determination, ideological legitimation, cohesion, material base, and foreign support distinguished the KMT on Taiwan from other authoritarian regimes as well as from its own botched efforts on the mainland.

These factors sufficed to ensure its *control* over Taiwan's territory, people, and resources—its overriding objective in the 1945–1950 period—but do not explain why it then shifted to a program to *develop* and industrialize the economy, or why this succeeded.

The initial motivation behind development was short term: to build Taiwan into a defensive bastion and to beef up its supplies and productive capacity for the imminent counterattack, after which Taiwan would revert to being one of the two-dozen-plus provinces of the Republic of China. It achieved the former goals rather quickly. Realizing that the sojourn on Taiwan would be lengthy, and under American pressure and tied assistance to develop Taiwan as a showcase of noncommunist development, the party-state then turned to promotion of agricultural and industrial growth. To the United States, Taiwan-as-symbol evolved from freedom's embattled garrison to living proof of the superiority of a noncommunist route to relatively egalitarian prosperity. Also positively affecting state policies were Sun Yat-sen's writings on a strategy of state-led economic development with a role for foreign investment, which provided systematic ideological underpinnings most other noncommunist LDCs lack.

The decision to commit resources to build Taiwan and to allow the Taiwanese to participate as capitalists was not inherent in the KMT despite Sun Yat-sen's advocacy of a role for regulated private capital. While the debilitating factionalism of the mainland had been curbed, there were still sharp differences of opinion in the elite over questions of developing the economy, the suitable role for the state in the economy, and permitting the growth of a private sector. In Taiwan, as this would certainly mean a Taiwanese bourgeoisie controlling sizable resources, this was a difficult political decision. In a one-party system, all decisions are political; in this case, the ethnic issue made it even more contentious. Here, the Americans, with their control over the regime's life-support system and conditions governing their provision of aid, played a decisive role. They helped to create the initial developmental institutions, staff them with American-trained experts, and insulate them from political tampering. They saw to the fostering of a private sector and Taiwanese participation in it. American pressure and Chiang Kai-shek's decision to back the pro-(limited)free-enterprise developmentalists over the hard-line return-to-the-mainland statist ideologues in the early 1950s determined the shape the economy would assume—a mixture of official commitment to American free-market ideals and actual conformity to the Japanese state-led model in practice.

With development, this division in the party resulted in specialization, reducing the influence of the ideological generalists. Over subsequent years, bolstered by continuous success, the technocrats gained more influence and backing and institutions such as the planning agencies and MOEA upgraded their capabilities and responsibilities. The creators of the Taiwan miracle were primarily engineers by training who learned by doing. Economists entered the agencies later, and they still tend to be outside government. Economic planners rarely concerned themselves with welfare issues, leaving those to other bureaus or the party, and adopting the attitude that an expanded economic pie was the best way to solve such problems. Although KMT leaders such as Chiang Kai-shek, Ch'en Ch'eng, and Chiang Ching-kuo had military backgrounds and put the island under martial law, civilian rule was not challenged seriously. Party control of the gun in Taiwan contrasts with such Asian neighbors as Thailand, Indonesia, and the Philippines where the military has more or less clearly run the show. It more resembles Korea, which has civilianized its leaders. The decision after 1958 to take steps to open the economy to trade and DFI and the later one to establish EPZs likewise involved political struggle within the KMT, with U.S. pressure tipping the balance.

Stability through authoritarianism and a developmentalist state laid a foundation for Taiwan's growth, but also key was the mainlander party-state's grudging willingness to create a system that granted wide scope to succeed economically to a pragmatic people with ambitions and talents in that direction. Cronyism and corruption existed, but so did genuine opportunity. This sets Taiwan off from such Asian neighbors as the Philippines, Indonesia, and, to a lesser extent, Thailand.

The KMT's political domination and economic agenda plus American assistance created suitable conditions, but we have to examine Taiwanese society to understand why policies worked. Fifty years as a second-class race had accustomed the Taiwanese to repression and limited aspirations. The brutal Nationalist takeover reinforced this. In addition, the aristocratic elite had been easily separated from its assets and other community leaders physically liquidated. People were organized into various groupings run by KMT cadres or military officers. From the perspective of the masses, it appeared as reprised colonialist domination.

But there were major differences. The land reform really did distribute land to the tiller and introduce technology of benefit to the individual farmer. Taiwanese could start up enterprises without being coerced into taking outsiders onto the board. There were no foreign corporations to compete with. Government enterprises were restricting their activities, leaving the field more open. Higher educational opportunities were available once one mastered Mandarin. One could engage in political horsetrading at the local level and have a say over bread-and-butter issues. The opportunities in the city to start a company or find a job seemed boundless. Recognizing and accepting the benefits and limits of the system, the people responded positively and successfully.

Cultural characteristics played an important role. These included pragmatic assessment of channels for upward mobility; acceptance of a moralistic authoritarian state and arrogant bureaucracy with a pater familias's concern for the citizens' daily life as normal; ambition for self and family; high value on education and learning by copying exemplars; frugality; the family as an economic unit: and entrepreneurship.

The problem in Taiwan has not been a dearth of entrepreneurship, but rather a structure to let it prosper. The Japanese demonstrated the potential rewards but kept them off limits to Taiwanese. The Nationalists built a structure enabling these latent talents to thrive. It involved granting high official prestige to business success—turning Chinese tradition on its head. Stability became self-enforcing as people were too busy making a living to worry about big political issues, and they knew firsthand that politics was dangerous. Government-business relations in Taiwan differed substantially from Japan and Korea. Whereas in Japan, regularized consultations between MITI and industry representatives helped determine industrial policy, and Korea has seen a more brutish, commandist approach, in Taiwan planners retained an aloof posture. They met to formulate policy and then relayed their decisions and attendant mechanisms to implement it to the business community and watched what happened. Although cadres did meet with entrepreneurs to exert some pressure and picked some favorites, Taiwan's private sector has been much more anarchic and self-directed than its Japanese or Korean counterparts.

The KMT state controlled the way Taiwan became incorporated into the world system in a way few other countries have. When it took over, it faced no foreign interests obstructing the integration of society or consolidation of power. Local groups tied to the Japanese either fled or jumped to the Chinese side. No indigenous landed elites opposed manufactured exports. The state closely regulated exports and imports, either directly or by allocating American aid commodities. In the 1950s, because of its small market, economic instability, indeterminate future, backward industry, and paucity of resources, Taiwan had virtually nothing to offer foreign corporations, had any come sniffing around.

Aid and financial dependence were the initial forms of incorporation with the global economy. Government-regulated tariffs, trade prohibitions, and foreign exchange controls prevented haphazard commercial linkages between the business class and the outside. The first foreign investors either joined with the state or, in the case of Japanese and Overseas Chinese, were small and did not pose a threat of denationalizing local enterprises, disrupting the domestic economy, or weakening state power.

When the KMT, under intense U.S. pressure and after great internal debate, shifted to a strategy welcoming DFI and liberalized trade, the integrated domestic economy already had a sound foundation and the state could channel foreign capital into selected areas. Fortuitous timing assisted this strategy so that, by and large, TNCs kept to a limited number of sectors, accepted local suppliers, introduced appropriate technology, and agreed not to disrupt the domestic market.

A division of labor in the economy among TNCs, local capital, and the state, with distinct spheres yet numerous vertical and horizontal linkages, formed the dynamic base for Taiwan's development. TNCs dominated certain sectors, notably electronics, through ownership and technology licensing and others, such as textiles, through subcontracting and purchasing arrangements. Taiwan's situation of dependency passed from one characterized by aid and loans to the more common pattern of DFI and trade, but never to a point of usurping the state or denationalizing local industry. On the contrary, it reinforced the state and boosted domestic production. Capital reproduction had a vital external component, but the majority was accumulated domestically.

Until 1977 this strategy worked extraordinarily well, despite the fledgling political challenges of 1971–72 and economic crisis of 1974–75. Local society and TNCs responded to the incentive packages presented to them, and foreign markets easily absorbed Taiwan's exports. The standard of living rose rapidly, and between authoritarian penetration and control of society and numerous mobility channels outside politics, the regime faced only a handful of challenges, all disorganized. Intellectuals were subject to strict censorship and either lived abroad or retreated to their studies. The 1971 call for reforms was a harbinger of 1977, as a few foreign-educated intellectuals struck a responsive nerve, but in that case, the regime handily suppressed it. The social base for an opposition had not matured.

The state successfully responded to economic crises in 1958 and 1973, with American public and private counsel. It defused economic frustration before it turned into political action. The technocrats did not consult social groups prior to strategy shifts—they analyzed problems and options and devised incentives based on what they believed entrepreneurs and TNCs would respond to, and which ensured the survival of the regime and the island's status quo internationally. They continued to utilize direct instruments such as selective tariff rates, state investments, designated priority sectors, incentive packages, and credit allocation to these ends (Wade 1984).

As a bourgeoisie, proletariat, and modern intelligentsia emerged, the KMT incorporated them into party-dominated associations or controlled enough of their environment to prevent the formation of class consciousness or spontaneous organization. The class fluidity and safety valve of emigration defused frustrations. The party mediated class relations. Serving the interests of the bourgeoisie by constantly improving the investment climate, the state nonetheless maintained an aloofness from it and other classes in marked contrast to Japan and Korea. It acted as if it reflected a capitalist-led pact of domination, but in reality it did not absorb capitalists into the political elite. State cadres were a professional, self-reproducing stratum. The fragmanted bourgeoisie ineffectively opposed a number of state policies, such as import duties, high interest rates, ultraconservative lending policies, retention of state control of key upstream industries, pressure on family enterprises to list on the stock market, TNC investment in some sectors, and "voluntary" patriotic exactions.

Individuals might run for office but there were no class-based political movements or populist politics outside of party-manipulated elections for local posts. The KMT constructed an ideologically indoctrinated coalition where all members of society believed they had a stake in preserving the political status quo.

Taiwan avoided the several types of disarticulation noted by Evans (1979) as inherent in a dependent-development form of society:[2] 1) technology brought by TNCs was not capital-intensive and inappropriate, but labor-intensive, absorbing rather than unemploying labor and transferring easily adaptable knowhow; 2) while starting as enclaves in some cases, TNCs became firmly linked with local entrepreneurs, transferring skills and upgrading capacity; 3) deepening of industry came after a solid technical, industrial, and financial foundation was established, avoiding the debt burden and further TNC dominance; 4) there was no class fraction characterized by foreign consumption patterns based on imported or locally manufactured luxury goods.

Distribution of land, free-wheeling outlets for entrepreneurship, measures to restrict capital concentration, numerous opportunities for employment and self-generated income, the family nature of enterprises, homogeneous consumption patterns, the rural safety net for migrant workers, and no necessity to limit incomes to pay foreign debts all contributed to reducing income inequality and extreme social disintegration.

The KMT party-state fell victim to its own success. As the economy grew, industrialization progressed, and the economy internationalized, society became increasingly complex and difficult to manage. Businessmen and professionals required more freedom to pursue their careers in and outside the country and to enjoy direct channels to decision makers. The mass education system and open social mobility integrated the generation born after 1947, blurring the lines between the two distinct mainlander and Taiwanese societies of their parents. As mainlanders died and their sons migrated, their positions naturally fell to Taiwanese who were more inclined to stay on or return to their homeland. Younger, better educated people, often Taiwanese, began taking positions in the party and government. Party rank and file came increasingly from college-educated young people who joined primarily for careerist reasons and were reluctant to submit to democratic-centralist discipline, an anachronism in a complex industrial society.

Young Taiwanese had not personally experienced the February 28 Incident and in many cases had never heard of it. While fearful of KMT repression, they could not conceive of a comparable bloodbath at this stage of development. A large middle class took shape, in time less obsessed with survival and more with the quality of life. Society grew around the KMT; the party retained dominance while losing relevance in the day-to-day life of the people it ruled.

In the 1970s, as these internal social changes evolved beyond party control, the external environment became increasingly threatening. As the mainland counterattack became infeasible, the KMT's legitimation shifted to its ability to sustain economic growth and improve the business environment. By the mid-1970s, failure to control the inflation, recession, and diplomatic isolation hammered away at its legitimacy in the eyes of its citizenry. Embattled as it was internationally, the elite still refused to democratize the political system beyond token gestures. It stifled reform and crushed dissidents. It manipulated "interest articulation." Open discussion of the ROC's fate or leadership succession were taboo.

To survive economically, it would be necessary to liberalize the economy, permit large globally competitive, Taiwanese-owned conglomerates to emerge, and reduce state intervention. Politically, survival would entail absorbing Taiwanese into the state at the highest level and appealing to the masses on a new basis—the survival of Taiwan per se, not the return to the mainland. Obviously, forces in the party, especially the security systems, opposed this, so there were conflicting signals of opening and cracking down through the 1970s.

A Chung-li type incident was inevitable as Taiwan's dynamic social forces, desirous of political participation and a say in the nation's destiny, continued to clash with an ossified political regime. Where and when it erupted was not important. It signalled, for the first time, that the people's wishes would have to be actively considered in future political and economic policy making. The division of labor between mainlander party members monopolizing politics and economic policy and Taiwanese entrepreneurs and workers acting in a tightly restricted sphere began to be torn asunder.

After Chung-li, society began aggressively to press its interests against the state. The *tangwai,* through magazines, organizations, electoral campaigns, and demonstrations, articulate aspirations of a large segment of the middle class and bourgeoisie despite internecine squabbling. New faces invigorate moribund, tame bodies such as the Legislative Yuan and provincial and local assemblies, raising pointed questions about the dividing line between party and state, the necessity for martial law, prohibition of new political parties, mainlander hegemony, corruption, incompetence, a criminal underworld, lack of social welfare programs, and so on. Literary works express a new Taiwanese consciousness and pride, while also exposing the seamier aspects of society. Taiwanese abroad organize and exert external pressure, often through foreign press releases embarrassing to the government. Young party members demand changes in the KMT's gerontocratic centralist structure. Businessmen, through trade associations and elected officials, press for further liberalization plus mercantilist support in foreign markets. They also demand more freedom to do business, including with the mainland. Returned experts desire an environment similar to that in the West where they resided for years. The state is increasingly becoming an arena for social conflict on the Western pluralist model.

These political pressures have forced changes in the party and state. The KMT has become less commandist and more election-oriented, fielding candidates with popular appeal. It has ensured that elections are cleaner and more fair. It has accepted the existence of an opposition. It has held open trials for political crimes. It has sent its officials to the Legislative Yuan where they undergo rigorous interpellation and are increasingly accountable for their actions. The state pays increased attention to welfare matters. It has permitted greater leeway to travel abroad for business and pleasure.

In an increasingly threatening environment, nearly devoid of diplomatic identity, Taiwan's overriding mission is to survive. Achievement of this requires continued successful management and intensification of economic dependency. The burden of anticipating trends in the international division of labor and devising strategies to take maximum advantage of them falls on the state. Businessmen complain of state interference but look to it for guidance and assistance. But future economic transformations will require more private input and less state commandism as the technical, capital, managerial, and marketing requirements deepen.[3] Business, for its part, must shoulder more of the burden of seeking and exploiting global niches and doing its own R&D. Understandably, fearing that Taiwan's future is only short-term, it has little enthusiasm for this. TNCs pose a stumbling block to Taiwan's efforts to upgrade its dependency to a different position in the global division of labor. Taiwan needs their presence to prove its international existence, but their lukewarm response to its upgrading strategy threatens success. Ironically, the fragility rather than the intractability of its situation of dependency threatens Taiwan.

As the People's Republic reforms its stagnant economic system it poses possibly a greater threat to Taiwan's de facto independence than did its saber-rattling of the past. It appears to be following Taiwan's model of a reduced state role in the economy after achieving stabilization and building an industrial base and infrastructure, while maintaining an authoritarian political system.[4] Should the PRC reforms succeed despite entrenched bureaucratic opposition and even expand their scope, to many foreign observers, Taiwan's intransigent refusal even to talk to the Communists might fall on increasingly unsympathetic ears. Even the implacably antagonistic Koreas talk between outbursts of violence.

Although mainlander KMT hard-liners will continue their harrassment, the trends of democratization and Taiwanization must persevere if Taiwan is to endure as a viable unit. Cardoso, Evans, and other dependency writers saw authoritarianism as the outcome of dependency; the two reinforced each other. While this affinity appears obvious, it may have limits. In recent years, the trend in Latin America's dependency cases par excellence—Brazil, Argentina, Peru, Uruguay—has been turned toward redemocratization.[5] In the same way, Taiwan's authoritarianism (and Korea's too) has reached a crisis. The society accepts the need for discipline to maintain survival and growth, but by now the one-party mainlander hegemony seems only to maintain the fictional existence of the Republic of China. Although the regime successfully created a broad-based consensus for development, public acceptance of the legitimacy of the political structure faces increased challenges.

Can a Miracle Be a Model?

Too many unique elements shaped Taiwan's experience to make it a viable model, but it offers several lessons worth considering by other LDCs. Taiwan's specific situation of dependency evolved through a series of unique or nonduplicable phenomena:[6] colonized by a developmentalist racially and culturally similar neighbor; a postcolonial externally originating state with a developed bureaucracy, elaborated developmentalist ideology, and no ties to the island's society; an implacable foe with a radically different vision of development; an additional foreign occupying power reinforcing and reforming the state; geopolitical prior to economic incorporation into the world system; breathing space to consolidate power, revive production, and restructure society without obstructionist foreign actors; fortuitous timing; close ties to two core powers. There are also distinct cultural attributes that facilitated dependency.

Elements of Taiwan's experience of dependent development not so enmeshed in situational and cultural variables, however, can be emulated by other late industrializers. Above all is a developmentalist state.[7] The KMT state's horrendous debacle on the mainland, considerable autonomy from Taiwanese society, Orwellian repressive apparatus, U.S. backing, concentration of talent, and determination to do a better job this time certainly helped. But official commitment to development; creation of extraministerial agencies relatively sheltered from political struggles to guide development; investment in infrastructure and human capital; collection and analysis of data on the economy, social potential, and global situation and making such research widely available; strategic credit allocation; wide geographic dispersal of new industrial opportunities; fostering of agriculture; and land distribution are not beyond the means of most states with minimal competence and will power.

Surely, authoritarianism, autonomy, and large-scale state economic activity facilitated achieving this in Taiwan. The question is when to soften political control and selectively adopt more market-conforming tactics to sustain development, even if maintaining a highly regulated economy as a whole. The KMT has had trouble with this, but its relationships with Taiwanese society and with the People's Republic make this problem more, not less, difficult to resolve than elsewhere.

Another duplicable component is properly allocated foreign assistance. This may involve foreign advisers and tied aid to implement, an infringement of sovereignty, but possibly a temporary sacrifice worth making for the sake of the long run. In Taiwan, it boosted the position of prodevelopment elements in the leadership who used foreign counsel as a pretext for their policies. When the foreigners departed, they left with their protegés in control.

A further important factor is correct assessment of the cultural legacy and citizenry's talents, then nurturing the constructive aspects and erection of a structure to let these flourish. If the political system is crudely authoritarian and no outlets exist for people to channel their energies beyond corruption, collaboration, or taking to the jungles, development fails.

Given the reality of the world system and international division of labor, the pervasive presence of TNCs, the general economic and social failure of Soviet-style socialism, and the disaster of excessive self-reliance, the question becomes: What is to be done?

In Taiwan's case, these realities were compounded by no resources, no foreign exchange, overcrowding, and diplomatic isolation. The extremely difficult decision to open up to trade and investment and relinquish some controls, once the payoff began, brought about a new attitude on the part of the leadership I call dynamic dependency: assessing the economy and society's capabilities and needs and then linking to the world system in such a way as to utilize these and improve one's situation. Luckily, unlike most nations, Taiwan did not have a legacy of TNCs already linking its economy and society to the outside, disintegrating social cohesion. Nonetheless, through analysis, training, solicitation of specific external actors, and careful negotiations, other sectors—old and new—could be made to benefit positively from ties to the world system. This is not to prescribe that all LDCs rush to mass-produce zoris and transistor radios, or develop export-oriented economies. Taiwan's situation necessitated a perhaps excessive reliance on exports. The point is that informed, selective, and managed linkages need not be tantamount to turning one's nation over to foreign masters. This key aspect of Taiwan's experience is being assiduously studied by millions of compatriots across the choppy waters of the Taiwan Straits.

NOTES

Notes to Chapter 1

1. The GINI coefficient is a commonly used but controversial indicator of the degree of income concentration in a population. The lower the coefficient, the more equal the distribution. For a very technical discussion of the GINI coefficient, see Fei, Ranis, and Kuo (1979:part 2).

2. Examples are Chang (1968); Galenson (1979); Gregor, Chang, and Zimmerman (1981); Ho (1978); Hsing (1970); Kawano (1968); Kuo (1983); Li (1976); Lin (1973); Wang (1977–78); Wu and Yeh (1978); and the series edited by Yu (1975). The economists include several American-trained Chinese living in Taiwan or abroad who serve as consultants to the government. Amsden (1979) and Wade (1984) are two economists writing within a political-economy framework who identify the political and institutional bases of state economic activity. Although since its expulsion in 1980 Taiwan no longer exists as far as the World Bank is concerned (it is an "offshore reference cognate economy"), the bank's "new orthodoxy" of Third World development is clearly derived from Taiwan as much as anywhere else. See, for example, Hasan (1982, 1984).

3. Examples are Ch'en (1984); Crane (1982); Frank (1982); Landsberg (1979); Liu (1975); Wynn (1982); and Zenger (1977). The concepts of dependency and world systems are explained later in this chapter.

4. Recently, writers utilizing dependency and world-systems methodologies have produced balanced studies improving greatly upon works cited in note 3. Examples are Cumings (1984); Gates (1979); Hsiao (1981); and Simon (1980).

5. For examples, see Arrigo (1981); Chen (1982); Kagan (1982); Kerr (1965); Mendel (1970); Ong (1979); Peng (1972); and Shih (1980).

6. See Copper (1979 and 1981); Domes (1981); and Wei (1973 and 1976) for examples.

7. There are numerous overviews of modernization theory. One of the most informative, with an extensive bibliography, is J. Samuel Valenzuela and Arturo Valenzuela, "Modernization and Dependency," in *Comparative Politics* 10,4 (July 1978):535–57.

8. The essays in Bert Hoselitz, *Sociological Factors in Economic Development* (Glencoe: Free Press, 1960), are among the most determined efforts to relate pattern variables to the real world. But also see the vicious attack in Frank (1969b).

9. Some oft-cited examples include John K. Fairbank, Alexander Eckstein, and

L. S. Yang, "Economic Change in Early Modern China: An Analytical Framework," *Economic Development and Cultural Change* 9,1 (October 1960):1–26; Albert Feuerwerker, *China's Early Industrialization: Sheng Hsuan-huai and Mandarin Enterprise* (Cambridge: Harvard University Press, 1958); Francis L. K. Hsu, "Cultural Factors," in *Economic Development: Principles and Patterns,* ed. Harold F. Williamson and John A. Buttrick (New York: Prentice-Hall, 1954), pp. 318–64; and Levy (1953). For a recent reworking, see Rozman (1981). An attempt to explain China's underdevelopment from a world-systems perspective is Moulder (1977). Ironically, since the late 1970s, some scholars have taken the traditional East Asian values, once blamed for backwardness, as the cause of rapid growth. See, for example, Roderick MacFarquhar, "The Post-Confucian Challenge," *The Economist,* February 9, 1980, 67–72.

10. For the distinction between dependence and dependency, see Caporaso (1978).

11. My understanding of this has benefited greatly from discussions with Gary Gereffi. For an extended discussion, see his book (1983) and Palma (1978).

12. This is clearly seen in Gregor et al. (1981) and in the essay by the Taiwanese novelist and social critic, Ch'en Ying-chen (1984), in his effort to introduce the concept to the Taiwan reading public.

13. The classic statements are Wallerstein (1974 and 1979). Excellent critiques are Daniel Chirot, "Changing Fashions in the Study of Social Change," in *The State of Sociology,* ed. James Short, Jr. (Beverly Hills: Sage, 1981), pp. 259–82, and Theda Skocpol, "Wallerstein's World Capitalist System: A Theoretical and Historical Critique," *American Journal of Sociology* 82,5 (March 1977):1075–90.

14. Prominent examples are Volker Bornschier and Thanh-Huyen Ballmer-Cao, "Income Inequality: A Cross-National Study of the Relationships Between MNC-Penetration, Dimensions of the Power Structure and Income Distribution," *American Sociological Review* 44,3 (June 1979):487–506; Volker Bornschier, Christopher Chase-Dunn, and Richard Rubinson, "Cross-National Evidence of the Effects of Foreign Investment and Aid on Economic Growth and Inequality: A Survey of Findings and a Reanalysis," *American Journal of Sociology* 84,3 (1978):651–83; Christopher Chase-Dunn "The Effects of International Economic Dependence on Development and Inequality: A Cross-National Study," *American Sociological Review* 40 (December 1975):720–38; and Richard Rubinson, "The World Economy and the Distribution of Income Within States: A Cross-National Study," *American Sociological Review* 41 (August 1976):638–59.

15. See note 3. Crane's emphasis on the state and his critique of the world system approach represent an improvement.

16. This discussion is based on Cardoso and Faletto (1979), Palma (1978), and Cardoso's lectures at the University of California, Berkeley in the fall of 1981.

17. I employed Evans's approach in my Ph.D. dissertation (Gold 1981), examining the triple alliance in Taiwan's textile, electronics, and petrochemical sectors.

18. I agree with Barrett and Whyte (1984) in their response to Hammer (1984), criticizing her narrow conceptualization of "dependency." Both the colonial and aid periods clearly established structures of dependency, relying on economic as well as political means to do so.

19. See John Myer, "A Crown of Thorns: Cardoso and the Counter-Revolution," *Latin American Perspectives* 2 (Spring 1975):33–48, cited in Colin Henfrey, "Dependency, Modes of Production, and the Class Analysis of Latin America," *Latin American Perspectives* 8,3–4 (Summer-Fall 1981):17–53.

Notes to Chapter 2

1. Since their initial encounters with European and Chinese migrants in the

seventeenth century, the aborigines have been pushed progressively farther into the highlands and less populous areas; hence their other name, "High Mountain Peoples" *(Kao-shan-tsu)*. Under Nationalist party policy, they have been the object of assimilation.

2. Cheng Ch'eng-kung is commonly referred to as Koxinga, a distortion of "Kuo-hsing-yeh," Master of the Imperial Surname, an honor granted to him by the Ming dynasty for services rendered. On the nationalistic significance of his career, see Crozier (1977). A museum on Ku-lang-yü (Gulangyu), an island off Amoy, Fukien, celebrates his patriotism and publicizes the message that Taiwan should be reunited with the mainland.

3. See Hsu (1980b), Shih (1980), and Lamley (1972) for details.

4. See Meskill (1979:88–91) on this topic.

5. The best study of the literati on Taiwan is Harry Lamley, "The Taiwan Literati and Early Japanese Rule, 1895–1915," Ph.D. diss., University of Washington, 1964.

6. This discussion is from Knapp (1980:60–64) and Wickberg (1981).

7. "The terms of rent between *ta-tsu-hu* and *hsiao-tsu-hu* were typically fixed over a long period of time, whereas the length of tenure between *hsiao-tsu-hu* and their tenants changed every few years," at the expense of the tenants, to be sure. Discussion based on Myers 1972a:384.

8. See Meskill (1979:ch. 12) for a description.

9. The classic study of this important characteristic of traditional Chinese society is Ho Ping-ti, *The Ladder of Success in Imperial China* (New York: Columbia University Press, 1962).

10. The best sources for material on Liu Ming-ch'uan are Chu (1963), Kuo (1973), and Speidel (1976).

Notes to Chapter 3

1. My major sources for the Japanese period are Barclay (1954); Chang (1980); Chen (1973); Myers (1973, 1974); Shih (1980); Tu (1975); and Yi (1955). I also conducted interviews with scholars in Taiwan and with members of the five major families, discussed below. My article "Origins of the Taiwanese Bourgeoisie: Collaborator-Entrepreneurs Under Japanese Colonial Occupation," with detailed references, is forthcoming in *Authoritarianism and Dependency in East Asia: Comparing Taiwan*, ed. Edwin A. Winckler and Susan Greenhalgh.

2. Sources on the republic include Huang (1970); Lamley (1973); and Shih (1980).

3. See Chen (1973) for more details on this structure.

4. The following discussion is based on Tsurumi (1977:ch. 2).

5. This is the exact opposite of the model Frank (1969a) proposes.

6. Sources on political movements are Chen (1972); Hsu (1972); Shih (1980); and Tsurumi (1977). *Hsia-ch'ao* [China Tide] magazine featured several articles on Japanese-era peasant and worker movements and leaders in its 1976–78 issues before it was banned by the government.

7. See Hsiao and Sullivan (1983) for details on the Taiwan Communist party. Shih (1980) also discusses it.

8. One-fifth of the cultivated land was owned by Japanese, mostly sugar companies (Wickberg 1981:230).

Notes to Chapter 4

1. For references on the Nanking decade, see, inter alia, Lloyd Eastman, *The Abortive Revolution: China Under Nationalist Rule, 1927–1937* (Cambridge: Harvard

University Press, 1974); Lloyd Eastman, *Seeds of Destruction* (Stanford: Stanford University Press, 1984); Paul K. T. Sih, ed., *The Strenuous Decade: China's Nation-Building Efforts, 1927-1937* (New York: St. John's University Press, 1970); Hung-mao Tien, *Government and Politics in Kuomintang China, 1927-1937* (Stanford: Stanford University Press, 1972); and Arthur Young, *China's Nation-Building Effort, 1927-1937: The Financial and Economic Record* (Stanford: Stanford University Press, 1971).

2. An important study of U.S.-Nationalist relations prior to Taiwan is Barbara Tuchman, *Stilwell and the American Experience in China, 1911-1945* (New York: Macmillan, 1971). An indignant and gossipy account of Nationalist corruption and decline is Sterling Seagrave, *The Soong Dynasty* (New York: Harper and Row, 1985).

3. A list of the demands is contained in Ambassador Leighton Stuart's memorandum on Taiwan in Department of State (1967:933-35).

4. Works on the February 28 Incident include Kerr (1965); Mendel (1970); *Shen-keng tzu-liao-shih* (1983); and Shih (1980).

5. This is based on Shih (1980:875-78).

6. This committee has metamorphosed over the years and is now called the National Security Bureau (*Kuo-chia An-ch'üan-chü*), but its mission remains the same. Not officially an organ of state, it claims legitimacy under the exigencies of prosecution of the civil war.

7. On the rise of Chiang Ching-kuo, see Chiang (1984); Durdin (1975); and Winckler (1982).

8. On the institutionalization and effects of martial law, see Kagan (1982) and Peng (1971:473-74).

9. Wu's thoughts on these and other issues can be found in Chiang Nan, "Wu Kuo-chen—Pa-shih i-wang" [Wu Kuo-chen—Reminiscences at Eighty], *Taiwan yü shih-chieh* [Taiwan and the World] 12 (June 1984):30-36, and 13 (July-August 1984):38-41.

Notes to Chapter 5

1. See Schurmann (1974:part 1) for an excellent analysis of the world at the beginning of the cold war.

2. These numbered approximately 10,000 by 1957 (Kerr 1965:417).

3. See Shieh (1970) for the relevant documents.

4. Ch'ien (1950) offers a comprehensive description of the formal state structure. There are still few studies of Taiwan's political system. Jacobs (1971 and 1978) and Winckler (1981a, 1981b, and 1984) are perceptive examinations of how pieces fit together.

5. The National Assembly that elected Chiang Ching-kuo as president and the American-trained Taiwanese economist Lee Teng-hui as vice-president in 1984 had 1,064 members: 913 hundred KMT members, 83 from two small parties, and 68 nonparty members (*Free China Journal*, January 15, 1984:1).

6. See Chang (1977), Hsu (1977), and Lerman (1978) on life in the Provincial Assembly.

7. By nature, this is a very murky area. My list is based on Lo (1984), a pamphlet entitled "Basic Facts About the KMT Regime on Taiwan and Its Illicit Activities in the U.S." dated 1976, and my own experiences. Peng (1972) presents an extended description of interrogation, imprisonment, and surveillance at the hands of the Garrison Command. Much of the information about the security agencies would still be closeted were it not for their bungling maneuvers in the Henry Liu murder. It is possible that these agencies were trying to outmaneuver rival agencies to impress the president or, as in the Jerzy Popieluszko case in Poland or the Benigno Aquino case in the Philippines,

that certain hardliners opposed liberalizing trends and wanted to scare dissenters. Late in 1984, as Taiwan's security agencies moved to clean up the increasingly disruptive criminal underworld, ties between secret police and criminals came to light, further exposing their activities. As of July 1, 1985, "two major military intelligence agencies were merged into a single establishment under the direct command of the Chief of the General Staff" as a way to enforce close control over security operations (*FCJ*, July 7, 1985:1).

8. There were clashes with mainland forces over the offshore Ta-chen and other islands in 1954, when the KMT withdrew, and Quemoy and Matsu islands in 1958, when the Nationalists held firm. After those battles, the hot war mostly gave way to a propaganda war. A description of life on the offshore islands can be found in Donald Kirk, "Still Waiting for War," *New York Times Magazine*, November 28, 1976, pp. 60ff.

9. "Total military assistance over the fifteen-year period 1951–65 was approximately $2.5 billion" (Jacoby 1966:118).

10. The locus classicus for the concept "revolution from above" is Ellen Kay Trimberger, *Revolution from Above: Military Bureaucrats and Development in Japan, Turkey, Egypt and Peru* (New Brunswick, N.J.:Transaction Books, 1978).

11. This is an important and controversial concept in political science. The most commonly adopted definition is:

> Corporatism can be defined as a system of interest representation in which the constituent units are organized into a limited number of singular, compulsory, noncompetitive, hierarchically ordered and functionally differentiated categories, recognized or licensed (if not created) by the state and granted a deliberate representational monopoly within their respective categories in exchange for observing certain controls on their selection of leaders and articulation of demands and supports.

(Philippe C. Schmitter, "Still the Century of Corporatism?" in *Trends Toward Corporatist Intermediation*, ed. Philippe C. Schmitter and Gerhard Lehmbruch [Beverly Hills: Sage, 1979], pp. 7–52; quote on p. 13.) For a different use of the term, see Amos Perlmutter, *Modern Authoritarianism* (New Haven: Yale University Press, 1981).

12. The conservative aspect of land reforms is discussed in Roy L. Prosterman and Jeffrey M. Reidinger, "Land Reform Can Be the Marxist's Worst Enemy," *Wall Street Journal*, October 27, 1983, p. 26, and Al McCoy, "Land Reform as Counter-Revolution," *Bulletin of Concerned Asian Scholars*, 3,1 (1971):14–49.

13. JCRR was set up on the mainland in 1948.

14. For details on Taiwan's land reform, see Chen (1961); Hsiao (1981); Tang (1954); and Yang (1970).

15. See Gallin (1966); Ho (1978:165–70); and Yang (1970:chs. 5 and 8).

16. For a listing of these enterprises, see Shih (1980:711). They included enterprises in sugar, aluminum, fertilizer, alkali, shipbuilding, brickmaking, machinery, power, cement, paper, mining, printing, hemp, textiles, tea, food processing, banking, and finance.

17. For a discussion of this concept, see Chiang (1947:ch. 4) and Ts'ui (1959:ch. 22).

18. The definitive source on the AID program in Taiwan remains Jacoby (1966).

19. "We are further considering that some Taiwanese applicants should be given consideration. To date, mainland interests have been in such a position that the bulk of the textile installations have been granted to mainland interests and the Taiwanese have received the short end of the stick." (J. G. White, Report TA 23.2.1., July 7, 1952, p. 4.)

20. In 1984, it was the only private corporation of the three from Taiwan to make

the *Fortune* list of the 500 largest industrial companies outside the United States. It was ranked 202. The others were Chinese Petroleum Corporation (81) and China Steel Corporation (472) (*China Post*, August 4, 1984, p. 7). The firm's profitable American ventures are discussed in *Business Week*, August 1, 1983, p. 37, and *Forbes*, July 15, 1985, pp. 88–93.

21. In the 1980s, it has increased its lobbying functions, although most lobbying is done informally by individuals over golf or meals, or by industry associations, such as the Cotton Spinners Association. The KMT controls the association and separate trade associations through its Committee on Social Affairs and appointment of staff members in them. As the economy's planning capabilities improved, the associations supplied production estimates to the responsible state agency.

Notes to Chapter 6

1. Excellent case studies of denationalization can be found in Evans (1979) and Gereffi (1983).

2. See O'Donnell (1973) for the initial formulation and the essays in Collier (1979) for stimulating discussions of it. I understand "authoritarianism" as an intermediate type of political regime between democracy and totalitarianism, enjoying some limited pluralism and autonomous social organization, little political mobilization, and relatively institutionalized behavior even if the limits of the exercise of power by the elite are not clearly defined.

3. This is based on Jacoby (1966:33–35).

4. This ended up as $20 million when military expenditures were not held down (Jacoby 1966:135). This demonstrates resistance within the military to the liberalization and to support of a private sector, in addition to refusal to trim its budget.

5. See the interview with Li in *Tien-hsia tsa-chih* [Commonwealth], November 1, 1984, pp. 26, 29. Ironically, the term "*tzu-li keng-sheng*" is the same one used by the Communists under Mao to express a policy of virtually complete autonomy and independence from the world system.

6. Yen was born in Kiangsu in 1905 and received a B.S. degree from St. John's University, an American-run school in Shanghai. He served under Ch'en Yi in Fukien and Taiwan and was on the island during the February 28 Incident. He administered the confiscation of Japanese properties in Taiwan. He served as governor from 1954 to 1957 and held several economic posts before becoming vice-president of the Republic of China and eventually president for nearly three years when Chiang Kai-shek died in 1975.

7. *Tien-hsia tsa-chih*, p. 29

8. For more information about these programs, see Jordan Schreiber, *U.S. Corporate Investment in Taiwan* (New York: University Press of Cambridge, 1970).

9. *EPZ Concentrates* 15,7–8 (August 1980):59.

10. For more details, see Chalmers Johnson, *MITI and the Japanese Miracle* (Stanford: Stanford University Press, 1982), especially ch. 8, and Terutomo Ozawa, *Multinationalism, Japanese Style* (Princeton: Princeton University Press, 1979).

11. Product life cycle is a concept popularized in the United States through the work of Raymond Vernon. It states that products go through stages of origin, development, and decline, each of which has different requirements of technology, investment, skilled labor, etc. Japan's rapid postwar development has been characterized by careful analysis of the product life cycle by Japan's economic technocrats, who break the production process into stages and determine where production of which products is most cost-effective. As is noted above, in the mid-1970s, MITI decided that Japan could no longer make certain goods competitively and encouraged and assisted Japa-

nese manufacturers to shift production of those items offshore—first to Taiwan and South Korea—and concentrate instead on developing new products. That is, Japan would stay at the origin stage of the product life cycle and let newly industrializing countries such as Taiwan and Korea take over when Japan lost competitiveness. This concept is also at the root of recent discussions of a new international division of labor based on a nation's comparative advantage at producing particular goods at different stages of the cycle. References include Folker Fröbel, Jürgen Heinrichs, and Otto Kreye, *The New International Division of Labour* (Cambridge: Cambridge University Press, 1980); John Gerard Ruggie, ed., *The Antinomies of Interdependence* (New York: Columbia University Press, 1983); and Raymond Vernon, *Sovereignty at Bay: The Multinational Spread of U.S. Enterprises* (New York: Basic Books, 1971). A frequently cited, very perceptive essay is James R. Kurth, "The Political Consequences of the Product Life Cycle: Industrial History and Political Outcomes," *International Organization* 33,1 (Winter 1979):1–34.

12. For more information on the different activities of American, Japanese, and Overseas Chinese investors and their social effects, see Gold (1983).

13. This is based on Yoffie (1983:113–16).

14. In 1985, the MOEA moved to reallocate these quotas, selling them to the highest bidder and reinvesting the profits to upgrade the industry (FCJ, January 20, 1985:4).

15. Biographical information comes from a variety of sources, including hagiographies such as China Credit Information Service (1973); Hsin-ching Publishing Company (1982); Lai (1983), Li (1978); and interviews.

16. "Large" is defined as paid-up capital exceeding NT$20 million, assets valued at more than NT$60 million or more than 300 employees. See CEPD (1980a:14).

17. The best discussions of the *kuan-hsi ch'i-ye* phenomenon are in China Credit Information Service (1976) and Lai (1981). On *zaibatsu*, see William Lockwood, *Economic Development of Japan* (Princeton: Princeton University Press, 1953). On *chaebol*, see Leroy P. Jones and Il Sakong, *Government, Business and Entrepreneurship in Economic Development: The Korean Case* (Cambridge: Harvard University Press, 1980).

18. See Kuo (1983:81ff); Arrigo (1980); and Kung (1981) for more details and examples.

19. There have been very few studies of a labor movement (or its absence) in Taiwan in any language. See Walter Galenson, "The Labor Force, Wages and Living Standards" in Galenson (1979:384–447). For an establishment study from Taiwan, see Djang (1977). Critical essays from Taiwan include several articles in the April 25, 1983 issue of *Sheng-ken* [Cultivate]; Ye Chih-ch'iu, "Kung-hui ts'ang-sang-shih" [The Vicissitudinous History of Labor], *Hsia-ch'ao lun-t'an* [China Tide Forum] 1,4 (May 1983):25–32; Yang Ch'ing-ch'u, "Kuo-nei kung-jen hsien-chuang fen-hsi" [Analysis of the Current Status of Workers in the Country], *Hsia-ch'ao* [China Tide] 15 (June 1, 1977):39–42. After more than ten years of wrangling, the government finally promulgated a Labor Standards Law on July 30, 1984, but it still faced tremendous opposition. See *Far Eastern Economic Review*, September 6, 1984, pp. 109–10, and articles by Chang Hsiao-fen and Wu Li-kan in *K'ai-ch'uang tsa-chih* [The New Era] 2 (August 1, 1984):44–50.

20. "Figures available show that from 1960 to 1967, over 15,000 (close to one in 50) of them went abroad, and less than 5 percent (760 in all) of the overseas students had returned during the same years" (Tien 1975:623). By 1983, the return rate on 80,039 students going abroad from 1950 to 1983 had increased to 13.7 percent, approximately 11,000 people (*FCJ* May 27, 1984:3). In 1984, students from Taiwan in the United States outnumbered those from the former leader, Iran. The 21,960 students

accounted for 6.5 percent of foreign students in America (FCJ December 30, 1984:3).

21. The same thing was done for Kaohsiung in 1979 as it became economically crucial and was an entrenched stronghold of the opposition movement.

22. Mendel (1970:114–21) describes several cases from the 1960s. Also, see Kerr (1965:446–48); Ong (1979:183–85); and Shih (1980:1126–42). For the government's position, see *China Yearbook 1961–62*:16–18.

23. See Peng (1972) for a detailed account.

24. See Jacobs (1971:143–49) on political changes in 1969.

25. So-called because of the years he had spent on the mainland before returning to Taiwan after World War II. Shieh was born in 1907.

26. I attended a raucous and intense meeting at Tunghai University the evening of April 16. Audience members spoke from the floor after telling their name and being photographed. Speakers rivalled each other in making patriotic statements, including urging the government to send troops to the islands. The slogan "an inch of land, an ounce of blood" was written in blood on a banner. Students voted to hold a march in Taichung, but the party and government leaders of the school rejected this plan. They did agree to hold one on campus, which the students vetoed. In any event, windows were broken at the Taichung office of the U.S. Information Service. The students believed that Tiao-yü-t'ai was a very hot issue in the United States as well.

27. That is, there is only one China, of which Taiwan is an inalienable province. As two parties claim to run the legitimate government of all China, foreign countries can only have full diplomatic relations with one; the other is a bandit regime.

28. In 1971, four *Ta-Hsüeh* leaders published possibly the first macro-level study of Taiwan society, *Taiwan she-hui-li ti fen-hsi* [Analysis of Social Forces in Taiwan]. Hsu Hsin-liang and Chang Chün-hung, KMT members with bright establishment futures, abandoned the pseudonyms used for this book and actively contested elected office in 1977. The Hsu contest climaxed in the Chung-li Incident.

29. For details of this movement, see Chen (1982) and Huang (1976).

Notes to Chapter 7

1. *FEER*, May 22, 1981:46. Balassa (1981:384) questions whether this would have harmed export competitiveness. For a more recent analysis of wages in the manufacturing sector, see Wu Hui-lin, *Taiwan chih-tsao-ye tan-wei lao-tung ch'eng-pen pien-tung fen-hsi* [Analysis of Manufacturing Unit Labor Cost in Taiwan] (Taipei: Chung-hua Institution for Economic Research, Economic Papers No. 5, 1982); Wu Chia-sheng, "Taiwan ti-ch'ü chih-tsao-ye kung-tzu shui-chun chi kung-tzu chieh-kou chih fen-hsi" [Analysis of Wage Rates and Wage Structure in the Manufacturing Sector in the Taiwan Area], *Taiwan Yin-hang chi-k'an* [Bank of Taiwan Quarterly] 34,4 (February 1983):79–104.

2. See Balassa (1981:109–26) and Yoffie (1983). For a detailed examination of textile quotas, See Vinod K. Aggarwal with Stephan Haggard, "The Politics of Protection in the U.S. Textile and Apparel Industries," in *American Industry in International Competition*, ed. John Zysman and Laura Tyson (Ithaca: Cornell University Press, 1983), pp. 249–312.

3. There were about 8,500 troops on Taiwan at the time of President Nixon's China trip in February 1972, down from a high of 15,000 during the Vietnam War. These were reduced to 2,000 by mid-1975 and less than 1,000 in December 1978 (*NYT*, October 14, 1975:2; December 16, 1978:8).

4. The United States ended military aid in 1973 although it continued to supply Taiwan with military credits (*NYT*, October 14, 1975:2).

5. See Djang (1977:92–93).

6. In 1980, the MOEA still owned fourteen business enterprises in petroleum, power, sugar, steel, shipbuilding, engineering, aluminum, fertilizer, petrochemicals, machinery, chemicals, mining, alkali, and phosphates in addition to investments in other enterprises. To give an indication of their size, their combined sales for 1980 approximated the combined sales of the top 62 private firms. The combined sales of the top 4 (petroleum, power, sugar, and steel) approximated that of the top 42 privates, at least as publicly reported. Of the 52 companies reporting sales above NT$3 billion, 18 were government business enterprises, excluding the provincial Tobacco and Wine Monopoly. The Ministry of Finance owned several insurance companies and the TPG owned five enterprises in iron, paper, agriculture, ammonium sulfate, and textiles (China Credit Information Service, 1981:58, 16), as well as the Tobacco and Wine Monopoly. . The KMT had several of its own enterprises as well.

7. See Evans (1979:ch. 5).

8. Yu (b. 1914) is from the same county in Chekiang as the Chiang family and has been closely associated with them throughout his career. He served as Chiang Kai-shek's personal secretary from 1936 to 1944, studied at Harvard and the London School of Economics (without taking degrees), and worked primarily in financial jobs both in Taiwan and with the World Bank and International Monetary Fund. He is regarded as the "Chiang family banker." See *FEER*, June 7, 1984:123 and *Free China Review*, June 1984:5.

9. In 1978, the electronics industry accounted for 14.2 percent of exports and was second in value behind textiles. In 1984 it surpassed the perennial frontrunner. During the 1970s, the industry, by value, ranged from 70 to nearly 90 percent export dependent. See CEPD (1980a).

10. In 1981, under great foreign pressure, the government created the National Anti-Counterfeiting Committee to clamp down on the widespread practice of pirating everything from books and records to clothes, watches, auto parts, and personal computers. As noted earlier, businessmen see imitation as a form of flattery—as well as a way to cash in on a good thing—and a way of learning by doing. They are proud of their ability to produce excellent forgeries. When the computer copyright infringement crackdown began, some Taiwanese bragged to me that their ability to make such fine copies proved how much the economy had developed. *FEER*, May 24, 1983:62 ran an article on pirating in Asia as a whole. A September 1984 article in *Life* on counterfeiting in Taiwan "provoked the public in this country to anger" (*FCJ*, October 28, 1984:4). The People's Republic is going the same route. Reuters reported on "$4 million worth of counterfeit goods, including jeans and Swiss-brand watches," most of which were made in China, being seized in Hong Kong (*San Francisco Chronicle*, January 25, 1985:18). In one case with which I am familiar, the PRC is pirating an internationally famous Hong Kong trademark, refusing to allow its registration in China, despite formally close relations between the firm's chairman and the Communist government.

11. See *FCJ*, January 27, 1985:4 on recent trends of outward investment from Taiwan.

12. See Clough (1978:87–91); *FEER* (November 19, 1982:74–77); Mao (1976).

13. See *FEER* (July 9, 1982:28–29).

14. The government has vigorously denied having such a relationship with Israel as this might jeopardize its efforts to solidify relationships with Arab oil suppliers. See, for example, *FEER* (May 22, 1981:45). I attended a Passover Seder in Taipei in 1978 at which there were several Israelis who said they could not tell me what they were doing on the island but that they were in "electronics."

15. This figure served as the base for the amount of arms the United States could

continue to sell to Taiwan as understood under the terms of the U.S.-PRC Shanghai II Communique of August 17, 1982. See *FEER* (January 27, 1983:28).

16. See *FEER* (February 27, 1981:79–81, October 23, 1981:99–101, and February 19, 1982:51–52.

17. According to the leftist Hong Kong daily *Ta kung pao* of June 14, 1984, quoting a member of the Legislative Yuan, over \$3.645 billion had fled in 1983 alone. On the type of people emigrating to the United States, see *The Economic News*, June 7–13, 1982:1. In late 1981, the assignment to Taiwan of a quota of 20,000 immigrants a year, an amount previously shared with the People's Republic, only fueled the exodus.

18. By 1983, the IMF ranked it thirteenth. South Korea was fourteenth, Hong Kong fifteenth, and Singapore sixteenth. In 1983, Taiwan was the seventeenth largest trading nation and the eighteenth largest importer (*FCJ*, June 10, 1984:1).

19. Not surprisingly, this fueled a black market in highly desired Japanese consumer goods, such as VCRs. See *The Economic News*, June 7–13, 1982:1.

20. For discussion, see *FEER* (April 14, 1983:40–2).

21. Grindlays Bank of Britain; Banque de Paris et des Pays-Bas and Société General of France (whose parent company is 90 percent owned by the French government); European Asian Bank; Hollandsche Bank-Unie N.V. of the Netherlands, which is a joint venture of seven European banks (AIT, 1981:10).

22. See testimony by Robert P. Parker, president of the American Chamber of Commerce, Taipei, in *Hearings Before the Committee on Foreign Relations, U.S. Senate*, 96th Congress (February 1979):442–52 and Arnold (1985). In the mid-1970s, as the People's Republic began to step up its foreign trade, Taiwan and American businessmen established U.S.-ROC and ROC-U.S. Economic Councils to promote trade and engage in lobbying. The former was a direct response to the National Council on U.S.-China Trade, which promoted trade and investment with the mainland.

23. See Hsi (1981) and Kuo (1983:122–33).

24. In a classic article, Simon Kuznets predicted that income inequality would follow an inverse U-curve in developing countries, increasing as the economy grew and leveling off and then declining only much later. See "Economic Growth and Income Inequality," *American Economic Review* 45,1 (March 1955):1–28.

25. On the subject of Taiwan's burgeoning middle class and its political interest, see *Shih-pao tsa-chih* [Sunday Times Chinese Weekly], July 25, 1984 and August 1, 1984.

26. For discussions on income distribution in Taiwan, see Fei, Ranis, and Kuo (1979); Ke (1983); Ranis (1978); and Wu Yuan-li, "Income Distribution in the Process of Economic Growth in Taiwan," reprinted in Wu and Yeh (1978:67–111).

27. There were periodic attempts to clean the system up. See, for example, "E-hsing pu-hsi-pan hsing-ch'eng yin-su chi hsiao-mi pan-fa" [The Factors Behind the Formation of Evil Cram Schools and the Method of Eradicating Them], *Lien ho pao* [United Daily], November 6, 1977. Nonetheless, their owners were among Taiwan's richest businessmen, and the area in back of the Taipei YMCA and the Taipei Hilton, where they are concentrated, is jammed from early morning till late at night.

28. See *Conference on Population and Economic Development in Taiwan* (1976) and Kuo (1983).

29. Taiwanese constituted about 75 percent of the two million KMT members in 1983 (*FEER*, January 13, 1983:18).

30. In June 1984 Yu Kuo-hwa became premier. Even if Lee Teng-hui assumed the presidency upon Chiang Ching-kuo's departure, mainlanders could rest assured that one of their own, with military backing, held real power from the premier's office.

31. For an overview of the movement, see Wei T'ien-ts'ung, ed., *Hsiang-t'u wen-hsüeh t'ao-lun-chi* [Collected Discussion of Nativist Literature] (Chung-ho: Hai-wang,

1978). Two prominent writers have had their works translated into English. See Hwang Chun-ming, *Drowning of an Old Cat and Other Stories*, trans. Howard Goldblatt (Bloomington: Indiana University Press, 1980), and Yang Ch'ing-ch'u, *Selected Stories of Yang Ch'ing-ch'u*, trans. Thomas B. Gold (Kaohsiung: Tun-li, 1978). Several *hsiang-t'u* stories appear in Vivian Ling Hsu, ed., *Born of the Same Roots* (Bloomington: Indiana University Press, 1981).

32. Most of the writers did not participate directly in politics. Exceptions were Wang T'o and Yang Ch'ing-ch'u, both of whom were arrested in December 1979.

33. But it should be noted that not all non-KMT politicians see themselves as "oppositionists"; they just rely on sources of support outside the KMT. There are also some people who recklessly criticize the KMT as the thing to do and are disowned by the *tangwai* core. See Winckler (1982:115–16).

34. See Arrigo (1981); Chen (1982); Domes (1981:1015–21); and T'ang (1979).

35. There was also an ultrarightist group with a journal of its own, *Chi-feng* [Hurricane]. See Kagan (1982:51–52).

36. See Kaplan (1981) and *SPEAHRhead* 9, Northern Spring, 1981 for questions about the incident and trial.

37. See Copper (1981:1029–39) and *FEER* (December 12, 1980:8–9). For an opposing view, see *Formosa Weekly*, December 13, 1980.

38. The diversified Cathay group, founded by Taiwanese Ts'ai Wan-ch'un, has long been regarded in the public mind as engaging in shady practices, such as lending money to struggling firms and then converting the debt to equity and swallowing them up, and profiting excessively in the property boom of the late 1970s. It appears that funds from the group-owned Tenth Credit Cooperative had been illegally diverted to other group enterprises using employees' names as borrowers. A former Cathay employee confirmed this practice to me. A run began on Tenth Credit in the winter of 1985 and spread to the related Cathay Investment and Trust. A Control Yuan investigation caused some high-level party and government resignations and numerous arrests, including that of Tenth Credit Chairman Ts'ai Chen-chou, a KMT member of the Legislative Yuan. See *FEER*, March 7, 1985:50–51.

39. For speculation on Wang's political ambitions, see Hsieh (1985).

40. See Oswaldo Sunkel, "Transnational Capitalism and National Disintegration in Latin America," *Social and Economic Studies* 22 (1973):132–76.

41. For an opposing point of view, see Arrigo (1981); *FEER* (February 26, 1982:78–79); Gates (1981); and Wu (1980).

42. *Tangwai* members of the Legislative Yuan pressed the issue of the separation of party and state. See Ting Shu-yuan, "Tang-cheng ying-kai 'fen-li' ma? Cheng-chih ying-tang 'chung-li' ma?" [Should Party and State Be 'Separate'? Should Politics Be 'Neutral'?], *Hsien-wei-ching* [Microscope] 34 (May 19, 1982):3–8; "Hsüeh-che t'an tang-ch'ien ti tang-cheng kuan-hsi" [Scholars Discuss Party-State Relations at Present], *Huang-he tsa-chih* [The Yellow River Magazine] 34 (May 1982):8–13. Also see Ch'en Kuo-hui, "Hsien-ch'i Kuomintang ti kai-t'ou lai" [Strip Away the KMT's Cover], *K'ai-ch'uang tsa-chih* [The New Era] 2 (August 1, 1984):12–22.

Notes to Chapter 8

1. Refer to chapter 5, note 10.

2. Refer to chapter 1.

3. This began happening in May 1985. The Economic Revitalization Committee included representatives from government, business, and academia and marked the first institutionalized forum for state business dialogue. Scholars have served on CEPD and its predecessors, but most do not assume permanent government posts. Economists

cluster in the Institute of Economics of Academia Sinica and the new Chung-hua Institute for Economic Research, frequently offering consulting services to the state.

4. Visits to the mainland, especially the Minnan region of Fukien where most Taiwanese originated, confirm these similarities.

5. For a discussion of recent Latin American writings on this subject, see Alejandro Portes, "From Dependency to Redemocratization: New Themes in Latin American Sociology," *Contemporary Sociology* 13,5 (September 1984):546–49.

6. Many of these can be found in Korea, but Taiwan had more extreme instances of them.

7. The classic discussion of the state in late industrializing countries is Alexander Gerschenkron, *Economic Backwardness in Historical Perspective* (Cambridge: Belknap, 1962). The definitive recent discussion can be found in Johnson (1982).

Bibliography

Amnesty International. 1976. *Amnesty International Briefing: Taiwan (Republic of China)*. London: Amnesty International.

Amsden, Alice H. 1979. "Taiwan's Economic History." *Modern China* 5,3 (July):341–80.

Arnold, Walter. 1985. "Japan and Taiwan: Community of Economic Interest Held Together by Paradiplomacy." In *Japan's Foreign Relations: A Global Search for Economic Security*, ed. Robert S. Ozaki and Walter Arnold. Boulder: Westview Press, pp. 187–99.

Arrigo, Linda Gail. 1980. "The Industrial Work Force of Young Women in Taiwan." *Bulletin of Concerned Asian Scholars* 12,2 (April-June):25–38.

———. 1981. "Taiwan jen-min fan-k'ang yun-tung ti cheng-chih yen-pien" [Social Origins of the Taiwan Democratic Movement]. *Meilitao* [Formosa Weekly] (April-July).

Arthur D. Little, Incorporated. 1973a. *The Outlook for the Electronics Industry in Taiwan*. No. 4.

———. 1973b. *Perspectives on Industrial Incentives in Taiwan*. No. 5.

———. 1973c. *A National Industrial Development Overview: Guidelines and Strategy for Taiwan*. No. 13.

Balassa, Bela. 1981. *The Newly Industrializing Countries in the World Economy*. New York: Pergamon Press.

Barclay, George W. 1954. *Colonial Development and Population in Taiwan*. Princeton: Princeton University Press.

Barnett, A. Doak. 1954. "Formosa: Political Potpourri." American Universities Field Staff, East Asia Series 3(13).

Barrett, Richard E., and Martin King Whyte. 1982. "Dependency Theory and Taiwan: Analysis of a Deviant Case." *American Journal of Sociology* 87,5 (March):1064–89.

——— 1984. "What Is Dependency? Reply to Hammer." *American Journal of Sociology* 89,4 (January):937–40.

Caldwell, J. Alexander. 1976. "The Financial System in Taiwan: Structure, Function and Issues for the Future." *Asian Survey* 16, 8 (August):729–51.

Caporaso, James A. 1978. "Dependence, Dependency and Power in the Global

System: A Structural and Behavioral Analysis." *International Organization* 32,1 (Winter):13–43.

Cardoso, Fernando H. 1973. "Associated-Dependent Development: Theoretical and Practical Implications. In *Authoritarian Brazil*, ed. Alfred Stepan. New Haven: Yale University Press, pp. 142–76.

—— 1977. "The Consumption of Dependency Theory in the United States." *Latin American Research Review* 12,3:7–24.

—— 1979. "On the Characterization of Authoritarian Regimes in Latin America." In *The New Authoritarianism in Latin America*, ed. David Collier. Princeton:Princeton University Press, pp. 33–57.

Cardoso, Fernando H., and Enzo Faletto. 1979. *Dependency and Development in Latin America*. Berkeley: University of California Press.

Chang, A. T. 1972. "Two Different Approaches to Investment in a Capital Intensive Industry in the Republic of China." *Industry of Free China* 38,6 (December):18–28.

Chang Chün-hung. 1977. *Wo-ti shen-ssu yü fen-tou* [My Profound Thoughts and Struggle]. Taipei: Kao-shan.

Chang Han-yü. 1955. "Jih-chü shih-tai Taiwan ching-chi chih yen-pien" [Evolution of Taiwan's Economy During the Period of Japanese Rule]. *Collection of Writings on Taiwan's Economic History, No. 2*. Taipei: Bank of Taiwan, pp. 74–128.

Chang Han-yü and Ramon Myers. 1963. "Japanese Colonial Development Policy in Taiwan, 1895–1906." *Journal of Asian Studies* 22 (August):433–50.

Chang, Kowie. 1968. *Economic Development in Taiwan*. Taipei: Cheng Chung.

Chang Tsung-han. 1980. *Kuang-fu-ch'ien Taiwan chih kung-ye-hua* [The Industrialization of Taiwan Before Retrocession]. Taipei: Lien-ching.

Chen Cheng. 1961. *Land Reform in Taiwan*. Taipei: China Publishing Co.

Chen Ching-chih. 1973. "Japanese Socio-political Control in Taiwan, 1895–1945." Ph.D. dissertation, Harvard University.

Chen, Edward I-te. 1970. "Japanese Colonialism in Korea and Formosa: A Comparison of the Systems of Political Control." *Harvard Journal of Asiatic Studies* 30:126–58.

—— 1972. "Formosan Political Movements Under Japanese Colonial Rule, 1914–1937." *Journal of Asian Studies* 31,3 (May):477–97.

Chen, Edward Y. K. 1979. *Hyper-Growth in Asian Economies*. London: Macmillan.

Chen Gu-ying. 1982. "The Reform Movement Among Intellectuals in Taiwan Since 1970." *Bulletin of Concerned Asian Scholars* 14,3 (July-September):32–47.

Chen Shao-hsing. 1979. *Taiwan ti jen-k'ou pien-ch'ien yü she-hui pien-ch'ien* [Population and Social Change in Taiwan]. Taipei: Lien-ching.

Ch'en Ying-chen. 1984. "Kuei-ying chih-shih fen-tzu ho ch'uan-hsiang cheng-houch'ün" [Ghost Shadow Intellectuals and the Conversionist Syndrome]. *Chung-kuo shih-pao* [China Times] (April).

Chiang Kai-shek. 1947. *China's Destiny*. London: Dennis Dobson.

Chiang Nan. 1984. *Chiang Ching-kuo chuan* [Biography of Chiang Ching-kuo]. Los Angeles: Mei-kuo Lun-t'an Pao.

Ch'ien Tuan-sheng. 1950. *The Government and Politics of China*. Cambridge: Harvard University Press.

China Credit Information Service. 1973. *Kung-shang jen-min lu* [Taiwan Business Who's Who 500]. Taipei: China Credit Information Service.

—— 1976. *Taiwan-ch'ü chi-t'uan ch'i-ye yen-chiu* [Business Groups in Taiwan]. Taipei: China Credit Information Service.

—— 1981. *Chung-hua Min-kuo tsui-ta min-ying ch'i-ye* [Top 500 Companies in Taiwan]. Taipei: China Credit Information Service.

China Handbook Editorial Board. 1956. *China Handbook 1956-57*. Taipei.

Chinn, Dennis. 1979. "Rural Poverty and the Structure of Farm Household Income in Developing Countries: Evidence from Taiwan." *Economic Development and Cultural Change* 27,2 (January):283-301.

Chou Wen. 1973. "Taiwan chih fang-chih kung-ye" [Taiwan's Textile Industry]. *Taiwan Yinhang chi-k'an* [Bank of Taiwan Quarterly] 24,1 (January):95-124.

Chu, Samuel. 1963. "Liu Ming-ch'uan and the Modernization of Taiwan." *Journal of Asian Studies* 23 (November):37-57.

Chung-hua Min-kuo Kung-shang Hsieh-chin-hui Ch'eng-li Erh-shih Chou-nien Chinien T'e-chi Pien-yin Hsiao-tsu. 1971. *Kung-shang hsieh-chin erh-shih-nien* [Twenty Years of Promoting Industry and Commerce]. Taipei: Chung-hua Min-kuo Kung-shang Hsieh-chin-hui.

Clough, Ralph. 1978. *Island China*. Cambridge: Harvard University Press.

Collier, David, ed. 1979. *The New Authoritarianism in Latin America*. Princeton: Princeton University Press.

Conference on Population and Economic Development in Taiwan. 1976. Taipei: Academia Sinica, Institute of Economics.

Copper, John F. 1979. "Political Development in Taiwan." In *China and the Taiwan Issue*, ed. Hungdah Chiu. New York: Praeger, pp. 37-73.

—— 1981. "Taiwan's Recent Election: Progress Toward a Democratic System." *Asian Survey* 21,10 (October):1029-39.

Council for Economic Planning and Development. 1980a. *Chung-hua Min-kuo tien-tzu kung-ye pu-men fa-chan chi-hua, 1980-89* [Development Plan for the Electronics Sector, ROC, 1980-89]. Taipei.

—— 1980b. *Ten-Year Economic Development Plan for Taiwan, Republic of China (1980-1989)*. Taipei.

Crane, George T. 1982. "The Taiwanese Ascent: System, State and Movement in the World Economy." In *Ascent and Decline in the World-System*, ed. Edward Friedman. Beverly Hills: Sage, pp. 93-113.

Crozier, Ralph C. 1977. *Koxinga and Chinese Nationalism*. Cambridge: East Asian Research Center, Harvard University.

Cumings, Bruce. 1984. "The Origin and Development of the Northeast Asian Political Economy: Industrial Sectors and Political Consequences." *International Organization* 38,1 (Winter):1-40.

Davison, D. W. S. 1980 "Politics of the Left in Taiwan." *Bulletin of Concerned Asian Scholars* 12,2 (April-June):18-24.

Department of State. 1967. *The China White Paper, August, 1949*. Stanford: Stanford University Press.

Djang, T. K. 1977. *Industry and Labor in Taiwan*. Nankang: Institute of Economics, Academia Sinica Monograph Series, No. 10.

Domes, Jurgen. 1981. "Political Differentiation in Taiwan: Group Formation Within the Ruling Party and the Opposition Circles, 1979-1980." *Asian Survey* 21,10 (October):1011-28.

Dos Santos, Theotonio. 1970. "The Structure of Dependence." *American Economic Review* 60,2 (May):231-36.

Durdin, Tillman. 1975. "Chiang Ching-kuo and Taiwan: A Profile." *Orbis* 18,4 (Winter):1023-42.

Economic Planning Council. 1976. *The Republic of China's Six-Year Plan for Economic Development of Taiwan, 1976-1981*. Taipei.

Evans, Peter B. 1979. *Dependent Development*. Princeton: Princeton University Press.

Fei, John C. H., Gustav Ranis, and Shirley W. Y. Kuo. 1979. *Growth with Equity: The Taiwan Case*. New York: Oxford University Press.

Frank, Andre Gunder. 1969a. "The Development of Underdevelopment." In *Latin*

America: Underdevelopment or Revolution, ed. Andre Gunder Frank. New York: Monthly Review Press, pp. 3-17.

—— 1969b. "Sociology of Development and Underdevelopment of Sociology." In Latin America: Underdevelopment or Revolution, ed. André Gunder Frank. New York: Monthly Review Press, pp. 21-94.

—— 1982. "Asia's Exclusive Models," Far Eastern Economic Review, June 25, pp. 22-23.

Galenson, Walter, ed. 1979, Economic Growth and Structural Change in Taiwan. Ithaca: Cornell University Press.

Gallin, Bernard. 1966. Hsin Hsing, Taiwan. Berkeley: University of California Press.

Gates, Hill. 1979. "Dependency and the Part-Time Proletariat in Taiwan." Modern China 5,3 (July):381-408.

—— 1981. "Ethnicity and Social Class." In The Anthropology of Taiwanese Society, ed. Emily M. Ahern and Hill Gates. Stanford: Stanford University Press, pp. 241-81.

Gereffi, Gary. 1983. The Pharmaceutical Industry and Dependency in the Third World. Princeton: Princeton University Press.

Gold, Thomas B. 1981. "Dependent Development in Taiwan." Ph.D. dissertation, Harvard University.

—— 1983. "Differentiating Multinational Corporations: American, Japanese and Overseas Chinese Investors in Taiwan." Chung-kuo she-hui-hsüeh k'an [Chinese Journal of Sociology] (July):267-78.

Gordon, Leonard H. D. 1970. "Taiwan and the Powers, 1840-1895." In Taiwan: Studies in Chinese Local History, ed. Leonard H. D. Gordon. New York: Columbia University Press, pp. 93-116.

Greenhalgh, Susan. 1984. "Networks and Their Nodes: Urban Society on Taiwan." China Quarterly 99 (September):529-52.

Gregor, A. James, Maria Hsia Chang, and Andrew B. Zimmerman. 1981. Ideology and Development: Sun Yat-sen and the Economic History of Taiwan. Berkeley: Institute of East Asian Studies.

Haggard, Stephan, M. 1983, "Pathways from the Periphery: The Newly Industrializing Countries in the International System." Ph.D. dissertation, University of California, Berkeley.

Haggard, Stephan M., and Cheng Tun-jen. 1983. "State Strategies, Local and Foreign Capital in the Gang of Four," paper presented to the Annual Meeting of the American Political Science Association, Chicago.

Haggard, Stephan M., and Chung-in Moon. 1983. "The South Korean State in the International Economy: Liberal, Dependent or Mercantile?" In The Antinomies of Interdependence, ed. John G. Ruggie. New York: Columbia University Press, pp. 131-89.

Hammer, Heather-Jo. 1984. "Comment on 'Dependency Theory and Taiwan: Analysis of a Deviant Case.'" American Journal of Sociology 89,4 (January):932-37.

Hasan, Parvez. 1982. Growth and Structural Adjustment in East Asia. World Bank Staff Working Papers No. 529.

—— 1984. "Adjustment to External Shocks." Finance and Development (December):14-17.

Ho, Samuel P. S. 1978. Economic Development of Taiwan, 1860-1970. New Haven: Yale University Press.

Housing and Urban Development Department, Council for Economic Planning and Development. 1981. Urban and Regional Development Statistics, Republic of China, 1981.

Hsi Ju-chi. 1981. "She-hui fa-chan yü ching-chi fa-chan ti pi-chiao fen-hsi" [A

Comparative Analysis of Social and Economic Development]. In *Wo-kuo she-hui ti pien-ch'ien yü fa-chan* [Our Nation's Social Change and Development], ed. Chu Ch'en-lou. Taipei: Tung-ta, pp. 75-102.

Hsiao, Frank S. T., and Lawrence R. Sullivan. 1983. "A Political History of the Taiwanese Communist Party, 1928-1931." *Journal of Asian Studies* 42,2 (February):269-89.

Hsiao, Hsin-huang Michael. 1981. *Government Agricultural Strategies in Taiwan and South Korea*. Taipei: Academia Sinica, Institute of Ethnology.

Hsieh, Yung-ting. 1985. "P'ao-hsiao cheng-t'an ti Wang Yung-ch'ing" [Wang Yung-ch'ing Fires Shots at the Political Stage]. *Ch'ien-chin shih-tai* [Progressive Age] 23 (June):5-13.

Hsin-ching Publishing Company. 1982. *Taiwan ta ch'i-ye-chia fen-tou shih* [History of the Struggle of Taiwan's Large Entrepreneurs]. 2 vols. Taipei.

Hsing Mo-han. 1970. "Taiwan." In *Taiwan and the Philippines: Industrialization and Trade Policies*, ed. John H. Power, Geraldo P. Sicat, and Hsing Mo-han. London: Oxford University Press, pp. 135-324.

Hsiung, James, ed. 1981. *The Taiwan Experience, 1950-1980*. New York: American Association for Chinese Studies.

Hsu Hsin-liang. 1977. *Feng-yü chih sheng* [The Sound of the Storm]. Taichung: Kuang-yi.

Hsu Shih-kai .1972. *Nihon Tōchika no Taiwan* [Taiwan Under Japanese Rule]. Tokyo: Tokyo University Press.

Hsu Wen-hsiung. 1980a. "From Aboriginal Island to Chinese Frontier: The Development of Taiwan Before 1683." In *China's Island Frontier*, ed. Ronald G. Knapp. Honolulu: University Press of Hawaii and Research Corporation of the University of Hawaii, pp. 3-29.

——— 1980b. "Frontier Social Organization and Social Disorder in Ch'ing Taiwan." In *China's Island Frontier*, ed. Ronald G. Knapp. Honolulu: University Press of Hawaii and Research Corporation of the University of Hawaii, pp. 87-105.

Hu Tai-li. 1984. *My Mother-in-Law's Village*. Taipei: Academia Sinica, Institute of Ethnology.

Huang Ching-yuan. 1978. *Multinationals in the Republic of China: Laws and Policies*. Taipei: Asia and the World Forum.

Huang, Mab. 1976. *Intellectual Ferment for Political Reforms in Taiwan, 1971-73*. Ann Arbor: Center for Chinese Studies, University of Michigan.

Huang Shao-t'ang. 1970. *Taiwan Minshukoku no kenkyū* [Research on the Republic of Taiwan]. Tokyo: Tokyo University Press.

Jacobs, J. Bruce. 1971. "Recent Leadership and Political Trends in Taiwan." *China Quarterly* 45 (January-March):129-54.

——— 1978. "Paradoxes in the Politics of Taiwan: Lessons for Comparative Politics." *The Journal of the Australian Political Science Association* 13,2 (November):239-47.

——— 1980. *Local Politics in a Rural Chinese Cultural Setting: A Field Study of Mazu Township, Taiwan*. Canberra: Contemporary China Centre, Research School of Pacific Studies, Australian National University.

Jacoby, Neil H. 1966. *U.S. Aid to Taiwan*. New York: Praeger.

Johnson, Chalmers. 1982. *MITI and the Japanese Miracle*. Stanford: Stanford University Press.

Kagan, Richard. 1982. "Martial Law in Taiwan." *Bulletin of Concerned Asian Scholars* 14,3 (July-September):48-54.

Kao, Charles H. C. 1984. "The Role of Government in Taiwan's Economic Development," paper presented at Chinese Economic Bureaucracy Workshop, East-West

152   STATE AND SOCIETY IN THE TAIWAN MIRACLE

Center, Honolulu, Hawaii, July.

Kaplan, John. 1981. *The Court-Martial of the Kaohsiung Defendants*. Berkeley: Institute of East Asian Studies.

Kawano, Shigeto. 1968. "The Reasons for Taiwan's High Growth Rates." In *Economic Development Issues: Greece, Israel, Taiwan and Thailand*, ed. Committee for Economic Development. New York: Praeger, pp. 121–58.

Ke, Sun-jyi. 1983. "The State and Income Distribution in Taiwan: A Special Case?" paper presented at 1983 Association for Asian Studies Meeting, San Francisco.

Kerr, George H. 1965. *Formosa Betrayed*. Boston: Houghton-Mifflin.

——— 1974. *Formosa: Home Rule and Licensed Revolution*. Honolulu: University Press of Hawaii.

Knapp, Ronald G. 1980. "Settlement and Frontier Land Tenure." In *China's Island Frontier*, ed. Ronald G. Knapp. Honolulu: University Press of Hawaii and Research Corporation of the University of Hawaii, pp. 55–68.

Kublin, Hyman. 1959. "The Evolution of Japanese Colonialism." *Comparative Studies in Society and History* 2,1 (October):67–84.

Kung, Lydia. 1981. "Perceptions of Work Among Factory Women." In *The Anthropology of Taiwanese Society*, ed. Emily M. Ahern and Hill Gates. Stanford: Stanford University Press, pp. 184–211.

Kuo, Chi. 1985. "Ching-ke-hui shih chieh-pan ti kuo-tu chun-pei?" [Is the Economic Revitalization Committee a Preparation for the Transition?]. *Ch'ien-chin shih-tai* [Progressive Age] 23 (June):8–9.

Kuo, Shirley W. Y. 1983. *The Taiwan Economy in Transition*. Boulder: Westview Press.

Kuo Ting-yee. 1973. "The Internal Development and Modernization of Taiwan, 1683–1891." In *Taiwan in Modern Times*, ed. Paul K. T. Sih. New York: St. John's University Press, pp. 171–240.

Lai Chin-yi. 1983. *Taiwan ta ch'i-ye-chia fen-tou shih* [History of the Struggle of Taiwan's Large Entrepreneurs]. 2 vols. Taipei: Ku Nien-lai Publishing Company.

Lai Ying-chao. 1981. *Kuan-hsi ch'i-ye-fa pi-chiao yen-chiu* [Comparative Research on Laws on Business Groups]. Taipei.

Lamley, Harry J. 1970. "The 1895 War of Resistance: Local Chinese Efforts Against a Foreign Power." In *Taiwan: Studies in Chinese Local History*, ed. Leonard H. D. Gordon. New York: Columbia University Press, pp. 23–77.

——— 1970–71. "Assimilation Efforts in Colonial Taiwan: The Fate of the 1914 Movement." *Monumenta Serica* 29:496–520.

——— 1972. "Private Conflict: The Hsieh-tou Phenomenon in Taiwan and South China," paper prepared for Conference on Taiwan in Chinese History, Asilomar.

——— 1973. "A Short-Lived Republic and War, 1895: Taiwan's Resistance Against Japan." In *Taiwan in Modern Times*, ed. Paul K. T. Sih. New York: St. John's University Press, pp. 241–316.

Landsberg, Martin. 1979. "Export-Led Industrialization in the Third World: Manufacturing Imperialism." *Review of Radical Political Economists* 11,4 (Winter):50–63.

Lenin, V. I. 1939. *Imperialism: The Highest Stage of Capitalism*. New York: International Publishers.

Lerman, Arthur J. 1978. *Taiwan's Politics: The Provincial Assemblyman's World*. Washington: University Press of America.

Levy, Marion. 1953. "Contrasting Factors in the Modernization of China and Japan." *Economic Development and Cultural Change* 2,3 (October):161–97.

Li, K. T. 1976. *The Experience of Dynamic Economic Growth on Taiwan*. Taipei: Meiya.

Li T'ing-lan. 1975. *Ch'uang-tsao ts'ai-fu ti jen* [Creators of Wealth]. 6 vols. Taipei: Ching-chi Jih-pao.

Lin Cheng-chieh and Chang Fu-chung. 1977. *Hsüan-chü wan-sui* [Long Live Elections]. Taipei: Yü-li.

Lin Ching-yuan. 1973. *Industrialization in Taiwan.* New York: Praeger.

Little, Ian M. D. 1979. "An Economic Reconnaissance." In *Economic Growth and Structural Change in Taiwan,* ed. Walter Galenson. Ithaca: Cornell University Press, pp. 448–507.

Liu Chin-ch'ing. 1975. *Sengo Taiwan keizai bunseki* [Analysis of Taiwan's Postwar Economy]. Tokyo: Tokyo University Press.

Lo Ch'i-k'ai. 1984. "Chieh-k'ai An-ch'üan-chü ti shen-mi mien-sha" [Tear Off the Veil of Secrecy of the Security Bureau]. *Lei-sheng tsa-chih* [Voice of Thunder] 36 (December):16–23.

Mancall, Mark, ed. 1964. *Formosa Today.* New York: Praeger.

Mao Yu-kang. 1976. "Population and the Land System in Taiwan." In *Conference on Population and Economic Development in Taiwan.* Taipei: Academia Sinica, Institute of Economics, pp. 163–91.

Marx, Karl, and Frederich Engels. 1970. *The German Ideology.* New York: International Publishers.

Mendel, Douglas. 1970. *The Politics of Formosan Nationalism.* Berkeley: University of California Press.

Meskill, Johanna. 1979. *A Chinese Pioneer Family.* Princeton: Princeton University Press.

Moulder, Frances V. 1977. *Japan, China and the Modern World Economy.* Cambridge: Cambridge University Press.

Myers, Ramon. 1972a. "Taiwan Under Ch'ing Imperial Rule, 1684–1895: The Traditional Economy." *Journal of the Institute of Chinese Studies of the Chinese University of Hong Kong* 5,2:373–409.

——— 1972b. "Taiwan Under Ch'ing Imperial Rule, 1684–1895: The Traditional Society." *Journal of the Institute of Chinese Studies of the Chinese University of Hong Kong* 5,2:413–51.

——— 1973. "Taiwan as an Imperial Colony of Japan: 1895–1945." *Journal of the Institute of Chinese Studies of the Chinese University of Hong Kong* 6,2:425–51.

——— 1974. "Taiwan's Agrarian Economy Under Japanese Rule." *Journal of the Institute of Chinese Studies of the Chinese University of Hong Kong* 7,2:451–74.

Naito, Hideo, ed. 1937. *A Record of Taiwan's Progress, 1936 Edition.* Tokyo: Kokusai Nippon Kyokai.

O'Donnell, Guillermo A. 1973. *Modernization and Bureaucratic-Authoritarianism.* Berkeley: Institute of International Studies.

Ong Jok-tik. 1979. *Taiwan: K'u-men ti li-shih* [Taiwan: A History of Anguish and Struggle]. Tokyo: Taiwan Chingnienshe.

Palma, Gabriel. 1978. "Dependency: A Formal Theory of Underdevelopment or a Methodology for the Analysis of Concrete Situations of Underdevelopment?" *World Development* 6,7–8:881–924.

Peng Ming-min. 1971. "Political Offenses in Taiwan: Laws and Problems." *China Quarterly* 47 (July-September):471–93.

——— 1972. *A Taste of Freedom.* New York: Holt, Reinhart, Winston.

Pepper, Suzanne. 1978. *Civil War in China.* Berkeley: University of California Press.

Prybyla, Jan. 1980. "Some Reflexions on Derecognition and the Economy of Taiwan." *Taiwan: One Year After United States-China Normalization.* Washington: U.S. Government Printing Office, pp. 71–83.

Ranis, Gustav. 1978. "Equity with Growth in Taiwan: How 'Special' Is the 'Special

Case'?'' *World Development* 6,3 (March):397-409.

Rozman, Gilbert, ed. 1981. *The Modernization of China.* New York: Free Press.

Schive, Chi. 1978. "Direct Foreign Investment, Technology Transfer and Linkage Effects: A Case Study of Taiwan." Ph.D. dissertation, Case Western Reserve University.

—— 1979. "Technology Transfer through Direct Foreign Investment: A Case Study of Taiwan Singer." *Proceedings of the Academy of International Business-Asia-Pacific Dimensions of International Business.* Honolulu: University of Hawaii, pp. 113-22.

Schurmann, Franz. 1974. *The Logic of World Power.* New York: Pantheon.

Shen-keng tzu-liao-shih. 1983. "San-shih-nien-lai chung-ta cheng-chih an-chien" [A Major Political Case of the Past Thirty Years]. *Shen-keng* [Cultivate] 28 (February 25):25-26.

Shieh, Milton J. T. 1970. *The Kuomintang: Selected Historical Documents.* New York: St. John's University Press.

Shih Ming. 1980. *Taiwan-jen ssu-pai-nien shih* [Four Hundred Years of the History of the Taiwanese People]. San Jose: Paradise Culture Associates.

Simon, Denis Fred. 1980. "Taiwan, Technology Transfer and Transnationalism: The Political Management of Dependency." Ph.D. dissertation, University of California, Berkeley.

Skocpol, Theda. 1979. *States and Social Revolutions.* Cambridge: Cambridge University Press.

Speidel, William M. 1974. "Elite Response to Modernization in Late Ch'ing Taiwan," paper presented at Annual Meeting of Association for Asian Studies, Boston.

—— 1976. "The Administrative and Fiscal Reforms of Liu Ming-ch'uan in Taiwan, 1884-1891: Foundation for Self-Strengthening." *Journal of Asian Studies* 35,3 (May):441-59.

Sun Chen. 1976. "The Trend of Economic Development and Productivity in Taiwan." *Conference on Population and Economic Development in Taiwan.* Taipei: Academia Sinica, Institute of Economics, pp. 101-25.

Sun Yat-sen. n.d. *San Min Chu I, The Three Principles of the People.* Taipei: China Publishing Co.

Tai Hung-chao. 1970. "The Kuomintang and Modernization in Taiwan." In *Authoritarian Politics in Modern Society*, ed. Samuel P. Huntington and Clement Moore. New York: Basic Books, pp. 406-36.

Tang Hui-sun. 1954. *Land Reform in Free China.* Taipei: JCRR.

T'ang Kuang-hua. 1979. "Tang-ch'ien cheng-chih wen-t'i ti cheng-chieh chi chieh-chüeh chih tao" [The Obstructions and Path to Solution of Current Political Problems]. *Tsung-ho yue-k'an* [General Monthly] 129 (August):18-23.

Tien Hung-mao. 1975. "Taiwan in Transition: Prospects for Socio-Political Change." *China Quarterly* 64 (December):615-44.

Ts'ui Shu-ch'in. 1959. *San-min chu-i hsin-lun* [New Discourse on Three Principles of the People]. Taipei: Shang-wu.

Tsurumi, E. Patricia. 1977. *Japanese Colonial Education in Taiwan, 1895-1945.* Cambridge: Harvard University Press.

Tu Chao-yen. 1975. *Nihon teikokushugika no Taiwan* [Taiwan under Japanese Imperialism]. Tokyo: Tokyo University Press.

Wade, Robert. 1984. "Dirigisme Taiwan Style." In *Developmentalist States in East Asia: Capitalist and Socialist*, ed. Robert Wade and Gordon White. Institute of Development Studies Bulletin 15, 2 (April):65-70.

Walker, Richard. 1973. "Taiwan's Movement into Political Modernity." In *Taiwan in Modern Times*, ed. Paul K. T. Sih. New York: St. John's University Press, pp. 359-96.

Wallerstein, Immanuel. 1974. "The Rise and Future Demise of the World Capitalist System." *Comparative Studies in Society and History* 16, 4 (September):387–415.
———. 1979. "Dependence in an Interdependent World: The Limited Possibilities of Transformation within the Capitalist World-Economy." In *The Capitalist World Economy*, ed. Immanuel Wallerstein. Cambridge: Cambridge University Press, pp. 66–94.
Wang Tso-jung. 1977–78. "Wo-men ju-he chih-tsao-le ching-chi ch'i-chi" [How We Created the Economic Miracle]. *Chung-kuo shih-pao* [China Times].
Wei Yung. 1973. "Taiwan: A Modernizing Chinese Society." In *Taiwan in Modern Times*, ed. Paul K. T. Sih. New York: St. John's University Press, pp. 435–505.
——— 1976. "Modernization Process in Taiwan: An Allocative Analysis." *Asian Survey* 16,3 (March):249–69.
Wen Hsien-shen. 1984. "Ching-chien-hui ti kuo-ch'ü, hsien-tsai yü wei-lai" [Past, Present and Future of CEPD]. *Tien-hsia tsa-chih* [Commonwealth] (November):12–25.
Wickberg, Edgar. 1970. "Late Nineteenth Century Land Tenure in North Taiwan." In *Taiwan: Studies in Chinese Local History*, ed. Leonard H. D. Gordon. New York: Columbia University Press, pp.78–92.
——— 1981. "Continuities in Land Tenure, 1900–1940." In *The Anthropology of Taiwanese Society*, ed. Emily M. Ahern and Hill Gates. Stanford: Stanford University Press, pp. 212–38.
Williams, Jack F. 1980. "Sugar: The Sweetener in Taiwan's Development." In *China's Island Frontier*, ed. Ronald G. Knapp. Honolulu: University Press of Hawaii and Research Corporation of the University of Hawaii, pp. 219–51.
Winckler, Edwin A. 1981a. "National, Regional and Local Politics." In *The Anthropology of Taiwanese Society*, ed. Emily M. Ahern and Hill Gates. Stanford: Stanford University Press, pp. 13–37.
——— 1981b. "Roles Linking State and Society." In *The Anthropology of Taiwanese Society*, ed. Emily M. Ahern and Hill Gates. Stanford: Stanford University Press, pp. 50–86.
——— 1982. "After the Chiangs: The Coming Succession in Taiwan." In *China Briefing, 1982*, ed. Richard C. Bush. Boulder: Westview Press, pp. 103–21.
——— 1984. "Institutionalization and Participation on Taiwan: From Hard to Soft Authoritarianism?" *China Quarterly* 99 (September):481–99.
World Bank 1980. *World Development Report, 1980*. New York: Oxford University Press.
Wu Naiteh 1980. "Emergence of the Opposition Within an Authoritarian Regime: The Case of Taiwan," ms.
Wu Yuan-li and Kung-chia Yeh, eds. 1978. *Growth, Distribution and Social Change: Essays on the Economy of the Republic of China*. Baltimore: University of Maryland Occasional Papers/Reprints Series in Contemporary Asian Studies.
Wynn, Sam. 1982. "The Taiwanese 'Economic Miracle.'" *Monthly Review* 33,11 (April):30–40.
Yang, Martin M. C. 1970. *Socio-Economic Results of Land Reform in Taiwan*. Honolulu: University Press of Hawaii.
Yi Hsi-liang 1955. "Jih-pen chan-ling ch'i-chung Taiwan ching-chi fa-chan chih hui-ku [A Retrospective on Economic Development in Taiwan During the Period of Japanese Occupation]. *Chu-i yü kuo-ts'e* [Isms and National Policy], pp. 22–28.
Yoffie, David B. 1983. *Power and Protectionism: Strategies of the Newly Industrializing Countries*. New York: Columbia University Press.
Yu Tzong-hsien, chief ed. 1975. *Taiwan ching-chi fa-chan lun-wen-chi* [Essays on Taiwan's Economic Development]. 8 vols. Taipei: Lien-ching.
Zenger, J. P. 1977. "Taiwan: Behind the Economic Miracle." *Free Trade Zones and Industrialization of Asia*. Tokyo: AMPO, pp. 75–91.

Index

Aborigines, 23–24, 28–30, 136–37*n*1
Agency for International Development
(AID), 67–68, 70, 76–79, 139*n*19.
See also Investment aid and loans
Agriculture, 28, 36–38, 66–67, 85, 89–
90, 106
American Express, 98
American Institute, 99
An-ping, 24
Arrigo, Linda Gail, 117
Arrow Company, 81
Arthur D. Little, Incorporated, 94, 100

Banking and banks, 108–109, 110–11;
Asian Development Bank, 108; Bank
of Taiwan, 53, 68; Banking Law Revi-
sion, 108; Central Trust of China, 68;
First National Bank of Chicago, 98;
World Bank, 108, 110, 143*n*8. *See
also* Investment
Bolshevik Revolution, 41
Boxer Rebellion, 34
Business groups, 88, 141*n*17

Cairo Declaration, 49
Capitalists, 70–71, 83–84, 104–105; un-
der Japanese rule, 39–40, 137*n*1.
Cardoso, Fernando, 14–15, 17, 18, 122,
123, 130
Caribbean Basin Initiative, 109

Carter, Jimmy, 99, 115
Cathay conglomerate, 109, 118, 145*n*38
Central Executive Committee, 59
Central Reform Committee, 54, 59
Central Standing Committee, 54, 113
Chang Chün-hung, 117, 142*n*28
Chaebol, 89, 141*n*17
Chao Yao-tung, 101, 105
Ch'en Ch'eng, 54–55, 62, 67, 77–78, 91,
125
Chen Chi-li, 120
Ch'en Chün, 117
Ch'en Chung-ho, 40
Ch'en Li-fu, 59
Ch'en Mao-pang, 84
Chen Wen-cheng, 120
Ch'en Yi, General, 49–53, 59, 140*n*6
Cheng Ch'eng-kung, 24, 137*n*2
Cheng Ching, 24
Chiang Ching-kuo, 53, 54, 62, 63, 91,
92, 108, 113, 114, 116, 118, 120,
144*n*30
Chiang Hsiao-wu, 62, 120
Chiang Kai-shek, 5, 41, 48–59 *passim*,
62, 67, 70, 77, 124, 125, 140*n*6,
143*n*8
Chiang Kai-shek, Madame, 53
Chiang Nan. *See* Liu, Henry
Chi-feng (Hurricane), 145*n*35
China, 8, 27–30, 47–48; People's Repub-

lic of, 86, 92, 93, 98–100, 107, 108, 110, 118, 131, 142*n*27, 143*n*10, 143*n*15, 144*n*22. *See also* Ch'ing dynasty; Colonial rule
China Development Corporation, 78
China External Trade Development Council, 107
China National Association of Industry and Commerce, 74, 140*n*21
China Steel Corporation, 101, 105, 139–40*n*20
Chinese Petroleum Corporation, 134–40*n*20
Ch'ing dynasty, 24–29, 35, 36, 47, 48
Chou Ch'ing-yü, 117
Chou En-lai, 93
Chung-hsing Textile, 70
Chung-li Incident, 3, 5, 17, 115, 116, 122, 129–30, 142*n*28
Churchill, Sir Winston, 49
Class structure: colonial, 28–29; postcolonial, 88–90, 118–19, 129
Colonial rule: pre-Japanese, 23–26; Japanese: assimilation of Taiwanese during, 41–42; consequences of, 39–40, 44–46; consolidation of, 8, 16, 30, 34–40; economic development, 32–46; exclusion of Taiwanese from government, 39–40; forced assimilation during, 44; resistance of Taiwanese during, 35–36, 42–43; Sōtokufu, 35–41 *passim*, 44; structure of society, 35–40; World War II and, 43–44. *See also* State; Education
Communist Party: of China (CCP), 48, 63, 65, 93, 120; of Taiwan, 42; of Soviet Union, 48
Consultative Council (*hyogikai*), 41
Coordination Council for North American Affairs, 99
Council for Economic Planning and Development (CEPD), 102, 103, 105, 145*n*3
Council for International Economic Cooperation and Development (CIECD), 78, 83, 87, 91, 92; Economic Planning Council of, 92, 102

Council on U.S. Aid (CUSA), 68, 69, 70, 78
Counterfeit goods, 104, 143*n*10

Den Kenjiro, Baron, 41
Dependency. *See* Economic development, theories of
Diet Bill No. Sixty-Three, 35, 42
Dutch East India Company, 23

Economic development, theories of: Comprehensive analysis, 11–17 *passim*; Dependency theory, 9–10, 12–17, 133, 136*n* 18; Economistic theories, 8–9; Modernization theory, 11–12
Economic Planning Council, 92, 102
Economic Revitalization Committee, 118, 145*n*3
Economic Stabilization Board, 68–70
Education: colonial, 38–39, 41–42, 45; postcolonial, 112–113, 144*n*27. *See also* Students
Eisenhower, Dwight, 64
Electronics Research Service Organization (ERSO), 103, 104
European Economic Community (EEC), 109, 110
Evans, Peter, 15, 128, 130
Export orientation, 74, 81–82, 186
Export Processing Zones, 79–80, 83–86

Far Eastern Textile, 70, 88
Finance capital, *See* Investment
Foreign Exchange and Trade Control Commission, 68
Formosa Group (*Mei-li-fao*), 117
Formosa Plastics, 71, 88, 102, 118, 139–40*n*20
Fort Orange settlement, 23
Frank, Andre Gunder, 13, 14
Fulet Company, 104

Gang of Four, 98
General Agreement on Tariffs and Trade (GATT), 110
General Instruments, 79, 83, 86

General Motors, 105
General Political Warfare Department, 62
George, Henry, 48
GINI coefficient, 135*n*1
Gotō Shimpei, 36, 37
Government, branches of: Control Yuan, 61, 92, 117; Examination Yuan, 61; Executive Yuan, 60–61, 68, 78, 91, 92; Judicial Yuan, 61; Legislative Yuan, 60–61, 92, 117, 118, 130; Taiwan Provincial Government, 61, 63. *See also* Kuomintang
Great Depression, 41, 43
Gulf Oil, 101

Hong, C.C., 84, 104
Hong Ming-t'ai, 104
Hsia-ch'ao (The China Tide), 116
Hsiang-t'u (nativist) literature, 114, 117, 144*n*31, 145*n*32
Hsu Hsin-liang, 114, 115, 117, 142*n*28
Hsüan-chu wan-sui (Long Live Elections), 115
Hualong Corporation, 102
Huang Hsin-chieh, 113

IBM, 104
Import substitution 67–73 *passim*; in Latin America, 75
Income, distribution of, 5, 66, 112, 144*n*24
Industrial and Financial Committee, 68
Industrial Development and Investment Center, 78
Industrial Development Bureau, 102
Industrial Development Commission, 68
Industrial Technology and Research Institute (ITRI), 103
Industrialization: capital-intensive, 94–96, 100–106; comparison of Latin America and Taiwan, 75–76; colonial, 25–33, 36–46; direct foreign investment, 70–72, 74, 79–87; export-orientation, 74–87, 92; import-substitution, 67–73, 95; sectors of, 67, 70–71, 80–86, 88, 95, 101–105, 139*n*16,

143*n*9; statistics on, 4–5, 85–86, 98; vertical integration of firms, 88–89, 100, 103, 105–106. *See also*, Agriculture; State, role of, in economic development; Investment; Trade
Infrastructure, 8, 29, 30, 26, 45, 64, 94, 100–11
Intellectuals, 26, 38, 43, 127–28; KMT attempts to liquidate, 51, 64; political activity of, 93–94. *See also* Students
Intelligence Bureau, 62
International Monetary Fund (IMF), 108, 110
Investigation Bureau, 62
Investment: aid and loans, 67–73, 76–79; capital flight, 109, 143–44*n*17; China Trade Act, 79; Cooley fund, 79; Export Processing Zones, 79–80, 83–86; foreign, 74, 77–81, 86, 94–96, 107, 110–11, 126–28, 143*n*6; government incentives and controls, 77–80, 83, 87, 100–11; International Monetary Fund (IMF), 108, 110; local, 83–85, 87–89, 143*n*8; public versus private, 67–72, 145*n*3; Sino-American Industrial Agreement, 79; Statute for Encouragement of Investment, 78, 103; Statute for the Establishment and Management of Export Processing Zones, 79. *See also* Banking; Industrialization; State, role of, in economic development
Israel, 107, 143*n*14
Itagaki Taisuke, 40

Japan, 34–37, 43–44, 47, 93; Ministry of International Trade and Investment (MITI), 80, 81, 100, 102, 140–41*n*11; Twenty-one Demands, 35. *See also* Colonial rule
Joint Commission on Rural Reconstruction, 65, 66

K'ang Ning-hsiang, 92, 113, 117, 118
Kao Chun-ming, 117
Kao Yü-shu (Henry Kao), 91

Kaohsiung, 79, 80, 83–86 *passim*, 142*n*21
Kim Il-sung, 55
Kissinger, Henry, 93
K-Mart, 81
Kodamo Gentarō, 36
Koo, C. F. 71
Korea, 34, 41, 49, 55, 121
Ku Hsien-jung, 40, 71
Ku Hsien-yung, 35
Kung, H. H., 59
Kuomintang (KMT): armed forces, 63–64, 69, 106–107, 139*n*8; corporatist approach, 64, 139*n*11; crisis of confidence in, 100; democratization, 10, 118–21, 131–32; economic plans, 70, 77–78, 94, 100, 102; elections, 51, 61, 92, 117, 118; establishment of, 48; external threats to, 97–111; legitimacy of, 90, 129–31, 142*n*27; martial law under, 10, 54, 119–20, 125; Ministry of Defense, 54, 62; Ministry of Economic Affairs, 105, 141*n*14, 143*n*6; move to Taiwan, 53–59; National Security Bureau, 138*n*6; Nanking Regime (1927–1937), 43, 48–49; National Assembly, 60, 117, 138*n*5; offensive against CCP, 50, 52–58, 139*n*8; opposition to, 61, 91–95, 129, 130, 145*n*33; political oppression, 50–52, 56–57, 120; reform of, 57–59, 144*n*29; retreat from Japanese invasion, 49; role of mainland elite in, 8, 64–65, 92, 119; security-gathering agencies of, 54, 62–63, 120, 138*n*6, 138–39*n*7; Seventh National Congress, 59; structure of party, 59–64; Taiwan Garrison Command, 54, 63, 115, 116; Temporary Provisions during the Period of National Crisis, 60. *See also* Government, branches of; State; United States, KMT aid
Kuznets, Simon 144*n*24

Labor, organizations, 89, 141*n*19; supply of, 8, 89–90, 98, 111
Land, ownership of: 26, 29–30, 37–38, 45, 137*n*7; reform, 65–67, 71, 125. *See also* Agriculture
Land to the Tiller Act (1953), 65
Latin America, 11–13, 75–76, 87, 131
League of Nations, 43
Lee Teng-hui, 114, 138*n*5, 144*n*30
Lei Chen, 91
Lenin, Vladimir, 33
Leninism, 20, 48, 60
Li Kwoh-ting (K. T. Li), 77, 78, 103
Li Tsung-jen, 53
Liang Ch'i-ch'ao, 42
Liaotung peninsula, 34
Lin families, 26, 30, 39, 40
Lin Hsien-tang, 42
Lin Po-shou, 71
Lin Ting-sheng, 83
Lin Yi-hsiung, 120
Liu, Henry (Chiang Nan), 120, 138*n*7
Liu Ming-ch'uan, General, 29, 30, 36
Lü Hsiu-lien, 117

Manchu dynasty. *See* Ch'ing dynasty
Manchukuo, 43
Manchuria, 43, 49
Martial law. *See* Kuomintang, martial law under
Marx, Karl, 17, 18
Matsushita Corporation, 84, 104
May Fourth Movement, 115
Meiji empire, 32, 33, 35, 36, 38, 70
Method, historical-structual, 15–17, 122
Miao Feng-ch'iang, 104
Miao Yü-hsiu, 104
Microtek, 104
Ming dynasty, 23, 24
Mitac Computer Company, 104
Mobil Oil, 101
Multitech, 104

National Distillers and Chemical Corporation, 101
National Security Bureau, 62, 63
National Security Conference, 62
Nationalist party. *See* Kuomintang
Nineteen-Point Program of Economic and Financial Reform, 77, 78

Nissan International, 88
Nixon, Richard, 93, 110, 142n3

Oil crisis (1974), 97, 98, 101, 102, 106, 110
Opium War, 27
Orderly Marketing Agreements, 74
Organization of Petroleum-Exporting Countries (OPEC), 95

Pan American Airlines, 98
Pan-ch'iao clan, 71
Parsons, Talcott, 11
P'eng Meng-chi, 51
P'eng Ming-min, 91
People's Liberation Army, 53
People's Liberation Front, 114
Pescadore Islands, 22, 33, 49
Political Action Committee, 54
Political Warfare College, 63
Population, growth of, 111–12
Potsdam Declaration, 49
Potsdam life cycle, theory of, 140–41n11

Qume, 103

RCA, 86
Reagan, Ronald, 99, 109
Roosevelt, Franklin D., 49
Russia, 41, 43, 48, 107

Schools. See Education
Security Agencies, 62–3
Shanghai Communique, 93, 99, 143n15
Shantung, 34
Sharp Corporation, 84
Shieh Tung-min, 92, 114, 142n25
Shih Ming-teh, 117
Singer Sewing Machine Company, 85, 87
Skocpol, Theda, 18
Sony Corporation, 84
Soong, T. V., 50, 59, 68
Stanford Research Institute, 78, 82
State: control of banking, 108–109; defined, 17–19; relations with larger society, 19–20, 126–32, 143n6; role in Taiwan's economic development, 33,

36, 73, 75–78, 87, 96, 100–11, 118, 122–26. See also Colonial rule; Government, branches of; Kuomintang
Students: abroad, 141–42n20; apathy of, 90–91; in prerevolutionary China, 115–16; political activity of, 42–43, 93–94, 115, 142n26. See also Education
Su Tung-chi, 91
Sun Yat-sen, 48, 58, 65, 67, 77, 124; Three Principles of the People, 8, 48–49

Ta-Hsüeh (The Intellectual), 93
Tai Chi't'ao, 42
Taichung, 21
Tainan Textile Corporation, 71, 88
Taipai, 35, 91
Taisho Democracy, 41
Taiwan Agriculture and Forestry, 66
Taiwan Assimilation Society, 40, 41
Taiwan Cement, 66, 71
Taiwan Development Company, 44
Taiwan Electric Appliance Manufacturer's Association, 84
Taiwan Fertilizer Corporation, 67
Taiwan Garrison Command, 63
Taiwan Industry and Mining, 66
Taiwan Investigation Committee, 49
Taiwan Paper and Pulp, 66
Taiwan Political Review, 113
Taiwan Production Board, 54, 68
Taiwan Relations Act, 99, 107, 110
Tai-yuen Textile, 70, 88
Ta kung pao, 143n17
Tanaka Kakuei, 93
T'ang Ching-sung, 35
Tangwai, 116–20, 130, 145n32, 145n33
Tatung, 105
Ten Major Development Projects, 98, 100, 101, 106, 109
Teng Li-chün, 22
Three Principles of the People, 8, 48–49
Tokugawa shogunate, 32
Toshiba Corporation, 83
Toyota, 105
Trade and commercialization: colonial,

27–31, 37, 40, 45; controls on, 77, 80, 82, 94, 107, 109, 126, 141n14; postcolonial, 77, 82, 85, 98, 107–10, 144n18, 144n22. *See also* Industrialization, sectors of; Agriculture; Transnational corporations
Transnational corporations (TNCs), 10, 16, 80–87, 131, 141n16; in Latin America, 75–76. *See also* Investment; Trade
Treaty of Nanking, 27
Treaty of Shimonoseki, 33
Treaty of Tientsin, 27
Tripartite Intervention, 33–34
Tripartite Pact, 43
Truman, Harry, 55
Ts'ai Chen-chou, 145n38
Ts'ai Wan-ch'un, 145n38
Tunghai University, 21–22, 142n26
Two-Twenty Eight Incident, 50–52, 115, 129

Union Carbide, 101
United Bamboo Gang, 120
United Nations, Economic Commission for Latin America (ECLA), 11, 12, 93
United States: armed forces, 99, 142n3; China-Japan War and, 49; Congress of, 69, 76, 99, 110, 120; Customs Service, 104; Development Loan Fund, 76; formal ties with Taiwan broken, 99, 116–17; KMT aid, 8, 16, 52, 53, 55, 58–59, 65, 68, 69, 72, 73, 75, 77, 79, 124, 139n9; 140n4; 142n4, 143n15; Military Assistance Advisory Group (MAAG) 64; Mutual Defense Treaty, 64, 99, 107; ownership of Senkaku Islands, 93; People's Republic of China and, 86, 99; Seventh Fleet, 64.

See also Investment aid and loans; Kuomintang.

Vietnam War, 86–87
Vocational Assistance Commission for Retired Servicemen (VACRS), 63–64

Wallerstein, Immanuel, 13, 14
Wang, Bobo, 104
Wang Laboratories, 103
Wang Sheng, General, 114, 115, 120
Wang T'o, 117, 145n32
Wang, Y. C., 71, 88, 118
Weber, Max, 17
Wei Tao-ming, 51
Westinghouse, 83
Willys, 88
Wilson, Woodrow, 41
Wong Hsi-ling, 120
World War: First, 35, 40–43; Second, 45, 52, 67
Wu Kuo-chen (K. C. Wu), 55, 138n9
Wu San-lien, 71
Wu Tun, 120

Xerox Corporation, 104

Yang Ch'ing-ch'u, 117, 145n32
Yao Chia-wen, 117
Yen Chia-kan, 63, 78, 140n6
Yen Ch'ing-ling, 88
Yen, C. K. *See* Yen Chia-kan
Yin, K. Y., 68, 70, 77
Yu Kuo-hwa, 92, 102, 118, 143n8, 144n30

Zaibatsu, 37, 40, 41, 44, 89, 141n17
Zenith Corporation, 86